MW00461009

TURNING POINTS

STEVE RICHARDS

TURNING POINTS

CRISIS
AND
CHANGE
IN MODERN BRITAIN,
FROM 1945 TO TRUSS

MACMILLAN

First published 2023 by Macmillan
an imprint of Pan Macmillan
The Smithson, 6 Briset Street, London EC1M 5NR
EU representative: Macmillan Publishers Ireland Ltd, 1st Floor,
The Liffey Trust Centre, 117–126 Sheriff Street Upper,
Dublin 1, D01 YC43
Associated companies throughout the world
www.panmacmillan.com

ISBN 978-1-0350-1535-1

1 3 5 7 9 8 6 4 2

A CIP catalogue record for this book is available from the British Library.

Typeset in Adobe Garamond by Jouve (UK), Milton Keynes
Printed and bound by CPI Group (UK) Ltd, Croydon, CR0 4YY

Visit **www.panmacmillan.com** to read more about all our books
and to buy them. You will also find features, author interviews and
news of any author events, and you can sign up for e-newsletters
so that you're always first to hear about our new releases.

To the great Ruairi – one of the relatively few to be born while Liz Truss was prime minister . . . alive during the starkest and yet most ambiguous turning point of the lot.

CONTENTS

INTRODUCTION

Until the last decade the United Kingdom had an undeserved reputation of being a relatively calm country. While other equivalent nations struggled with unstable constitutions or corrupt governments, Britain apparently soldiered on, regularly electing Conservative administrations while allowing Labour to rule every now and then. With good cause that perception of solidity has changed over recent years. A country that has had three prime ministers and four chancellors in the space of twelve months, as the UK did in 2022, is not a model of stability. Indeed, the UK has been challenging the picture of smooth government since 2010 with a rare peacetime coalition at Westminster, the rise of the SNP, Brexit, the ascendancy of Jeremy Corbyn, Boris Johnson's haphazard regime, and the brief tenure of Liz Truss. At times, the experience of the UK has made the politics of Italy seem tediously straightforward.

But was this picture of solid stability ever justified? We could debate for many hours what were and were not significant turning points in the UK since 1945, but most would accept that there have been several phases when seismic change seemed possible or desirable and not solely since the 2008 global financial crash. When

I have discussed with friends and colleagues the theme of this book they have responded by saying something like, 'Of course, you will include "X"', or 'Surely you will include "Y". That was a momentous event.' Sometimes the suggestions coincided with those explored in the book. Sometimes they did not. A supposedly stable country before the 2008 crash, in fact, seems to have gone through quite a few potentially volcanic challenges since the end of the Second World War.

Partly the way news is reported makes some dramas seem more significant than they were. In terms of noise and frenzy, we appear to be hurtling towards turning points most of the time. The ubiquitous headline 'Breaking News' is one of the great media distortions. Many of the stories that lead bulletins or are on the front pages have few real consequences (even fewer are of consequence that generate uproar on Twitter).

I worked as a political correspondent in the 1990s at the BBC. Its generously staffed headquarters at Millbank was full of people rushing around from early in the morning until late at night as if another world war was about to break out when, in reality, some Conservative MPs might have been rebelling over a road closure. Viewers would have assumed that they were living through a turning point as they watched. They were not. In a frenzied way they were being told about a rebellion that meant virtually nothing even at the time. At least once a week there was speculation that John Major was about to fall as some new crisis or other surfaced. He never did until the election of 1997. This was before Twitter raised the political temperature.

Conversely there are themes that drive deep change over time. They include the so-called technological revolution, demographic trends and climate change. There is no clearly defined turning point in these most significant policy areas: governments adapt or fail to do so over a long period. In all three, it is hard to make the case that British governments have risen to the demands or addressed the possibilities that arise from these three big themes. Even so there is and will continue to be constant change, some of it veering towards the apocalyptic, arising from the climate crisis, growing elderly populations in advanced countries and the potential of technology. In these areas, no single year or event will mark a turning point.

The ten turning points I explore in this book can be dated precisely. They take three different forms. There are general elections: the ones held in 1945, 1979 and 1997. The first two brought about historic and enduring change, especially the second. The 1997 election led to a less vivid transformation of the country. I recall sitting next to the BBC's Evan Davis at the launch of Labour's manifesto. He observed to me that Tony Blair's message was essentially: 'Everything in this old castle is broken. We plan to change the ashtrays.' Nonetheless, in some important respects the New Labour era also marked a break with the immediate past. At the very least there was a change in the governing party after eighteen years of Conservative rule.

There are also three turning points relating to foreign affairs, all of which triggered urgent questions about the UK's place in the world: the Suez crisis in 1956, the war in Iraq in 2003 and the Brexit referendum in 2016. All three were also intense domestic sagas. The questions were far from answered at the time or arguably since.

Two global crises are explored in a single chapter: the 2008 financial crash and the Covid pandemic that spread like wildfire in 2020. Both brought about a revived dependency on the state after a long period in which government activity was viewed with suspicion, at least after Margaret Thatcher had cast her spell. In the first, the banks and those that used them pleaded for the government to intervene financially on a mind-boggling scale. This was nothing compared with the costs of supporting virtually every business during the pandemic, an emergency that also highlighted the value and fragilities of the NHS and the lightly regulated, underfunded social-care sector.

An external force was also a factor in another turning point, which tormented three prime ministers in the 1970s. In different ways Edward Heath, Harold Wilson and James Callaghan left office after struggling to adapt to the daunting consequences of a sudden quadrupling of oil prices in 1973. The costs of imported energy soared as miners in the UK were becoming more muscular and Margaret Thatcher hovered in the wings. She did not realize she was hovering in 1973, but that was when the stage was cleared for her leadership.

In their incomparably different ways Clement Attlee and Margaret Thatcher were resolute in their sense of mission but their exertion of political will was by no means unusual. Two turning points were also the product of resolute determination. Roy Jenkins's social reforms in the late 1960s remained in place throughout the subsequent decades. They were followed much later by civil partnerships and the legalization of gay marriage. These life-changing reforms were introduced in spite of much noisy protest from opponents at the time, yet any attempt at revision failed dismally. In contrast the wilful impatience of a newly elected prime minister, Liz Truss, and her chancellor, Kwasi Kwarteng, to unveil an entirely new set of economic policies within days led to the quickest turning point in modern times. Almost as speedily the policies and ideas on which they were based were scrapped. Truss and Kwarteng fell too.

In the coming pages I seek to explore why these turning points arose and whether the lessons were learnt by the main political parties, the media and beyond. In each case, did the UK really change deeply and move on strengthened and emboldened? Or were the turning points a mere punctuation mark before the old familiar patterns reasserted themselves? To what degree are big personalities the main factor in explaining turning points since 1945, and how much is down to what James Callaghan called a 'sea change' during the 1979 election – a period in which leaders were almost powerless against underlying forces? Why do there seem to have been more seismic events in recent years? We seem to live in the age of constant crisis. As the comedian Stewart Lee observed during his live shows in the spring of 2022, 'It's nice to be here in the short break between the global pandemic and the start of World War Three.'

I

LABOUR WINS A LANDSLIDE

The Labour government that was formed in 1945 was a dramatic break with the past while being reassuringly familiar. Labour had not won an overall majority before, let alone a landslide on this scale. Here was a drastic change in the political landscape. During the first half of the twentieth century, Conservative governments tended to rule with interruptions from the Liberals in the early decades and then by fleetingly insecure Labour administrations without an overall majority. For the first time Labour had total command in the House of Commons.

Yet the new prime minister, Clement Attlee, and his cabinet took full charge as fully formed politicians with considerable experience of power. In the preceding years they were defined by mighty political battles, internal struggles, a formal schism in their party, economic storms and then the Second World War. Such definition based on wide experience became increasingly rare towards the end of the twentieth century and the start of the twenty-first.

Unusually Attlee and his senior ministers were developed ideologically too. Unlike some subsequent Labour governments, they were confident about the ideas and values on which their policies were based. It would not have been a Labour administration without intense division and internal tensions, but there was a broadly clear and coherent sense about their purpose in power. They looked to new forms of centralized planning to bring about social and economic change. They disagreed over the precise forms the planning should take but their central vision of a more active state bound them together in a common project. As importantly, they were not intimidated about the prospect of government. For Labour in the 1980s and again after 2010, winning and exercising power seemed almost mystical in its tantalizing distance.

In contrast Attlee had been deputy prime minister during the war, carrying out some of the more arduous administrative tasks that had passed Churchill by; the duo, a partnership of almost comically contrasting personalities, became bound by mutual respect while running the coalition. By 1945, not even Attlee's deepest critics in the newspapers or in the Conservative Party could argue credibly that he was not suited for government, an allegation regularly made about Labour leaders. He had governed at the toughest of times.

The new foreign secretary, Ernest Bevin, had been there too, as an authoritative, widely respected minister of labour and national service. Before that he had been general secretary of the Transport and General Workers' Union, the biggest union in the world and one that he had played a central role in forming. The new chancellor, Hugh Dalton, had been president of the Board of Trade in the wartime coalition. He had written two well-regarded books on economics and inequality before becoming an MP in 1923.[1]

Dalton's successor at the Board of Trade, Stafford Cripps, had been leader of the house in the coalition. Before that he was ambassador to the Soviet Union, the thorniest of diplomatic roles. The new health and housing minister, Aneurin Bevan, was not in the wartime government, but had been a prominent MP since 1928 and a leading figure in the general strike two years before that. Herbert Morrison had risen through local government, leading the Labour group on London County Council, ultimately becoming Churchill's home secretary.

While the senior Conservatives in the coalition, Churchill and Anthony Eden, had focused on the direction of the war, the Labour ministers had more domestic remits in the government and as a result greater direct engagement with British voters. Voters had got to know them as ministers, in striking contrast to the 1930s when they were only part of a diminished opposition party, far away from power. In terms of experience, only the Labour cabinet in February 1974 could compete. Yet unlike the 1974 government, Labour seemed dazzlingly fresh and novel. For the first time, here was a cabinet of exclusively Labour ministers with an overall majority that gave them room to act. The parliamentary context was the basis for much hopeful optimism. In 1974, an equally experienced cabinet ruled but with no governing majority at first and burdened by familiar divisions. There was no sense of a fresh beginning in 1974. In 1945 there was a freakish juxtaposition: an experienced government that was also new.

With the exception of the reticent Attlee, the big personalities would have flourished in an age when television became dominant for reporting politics, even if at the time only Morrison was gripped by the need to convey messages deftly through the media. They were a group of compelling, complex politicians with a profound sense of the past as well as hope for the future. They opened an era when the Labour front bench, in power (or later opposition), was crammed with charismatic politicians of depth. This did not necessarily mean electoral wins for the party or the successful implementation of policy, but from 1945 and for decades to come,

Labour fielded formidable front-bench teams. Without intending to, Churchill did the Labour Party a huge favour by inviting them to form a government with him in 1940. He turned a diminished party into a governing force.

Even without that invitation the senior Labour ministers in 1945 had reflected about ideas, and the policies that arose from them, during the economic crises in the years that preceded the war. Attlee had written a meaty book in 1937 when still a relatively new and vulnerable party leader. *The Labour Party in Perspective* challenged ideas fashionable at the time in arguing that Labour should form a popular front with the Communist Party, the Independent Labour Party and other radicals. He also opposed an alliance with disillusioned Tories, including Churchill. Instead, he positioned Labour as a vehicle for change in the near future and as part of his argument raised several ideas that would shape his later government. Arguably Attlee was one of the least interested in the power of ideas amongst his senior team, but he was more ideologically engaged than his managerial demeanour suggested.

In some respects, therefore, the election of the first Labour government with a majority was not a turning point at all. Labour has often struggled to win elections from opposition but in 1945 Attlee contested an election as the outgoing deputy prime minister. In some respects the election outcome also marked a continuation of the recent past in terms of policy and ideas.

Deeper currents were in play as they tend to be during phases of historic change. Most obviously, the war had necessitated a collective resolve and a degree of government activity that helped to make Labour's radical ambition seem more like a natural development than a reckless divergence from a conservative consensus. The climate also favoured a move leftwards after the war. Successive governments had failed to make 'a land fit for heroes' following the First World War. They could not fail again. The state had no choice but to become much more active, no matter which party won in 1945.

The Build-up to 1945

The Beveridge report on the future of welfare was published in December 1942 and there could have been no better prelude to a Labour government. There was not such groundswell before 1964 and 1997 when Labour won overall majorities from opposition. Those later victories were followed by a deep insecurity within the governments: Labour ministers considered themselves to be imposters disturbing the natural order. But by 1945 there was a match of sorts between prevailing ideas and the new government.

The Beveridge report came eleven years after a traumatic schism in the Labour Party. In 1931, the Labour prime minister, Ramsay MacDonald, had felt it necessary to follow fashionable orthodoxy in the midst of a deepening economic crisis. He was leading a minority Labour government that could not agree by how much public spending should be cut. Even if his government could reach a unified conclusion, it faced defeat in the House of Commons. MacDonald was trapped. When he could secure no agreement, he turned to the Conservatives and led a national government. Most Labour MPs opposed the fiscally conservative economic consensus presented by the national government, and so the party became a smaller parliamentary force for the rest of the 1930s.

By 1942, during an even greater crisis, the argument about what the state should do and the level of public finance required made the stressful, draining rows of 1931 seem like ancient history. Beveridge proposed to spend money, not cut it. His remit was to come up with plans to reform threadbare welfare provision. Beveridge, who had as big an ego as any of those who were to form the Labour government, did much more than that. Famously he identified the 'five great evils', Want (poverty), Ignorance (education), Disease (health), Squalor (housing), Idleness (unemployment), and with a great flourish, he demanded government action to address them all.[2]

Beveridge was an unusual figure, combining a passion for forensic detail with exuberant showmanship. His persistent use of capital letters in his report helped to convey an evangelism that gave the most complex recommendations an almost tabloid dimension. When his report was published he made a magisterial BBC broadcast as if he were a chancellor of the exchequer explaining a recently delivered budget. To the unease of Conservative ministers, he spelt out his plans almost as if they were already government policy:

> Disability benefit will be replaced by an industrial pension . . . proportionate to the earnings lost . . . the scheme provides benefits to meet other needs . . . including maternity, [and] training for new occupations . . . pensions will be conditional on retirement at work . . . those who need more than contributory pensions will have their needs met . . . the provisional rate of benefit is £2 a week . . . of course the security plan will mean a lot of money . . . amounting to £700m in 1945 . . . those are large figures but they're not large figures compared with total national income . . . the total addition from taxes and rates is at most £86m . . .[3]

On he went, as if the proposals were soon to be implemented. Beveridge was wily too, describing his report repeatedly as 'the security plan' at a time when those watching and reading felt deeply insecure on so many levels. He also mischievously sought to win over Churchill by linking his own ideas with those of a former wartime prime minister: 'I am seeking the completion of what Lloyd George began thirty years ago when he introduced health insurance . . . and what Churchill began as president of the Board of Trade with the introduction of unemployment insurance . . . I'd like to see him complete his plan . . .'[4]

Those references to Lloyd George and Churchill, both also carrying big egos, were not only clever politics. They were also a reminder that Beveridge was not an aberration, but part of a pattern of reform going back several years. As such, he inadvertently foreshadowed the ambiguity of the Labour government: one that followed trends from the past while being daring and fresh in its radical verve.

In spite of his revolutionary fervour, Beveridge was a Liberal. He was closest to the radical instincts of Lloyd George, another figure who helped to pave the ideological route towards 1945, as he suggested in his broadcast. The tone of the report reflected his liberalism as much as his recognition that the state must accept far greater responsibilities. It argued that policies for welfare 'must be achieved by cooperation between the state and the individual'. The state 'should not stifle incentive, opportunity, responsibility; in establishing a national minimum, it should leave room and encouragement for voluntary action by each individual to provide more than that minimum for himself and his family'. In celebrating the role of the state and the need for an individual to be responsible, Beveridge had hit – philosophically at least – on what Tony Blair might have later called a 'third way'.[5]

Although there were echoes with previous reforms, Beveridge's proposals marked a huge leap from the past. He was opposed to 'means-tested' benefits and supported a flat-rate universal contribution in exchange for a flat-rate universal benefit. In this respect he opted for simplicity and sought to avoid the complexities relating to income and when benefits may or may not apply. He also argued that a free national health service was as crucial as a new welfare state. In doing so he was leading the UK down a distinct path: his social security system proved very different from those of equivalent European countries. In return for national insurance contributions, it provided only a minimum guaranteed income, rather than the earnings-related income that much of Continental Europe adopted.[6]

The distinctiveness was less noticeable at first than the sweep of the ambition. On the day of publication such was the excitement there were long queues to buy it. Seventy thousand copies were sold and it was a bestseller. Although it may seem inconceivable today that a government report could generate such excitement, the ideas and the policies symbolized light amidst the wartime gloom.

But here is the first example of many that show Labour's win in 1945 marked a turning point and was not merely part of a new consensus formed during the war and before. Labour welcomed the Beveridge report more or less unequivocally, in some cases wondering only whether it should have gone further. The Conservatives were less sure. Churchill's chancellor, Sir Kingsley Wood, was alarmed at the spending implications and made no commitment to implement the report. There was nothing inevitable about the formation of an extensive welfare state in 1945. Nor was the NHS by any means a probable consequence. Following the publication of the report the coalition issued a commitment to ensure that in the future there would be 'a publicly organized and regulated service [so] that every man, woman and child who wants to can obtain – easily and readily – the whole range of medical advice and attention.'[7] The pledge was vague even if the direction of travel was clear. How could they 'obtain' help? What form would the 'medical advice and attention' take? The Conservative wing in the coalition felt compelled to address the shortcomings of health provision in general terms, part of a helpful backdrop for the Labour government a few years later. But the NHS was opposed at the time by the Conservatives.

Churchill was one of those doubtful about the scale of Beveridge's ambition. He gave a broadcast on 21 March 1943 entitled 'After the War', when he warned the public not to impose 'great new expenditure on the state without any relation to the circumstances which might prevail at the time' and said there would be 'a four-year plan' of post-war reconstruction 'to cover five or six large measures of a practical character' which would be put to the electorate and implemented by a new government. These measures were 'national compulsory insurance for all classes for all purposes from the cradle to the grave'; the abolition of unemployment by government policies which would 'exercise a balancing influence upon development which can be turned on or off as circumstances require'; 'a broadening field for state ownership and enterprise'; new housing; major reforms to education; and largely expanded health and welfare services.[8]

He was ready to announce a significant shift to a bigger and more active state in theory but his carefully calibrated words had several qualifications and ambiguities. He did not commit to universal health provision and the warning at the beginning about the pressures on public spending hinted at severe limits about how ambitious he would be once the war was over. The Conservatives' partial resistance to the prevailing tides went well beyond Beveridge. There were also some doubts on the Conservative side about Rab Butler's

Education Act passed in 1944, another significant prelude to the Labour government. Butler was a subtly intelligent Conservative. He was the most willing to recognize and adapt to changing times and became a key figure in the Tory revival after 1945. Again the wariness on the Conservative side was partly about cost. The central proposition of the Butler act was to raise the school leaving age, a measure that would require more teachers, classrooms and resources.

There were other potential causes of internal dissent too in relation to Butler's plans. With characteristic stealth and sensitivity, Butler had challenged the dominance of church schools by proposing to give more power to local authorities. The need to reform education had been recognized by Liberal and then Labour MPs since the end of the First World War. In 1918, Lloyd George, the Liberal prime minister, had passed an act aimed at raising the school leaving age and giving more responsibility to local authorities. Lloyd George's changes were never implemented, largely due to resistance from parts of the Conservative Party after the First World War and throughout the 1920s and 1930s.

But by the outbreak of the Second World War, Butler had become used to challenging orthodoxies in his party. While for some Conservatives, education was still seen as a religious responsibility, churches did not have the resources or inclination to meet the demand for school places. Churchill wanted Butler to focus on ensuring schools made do in wartime conditions. But Butler insisted that the education system needed to adapt more fundamentally. He was much less demonstrative than Churchill but far more ambitious, at least in terms of domestic reform. Butler looked beyond the boundaries of the Conservative Party, calculating rightly that in the national wartime government he would have the support of Labour ministers including the deputy prime minister and Labour

16

leader, Clement Attlee. In making the case for more secular education and a school leaving age of fifteen, rising to sixteen, Butler cited
the left-wing political philosopher R. H. Tawney, as much as more
conservative advocates of change.

The most enduring reform of the 1944 act established secondary
education at the age of eleven, while abolishing fees for state secondary schools. The act also renamed the Board of Education as the
Ministry of Education, giving it greater powers and a bigger budget.
The legislation marked both a move towards greater centralization
and, at the same time, an assertion of localism with councils acquiring more responsibility for schools. The act hinted at a much bigger
vision of how to manage a public service through assertive central
and local government. The hint was not followed through. Following decades of confused corporatism in the 1960s and 1970s, the
Thatcher governments from 1979 opted for weaker central government and moribund local government. By then, Butler's one-nation
Conservatism was out of fashion. But it was not wholly in fashion
when the act was passed in 1944.

It took the 1945 Labour government to fully implement Butler's Education Act with his legislation providing the template
for Labour's education policy. The new education secretary, Ellen
Wilkinson, from the left of the party, decided from the beginning
that funding the revised school leaving age and substantially restructuring the management of schools was sufficiently ambitious in itself.
During her brief tenure – she died in office – Wilkinson was criticized for not going much further but it was the Labour government
that found the resources to ensure more pupils could fulfil their
potential by staying on in school.

As with health and education so it was in other major policy areas.
An incoming Labour government was given a route map of sorts

from the recent past. The Emergency Medical Scheme introduced during the war led to much greater dependence on state funding for health provision: up to 90 per cent of funding for voluntary hospitals, for example. There was an obvious need for clearer forms of accountability given the higher levels of public spending. The need was met after 1945 by the establishment of the NHS with clear lines of accountability going back to the health secretary and the wider government.

Another dominant issue during the 1945 election was housing. It is usually a policy area overlooked as parties bid for power, but the issue could not be cast to one side after the war. Beveridge chose to describe it as 'Squalor'. There have been many housing crises after 1945 in the UK and yet they have never played such a big part in any subsequent election campaign. In 1945, there was a loud clamour for more and better homes. Again, the past provided a limited guide. The Housing and Town Planning Act passed in 1919 required local authorities to address housing needs with central government providing the bulk of the money. As with Butler's Education Act a new complex dance was taking shape between central and local government. But how was central government going to raise the money for a massive housebuilding programme? How would it be coordinated from the centre but with the added local dimension provided by councils? These questions were partially answered by the 1945 Labour government.

Perhaps the issue over which there was strongest consensus between the parties was employment, or the social and economic evil of unemployment. While the Conservatives and their newspapers were somewhat ambivalent about the other new social projects emerging, they recognized the virtue of full employment and accepted

18

that governments had a responsibility to achieve this objective, a consensus that remained in place until 1979. The wartime coalition and the 1945 government were the first of several administrations in the UK that were shaped by the 1930s. They ruled with an assumption that the high levels of unemployment during the Great Depression were an economic and social disaster.

In 1944, the coalition published an employment white paper that declared the government accepted 'as one of its prime aims and responsibilities the maintenance of high and stable levels of employment.'[9] It was finally catching up with Lloyd George, who had been arguing for government action to address unemployment since the economic crisis of 1929. But even on this issue there was debate regarding how best to protect and generate employment amidst the huge post-war economic storms. A Labour government had the political space to act, but had to decide on the means. They also had to work within a dire economic context, one that might have intimidated a less talented and ambitious administration to near paralysis. Subsequent Labour governments had a tendency to limit their reforming zeal in order to prove to a sceptical media and electorate that they were economically prudent: Attlee decided from the beginning that wholesale reform was essential in spite of the economic challenges.

In August 1945 the new prime minister received a letter from the Treasury that had been written by the most prominent economist of his generation, J. M. Keynes. The message was far more alarming and its composer a thousand times more authoritative than equivalent notes received by other incoming governments. In 2010, the outgoing Labour chief secretary to the Treasury, Liam Byrne, famously wrote jokingly that 'I'm afraid there is no money'. In 1964 the departing chancellor, Reginald Maudling, left a note to the new chancellor, James Callaghan, declaring: 'Good luck, old cock . . . Sorry to leave it in such a mess.' Both those frivolous messages had a whiff of truth about them. In each case the British economy was tottering, as it often is.

But compare those jocular warnings with Keynes informing Attlee that he faced a 'financial Dunkirk'. The war had cost the UK one quarter of its national wealth. With industry geared to arms production, exports had fallen to one third of what was needed to pay for imports. To Attlee's anger and alarm, financial aid from the US had been cut as soon as the war ended. There is much talk of 'boldness' in politics, usually when leaders are being cautious. In the first summer of his premiership Attlee made a genuinely courageous decision. He resolved to deliver the government's programme of reform and to retain the UK's status as a world power.

He sent Keynes to Washington to negotiate a new aid package. The economist succeeded in securing a loan of several billion dollars but with tough terms attached. Like the Labour government's loan from the International Monetary Fund in 1976, the deal triggered deep internal tensions, as the US told the UK to end exchange controls in the UK. The pound would be freely convertible to dollars by July 1947. The loan bought Attlee some time, but the 1947 deadline was a ticking bomb. No wonder the government moved fast. This seemingly modest, reticent leader presided over a government that passed 347 acts over the following four years.[10] It makes Thatcher's counter-revolution in 1979 seem snail-like.

Aside from the fraught economic situation, there were plenty of other reasons why Attlee's government might have been more cautious than it chose to be. The new government was seeking to change a country that had stood apart from most other European equivalents. As the historian David Marquand has highlighted, there was a fundamental cultural challenge to Labour's ambitions: 'Britain has lacked a state tradition of the sort which has shaped the politics of most other European nations. Part of the reason is that the doctrines and still more the ethos of early ninteenth-century market liberalism were more deeply embedded in her culture than in other European cultures'.[11]

A party's recent past is as important as the wider political culture. Following the 1980s when Labour was slaughtered in four successive elections, Tony Blair responded by being more fiscally conservative than his predecessors and declaring his willingness to work with those from other parties. The opposite applied in 1945. The traumas of the schism in 1931 when Labour's leader MacDonald formed a national government with the Conservatives and adopted a fiscally conservative economic policy were still fresh in the minds of the 1945 cabinet. In response the government was more determinedly tribal and there was an opportunity to mark a break with 1931 by being radical. For Blair in 1997, by contrast, there was a chance to be 'new' by adapting to the orthodoxies in fashion after eighteen years of Conservative rule.

Winning a Landslide

Before Attlee and his colleagues could contemplate their reforms, they had to win an election. There is a widespread view that victory was inevitable before the campaign got under way. This is not the case. There was certainly some polling evidence before the campaign that Labour was striding ahead in terms of popularity. But the inevitability of victory is impossible to prove. There have been other periods when the currents pointed leftward but the Conservatives won the election. The 2008 financial crash, which raised urgent questions about the nature of global capitalism, was followed by a Conservative victory in 2010. A fresh consensus between the Conservative and Labour parties about the potential benevolence of the state in the 2017 general election was followed by a landslide Conservative victory in 2019. In 1945, Labour faced big challenges in the election even if their pathway had opened up during the war and the economic crises of the 1930s.

One significant challenge was Churchill. In 1945 he was arguably the most formidable Conservative opponent a Labour leader could face. He was already a legendary figure. Attlee was a tentative campaigner and compared with the exuberant Churchill appeared to be retiring in his public projection. As is often the case with Labour as an election approaches, senior colleagues had their doubts about their leader: the party chair, Harold Laski, urged Attlee to resign shortly before the start of the campaign, claiming that his leadership was 'a grave handicap to our hopes of victory in the coming election. You should draw the inference that your resignation of the leadership would now be a great service to the party.' The terse reply has become justly famous: 'Dear Laski, Thank you for your letter, contents of which have been noted. CR Attlee.'[12]

As the campaign got under way, Labour's would-be chancellor Hugh Dalton assumed the Conservatives would win, an assumption that can often be self-fulfilling. Attlee himself expected a small overall majority for the Conservatives. He sensed that Churchill was bound to win, just as Lloyd George had won the 1918 election, a so-called 'khaki election'. Even on election day, most of the newspapers calculated that Churchill would win. The leader in the *Daily Express* proclaimed joyfully: 'There are reasons for expecting that, by tonight, Mr Churchill and his supporters will be returned to power.'[13] Throughout the war, Churchill had high levels of support. His personal ratings in opinion polls never fell below 78 per cent, and for most of the time were well over 80 per cent. Leaders with such spectacular ratings tend to win elections.

Labour victories in UK elections are never inevitable but in this case Attlee judged the mood music better than Churchill. He was not easily provoked and remained genuinely calm, quite a feat when the stakes were so high. Churchill enjoyed elections but was never an especially effective campaigner. His love of vivid language, so potent in the war, led him to sound over the top in the 1945 campaign, not least when he declared even before the dissolution of parliament that 'a Labour government would have to fall back on some form of Gestapo.'[14] The assertion would have been preposterous in any circumstances but was even more so as he was referring to a party led by Attlee, his reliable deputy prime minister for five years.

There was also another unexpected dimension to Labour's victory. In spite of himself, Attlee could be quite an effective communicator. He was never exuberant. He was not an orator who could cast a spell over an audience. He had no great interest in the art of communication. But occasionally he could cut through with the clarity of his thinking and his framing of arguments.

Attlee is the only Labour leader who has successfully reclaimed the term 'freedom' from the Conservatives. In the 1980s Neil Kinnock and his deputy, Roy Hattersley, tried to do so as Margaret Thatcher seized 'freedom' and defined her entire political project around 'liberating' the people from the state. In 1988 Hattersley published a well-argued and elegantly written book, *Choose Freedom*, in which he argued that the state could be the agent of freedom and not its enemy. He was railing against the mood of the times. Attlee was not as good a writer as Hattersley or an orator like Kinnock, who delivered several powerful speeches on the theme of freedom in the 1980s, but he had a crisp lucidity and was an instinctive reader of the political rhythms.

He knew that in order to win, especially after a momentous war in which the country's very freedom had been threatened, he needed to win the wider argument over the term. He did so in his response to Churchill's 'Gestapo' onslaught with an uncharacteristic verve. Future Labour leaders did not turn to Attlee for guidance as to how to frame an argument, but perhaps they should have done. For once, a Labour leader won the case about 'freedom':

> There was a time when employers were free to employ little children for 16 hours a day . . . free to employ sweated women workers on finishing trousers at a penny halfpenny a pair . . . free to neglect sanitisation so that 1000s died of preventable diseases . . . every attempt to remedy these crying evils was blocked by the same plea of freedom for the individual. It was in fact freedom for the rich and slavery for the poor.[15]

It was only through the 'power of the state' that people had become free.

Attlee recognized the significance of the argument he put across as he cited the words with a hint of pride in his modest memoir, published after he had retired. Given that some of the historic reforms that were implemented were lucky to get half a sentence in his autobiography, here is evidence that Attlee sensed his famous election victory was won partly by making a fundamental case and then by advocating policies that arose from it. Future Labour leaders who lost elections might have fared better if they had been as nimble as Attlee in claiming the vote-winning term 'freedom' for their party.

The drafting of the 1945 manifesto was skilfully coordinated by Morrison, the only senior party figure fascinated by the importance of projection and presentation. The document, *Let Us Face the Future*, was an artful combination of radical fervour at a time of historic change and a careful pitch to the widest possible electorate. In the best possible way it was cunning. At the end there was an overt appeal to 'progressives', including non-Labour voters. Blair also reverted to 'progressive' as his favoured term to describe his leadership in the build-up to his 1997 landslide victory on the back of a much more cautious manifesto than the one in 1945. But the Labour leadership in 1945 also sought to portray their more radical ideas as practical as well as ideological.

Labour's Call to all Progressives

Quite a number of political parties will be taking part in the coming Election. But by and large Britain is a country of two parties.

And the effective choice of the people in this Election will be between the Conservative Party, standing for the protection of the rights of private economic interest, and the Labour Party, allied with the great Trade Union and cooperative movements, standing for the wise organisation and use of the economic assets of the nation for the public good. Those are the two main parties; and here is the fundamental issue which has to be settled.

The election will produce a Labour Government, a Conservative Government, or no clear majority for either party: this last might well mean parliamentary instability and confusion, or another Election.

In these circumstances we appeal to all men and women of progressive outlook, and who believe in constructive change, to support the Labour Party. We respect the views of those progressive Liberals and others who would wish to support one or other of the smaller parties of their choice. But by so doing they may help the Conservatives, or they may contribute to a situation in which there is no parliamentary majority for any major issue of policy.

In the interests of the nation and of the world, we earnestly urge all progressives to see to it – as they certainly can – that the next Government is not a Conservative Government but a Labour Government which will act on the principles of policy set out in the present Declaration.[16]

While Labour was beginning to learn to be more agile in election campaigns the Conservative Party was suffering from exhaustion and, equally important, a perception that it was tired. One way or another the Conservatives had been in power since 1931. They had been the dominant governing force during the years of unemployment that were a recent memory as voters looked to a better future.

During general elections Labour is often seen – or portrayed – as 'weak' on matters of defence. While such arguments can be shallow to the point of absurdity, they also matter, symbolizing a party's 'fitness to govern'. To some extent, even with Churchill at the helm, the theme strangely worked against the Conservatives in 1945. Some of their number had been appeasers, supporting Neville Chamberlain, Churchill's predecessor, in his attempts to avoid another war by determinedly misreading Hitler's willingness to negotiate and compromise in the late 1930s. While Churchill had prevailed and became the victorious war prime minister, he led a party in which he had been in a minority on the backbenches until the fall of Chamberlain in November 1940. In contrast the Labour leadership had opposed Chamberlain's foreign policy and had joined Churchill's war cabinet. The likes of Ernest Bevin, soon to be foreign secretary, had proven themselves to be more Churchillian than Churchill:

> The Parliament of 1935 had a big Conservative majority, and the policy pursued by the Conservative government landed this country into war. It was due to the action of the Labour Party that this Conservative Government resigned. Mr Churchill, who had opposed his own Party, formed an all-Party Government which successfully brought us to victory. Now, a new Parliament must be elected. The choice is between that same Conservative Party, which stands for private enterprise, private profit, and private interests, and the Labour Party, which demands that, in peace, as in war, the interests of the whole people should come before those of a section. Labour puts first things first: security from war, food, houses, clothing, employment, leisure, and social security for all, must come before the claims of the few for more rent, interest and profit. We have shown that we can organise the resources of the country to win the War; we can do the same in peace.[17]

Most of the usual factors that stop Labour from winning elections in the UK were not in play. Labour were not easily portrayed as 'soft' on defence. They were evidently ready for government as they had been governing. Although Churchill and the Tory newspapers sought to portray them as extreme and dangerous, those claims did not strike a chord with the electorate. The modest personality of Attlee was an asset and not a problem. Not even Beaverbrook or other Tory-supporting propagandists could portray him credibly as a dangerous, fuming revolutionary. Labour won 393 seats compared with 213 for the Conservatives. The party had an overall majority of 145.

Attlee, the Team Manager

Attlee was a deft leader of his cabinet, at least until towards the end of his premiership. He was much less self-absorbed than some prime ministers and showed no sign of concluding loftily that he alone was fulfilling a historic destiny in which other ministers played minor walk-on parts. Aneurin Bevan had been one of his most persistent critics on the backbenches. Yet Attlee recognized the obvious advantages of securing such a passionate, articulate figure inside the tent. All leaders make such calculations. But Attlee was also self-confident enough to see that Bevan had the drive to deliver and the strength to take on the medical profession. He gave him the huge brief of health and housing.

When senior party figures put pressure on Attlee to resign, as they did on a fairly regular basis, they often had Ernest Bevin in mind as a successor. Attlee was fully aware of this, but still made Bevin his foreign secretary, a post where the occupant can easily burnish leadership credentials especially in the context of 1945. Attlee also made other calculations in promoting potential rivals. Morrison had stood against Attlee in 1935 and was no fan of the Labour leader. But Attlee knew he was a highly effective administrator with a background as an innovative leader of London County Council in the 1930s. He made him leader of the house, responsible for coordinating the government's huge legislative programme. This was the opposite approach to more recent prime ministers. Boris Johnson, in particular, appointed ministerial teams on the basis of how dotingly subservient they would be. Attlee's method, appointing big figures, led to more effective government.

Most of the time, Attlee prevailed in cabinet even when there were formidable dissenting voices. As for his own position as leader, when Stafford Cripps suggested amidst economic turmoil in September 1947 that he stand down in favour of Bevin, Attlee knew precisely what to do. He offered Cripps a new job as minister for economic affairs. Cripps was delighted, accepted the post and Attlee pressed on. He managed the scheming egos and got the best out of them in terms of policy implementation.

Attlee's cabinet were in their sixties and seventies, significantly older than governments in later decades but fairly typical then. Their collective age gave them the huge advantage of weighty experience. But, on the other hand, some ministers were quite often ill, exhausted and burdened by the demands of power. The education secretary, Ellen Wilkinson, died after suffering from bad health. There was speculation then and since that she had killed herself. Attlee took time off occasionally. Bevin died in 1951 while still a minister; he had reluctantly accepted the undemanding post of lord privy seal because he was ill. Others stood back from various crises to recover from illness in a way that rarely happens in modern cabinets of bewildered but youthful energy.

In October 1946 Herbert Morrison summed up the essence of the government's key objective, one that united the entire cabinet: 'Planning as it's taking shape in this country under our eyes is something new and constructively revolutionary.'[18] He was making a broad but important point. A British government planning ambitiously on several different fronts did mark a new era. The war provided the backdrop to this leap forward and the nationalization programme that followed the 1945 election. As far as Labour had a strategy for planning from the centre, it was largely to renew and continue the physical and financial controls of wartime, to help exports, to direct industry towards development areas and to direct the use of vital raw materials. The assumption behind public ownership was that it would lead to greater efficiency compared with the fragmented industries of the private sector. The aim was to coordinate production, distribution, investment and pricing policies within and across different sectors. The greater integration and central planning would lead to economies of scale along with the modernization of working methods and machinery. The government would lead from the front as it had during the war.

Deputy Prime Minister Morrison coordinated the various nationalizations. He had an expedient vision in which 'competent business people will be appointed to manage the undertaking, with a considerable degree of business freedom . . . but it'll be a public concern . . . the spirit of public interest must run through it . . .'[19] The railways, coal, electricity, gas, iron and steel were taken into public ownership. So was the Bank of England. Production targets were set across the economy. The model was accepted with little debate within the government or beyond.

Public ownership was implemented with impressive speed and yet the pace left many unresolved questions. Pricing policy was set below market levels. There were relatively cheap train fares and energy. The notion that government should set prices lower than the market went out of fashion from 1979, but became a big theme again when energy costs soared in 2022 and the self-proclaimed Thatcherite chancellor at the time, Rishi Sunak, spent billions subsidizing fuel bills. Suddenly a new political generation understood the pressure on ministers in the post-war era to make essential services more affordable. Labour relations were fairly harmonious in the early years of public ownership. Better working conditions were introduced for miners and after 1948 the new National Coal Board began an impressive record of much-needed capital investment.

At the same time the welfare state expanded beyond recognition, the changes being based largely on the Beveridge report. Within a year of the election, the National Insurance Act provided financial protection in the event of unemployment and sickness, and established minimal working conditions for the employed. The elderly received pensions. The Industrial Injuries Act provided financial relief for those who were temporarily absent from work due to injury and for those absent long-term. Later the National Assistance Act provided financial assistance for the unemployed. On the key election issue of housing, by the time it left office the government had built more than a million homes. New towns were planned to reduce overcrowding. These were major achievements, especially in light of more recent governments post-1979, who struggled to build more than a clutch of affordable properties here and there.

In 1931 Labour ministers were arguing about which areas of public spending should be cut. In 1945 they were investing on all fronts. The great enduring innovation was the introduction of the National Health Service in 1948 only three years after the election, a triumph of vision, will and remarkably fast pace of implementation.

Inevitably the focus at the time and since was on the theatre of Bevan's crusade against those who altogether opposed the concept of a state-financed NHS. Bevan's biographer and close friend Michael Foot described Bevan's challenge as 'nothing less than to persuade the most conservative and respected profession in the country to accept and operate the Labour government's most intrinsically socialist proposition.'[20] For evidence Foot cited Alfred Cox, the former secretary of the British Medical Association, who wrote in the *Health Journal* in April 1946: 'It looks to me uncommonly like the first step, and a big one, towards National Socialism practised in Germany'.[21]

With the support of the Conservative opposition in parliament the BMA refused to negotiate with Bevan at first. The consultants proved to be more flexible. As Bevan famously noted he 'stuffed their mouths with gold'.[22] But with unyielding focus, passionate spirit, prime-ministerial support, that huge Commons majority, and the support of most voters, Bevan triumphed. The NHS formally opened on 5 July 1948. In a land where 'freedom' was a contentious term people were 'free' to fall ill and not worry about the possible costs and availability of treatment.

A population accustomed only to a tentative relationship with the state before the war suddenly had free access to doctors, dentists, opticians and hospitals. Attlee framed the argument in favour of investment in his reforms with a striking persuasiveness. In the Commons when faced with questions about the cost of the national insurance bill that took legislative form in 1946 he declared with a resolute flourish:

> The question is asked – can we afford it? Supposing the answer is 'no', what does that mean? It really means the sum total of the goods produced and the services rendered by the people of this country is not sufficient to provide for all our people at all times, in sickness, in health, in youth and in age, the very modest standards in life that are set out in the national insurance bill.[23]

This was an astute argument, connecting the work and productivity of voters with the reward of decent standards to be introduced and maintained by the state. Voters are not known for making connections between what they do and the capacity of the state to deliver. Attlee made the connections for them. He was a far more effective communicator than his reputation suggests.

Ministers had no choice but to move with speed. The challenges highlighted in the Beveridge report were urgent and could not be addressed after endless policy reviews. Soon after Labour's landslide victory in 1997, David Blunkett, the new education secretary, joked privately: 'We've hit the ground reviewing.'[24] That option was not available to a government in post-war Britain. Here was the first Labour government with a majority and it was a landslide. There would be no problems getting legislation through the House of Commons. When MacDonald agonized what to do in 1931 he had no such luxury, leading a minority Labour administration. One of the questions MacDonald had had to ask when considering all options was whether or not any route would command a majority in the Commons. Attlee faced many pressures. He did not have to ask that question, at least in his first term.

The Pace of Change and Consequences

Because ministers moved with such commendable speed they had little time to reflect on unresolved questions about how best to plan an economy. What were the most efficient forms of public ownership? How to make those responsible for delivery accountable for their actions? When planning takes place from the centre, how to address varying local demands? What is the most effective way of measuring value for money and how to assess how much money is required for nationally funded services in the short term and to plan for the longer term? They are still unanswered today.

If there had been time, perhaps there should have been more 'hitting the ground reviewing'. Ministers agreed that the government should plan and organize like no peacetime government had done before. But what form should the planning take? In 1937 the economist and future Labour MP, Douglas Jay, argued in *The Socialist Case*: 'in the case of nutrition and health, just as in the case of education, the gentleman in Whitehall really does know better what is good for people than the people know themselves'.[25]

Soon the notion that 'Whitehall knows best' got bound up lazily in the eternal 'freedom' debate, with Conservatives seizing on the notion that Labour governments arrogantly thought they knew what was best for the people whereas the Conservatives 'trusted' the people with their 'freedoms'. Yet Jay was hinting crudely at what is an unavoidable question arising from state activity. A government raises money and therefore has a responsibility to ensure it is spent wisely. What is wise and not wise is subjective but 'Whitehall' has a role in deciding what is 'good for people' if it is providing the resources for public services. The issue of accountability, which institution or institutions are responsible for what, was an unavoidable area of contention within the government.

The setting up of the NHS was emblematic. With a spectacular flourish and determined focus, Bevan, with the support of Attlee, resolved to introduce a nationally available system of free healthcare with costs to be met by taxation rather than the insurance model applied in parts of Europe. All hospitals would be nationalized. The bill was published in March 1946 and was implemented after a further energy-draining two years. Bevan's epic battles took many forms. They included a significant internal debate with Morrison, who fought for control of hospitals by local authorities so that health provision was more accountable at a local level. With his background on London County Council, Morrison was an advocate of what later became known as 'localism', power being devolved away from the centre. When the 2010 coalition published its controversial health white paper, a document longer than Bevan's mighty equivalent that set up the NHS in the first place, there were proposals to devolve some powers to local authorities. The Liberal Democrat deputy prime minister, Nick Clegg, supported the disruptive and reactionary white paper, naively extolling the introduction of new powers for local authorities and failing to recognize the degree to which the wider proposals undermined the entire basis of the NHS.[26]

The problem with Morrison's arguments in 1946, and Clegg's later, was that as central government was raising the cash for the NHS it was not clear how local authorities would play a clear and accountable role in the provision of healthcare. Bevan had a more coherent vision though not wholly so. The NHS would be run from the centre. Regional boards were appointed that had considerable powers in terms of delivery and standards, but the responsibility for raising the money and distributing it still lay with central government, after a negotiation between the Department of Health, the Treasury and Number 10. From the beginning the division of power meant that the NHS proved especially hard to control financially as executive direction lay with the regional boards rather than the Department of Health which was negotiating the financial package.

There was reasoning behind Bevan's structuring of the NHS. He inherited a chaotic overlapping provision of local government and voluntary sectors. Meanwhile the Emergency Medical Scheme introduced during the war had already led to much greater dependence on state funding for voluntary hospitals. Like all health secretaries who succeeded him Bevan wrestled with the issue of accountability. He opted for a relatively simple nationalization. The voluntary hospitals became state-owned and therefore the government would be accountable ultimately for all health provision and the financial obligations. The delegation of day-to-day responsibilities would lie with regional and local bodies appointed by the minister. In the end if the minister disapproved he or she could change the composition of the devolved bodies. But Morrison continued to put an alternative case, arguing, 'it would be disastrous if we allowed local government to languish by whittling away its most constructive and interesting functions'.[27] Bevan prevailed but the debate was never fully resolved.

Bevan's other challenge was housing. Although more than a million homes were built while Labour was in power the government was criticized for not moving even faster. As Conservative housing minister in the early 1950s, Harold Macmillan managed to build at a faster pace of around 300,000 a year. As with other initiatives in which the Labour government was exerting centralized direction there were thorny problems over who controlled what, and who was accountable to whom.

In his role as the government's first chancellor Dalton decided on the level of money for new homes. Meanwhile the Ministry of Works directed the building industry, as the Ministry of Labour coordinated the number of workers required to build them. Construction material was arranged through the Ministry of Supply. Stafford Cripps as president of the Board of Trade was responsible for regulating employers. Councils were the local agents closest to where the houses were being built. Bevan was responsible in cabinet for housing, but the agencies and departments involved in delivery were many.

The various departments and ministers were not always dancing together and sometimes were not on the dance floor at all. Bevan was focused on the NHS as well as seeking to be the initiator of the housebuilding programme. The Labour government hailed the virtues of planning from the centre but had no time to work through and assess the best way of achieving delivery. The subsequent Conservative government, in which Harold Macmillan had the housing portfolio as a single cabinet post, improved matters. Macmillan's elevated position was unusual. Since 1945, housing has mostly been part of a much wider cabinet remit, one reason amongst many that not enough houses have been built.

There were similar blurred lines of responsibility following the full implementation of the 1944 Education Act. A new complex relationship arose between state and local government over the provision of education, the standards, the structures and the funding. Again it has never been fully resolved.

Even sympathetic historians of the Labour government are not especially exuberant about its nationalization record, pointing out that ministers more or less lost interest after the late 1940s. The key industries had already been brought into public ownership. Attlee and his senior ministers became swamped by economic crises and new challenges. After Labour left office in 1951, there were many internal rows over the purpose of a future Labour government and on specific issues such as nuclear disarmament. There was not much focus on ownership despite there being important lessons to explore. Arguably the financial and business guidelines of the nationalized industries were too restrictive and too many complacent establishment figures were appointed to nationalized boards, including peers, retired generals and other non-specialists. No workers were appointed. There was little planning to relate the activities and targets of nationalized industries to the wider economy. To what degree could public ownership boost overall productivity and growth in the longer term? Amid an ongoing economic emergency, the longer term seemed far away and fire-fighting took precedence.

Partly the verdicts on the 1945 Labour government's nationalization programme reflect the context in which they were written. By the 1980s public ownership was out of fashion amongst many in the Labour Party and some of the early verdicts of Thatcher's privatization were prematurely glowing.

It was during the 1980s, at the height of Margaret Thatcher's counter-revolution, that the historian Correlli Barnett made a wider argument in 'The Audit of War'. He suggested that Attlee and his ministers had made a fundamental error in not prioritizing economic reconstruction over social reconstruction. He described the choices made as: 'Social goodies rather than industrial reconstruction', despairing of Beveridge's influence in particular.[28]

In an illuminating and largely sympathetic account of the 1945 government a year after Thatcher's 1983 landslide election victory, Kenneth O. Morgan outlined the successes of the nationalized industries but concluded they served an extremely limited purpose: 'Without nationalization, above all, the morale and impetus of the 1945 Labour government could not have been sustained. For most members of the party and the movement that was its ultimate justification'.[29]

But in the years that followed Thatcher's victories in 1983 and 1987, and beyond the Conservatives' removal from power in 1997, the chaotic consequences of replacing state monopolies with private ones played out more vividly. The energy markets did not work effectively with companies of varying size gambling on the price of gas. When prices started to soar in the 2020s, it was a Conservative government that made use of a price cap, an intervention in a failing market that they had ferociously opposed when advocated by the Labour leader, Ed Miliband, in the run-up to the 2015 election. The privatized railways became even more expensive and unreliable under their fragmented ownership. Water companies were busy pumping sewage into rivers, to the alarm of even free-market, right-wing Conservative MPs. The rushed experiment in state ownership from 1945 looks more substantial in the light of the alternative chaotic arrangements in which governments had to constantly intervene in markets that did not work. By 2022, the transport specialist Christian Wolmar dared to publish a counter-intuitive book arguing that the nationalized British Rail was nowhere near as bad as its caricature suggested.[30]

Barnett presented a false dichotomy, as if there was only a crude choice between social welfare and economic growth. He was correct to observe that the economy tottered along weakly from one crisis to another after 1945. Industries that had suffered from underinvestment for decades – Barnett was also right about that – were having to adapt to the new challenges of peacetime production. Likewise, the spending demands on health and welfare provision inevitably began to exceed the original estimates. However, no government elected after the trauma of the Second World War would have had the choice of pushing Beveridge entirely to one side, or delaying the urgent need to address the iniquitous arrangements for healthcare and housing. Meeting these needs cost money. The scale of government investment contributed to economic growth of around 2.5 per cent per annum in the years of the Labour government.[31]

The space for such critiques as Correlli Barnett's was available because ministers in the Labour government made no great persistent case about why they were planning from the centre in the way that they chose to do. That is partly because they were not entirely sure of the answer. There was no blueprint for nationalization. Manny Shinwell, the minister responsible for nationalizing the mines, noted that he had to more or less make it up from scratch. As ministers often do, Morrison returned to his own past experience, in his case at London County Council when he organized the Underground and the buses under a single authority. Bevan had a clear sense of responsibility for delivery at all levels in the NHS and yet he had no choice but to give power to regional boards that were accountable to him rather than the voters or patients in the areas they were in charge of. He could not deliver it all from the centre, keeping an eye on every hospital. Meanwhile local authorities, excluded from the NHS, acquired responsibility for schools, but central government provided much of the funding. As well as questions about who was accountable to whom and who was responsible for what, there were other persistent issues. How to empower employees or users of the new publicly owned services? What happened when demand outstripped the amount governments were willing to spend?

Quickly the Labour government had to face the consequences implicit in the questions. The 1950 election was a dull affair. Ministers were exhausted. They had faced a series of economic crises, including devaluing the pound a few months before the campaign that took place in a cold and wet February. Cripps had succeeded Dalton as chancellor. He had resigned after inadvertently leaking a small item in his budget, a comically small violation of integrity in light of how most of a budget's contents are regularly leaked now. Cripps became the dominant figure in the government, pursuing a nuanced economic policy that included more rationing and tight controls on public spending and yet continued support for some social programmes amidst the impossible economic constraints.

Bevan remained close to Cripps. He much preferred him to Cripps's successor Hugh Gaitskell, appointed after the 1950 election, which Labour won with a tiny majority of five seats even though their share of the vote went up by 1.25 million.

During Gaitskell's brief reign as chancellor there was a totemic split within the cabinet. Bevan and Wilson resigned over his plans to introduce prescription charges to pay for increases in defence spending. In doing so they highlighted one of those great unresolved issues in relation to the NHS, the appropriate level of funding. On the whole governments have opted for spending levels significantly below the European average. Only the Labour government after the 2001 election managed to reach the EU average.

The division over Gaitskell's budget was far from short-lived. For years to come Labour were divided about spending levels and the importance of defence budgets. In this case Bevan and Wilson were proven right. Gaitskell's spending plans for defence were never realized. Subsequent Conservative governments spent much less. Attlee and Bevin were resolved to maintain Britain's place as a world power, authorizing in secret the development of independent nuclear weapons and being central to the development of NATO, which included a commitment to relatively high levels of defence spending. In planning to spend more than his Conservative successors deemed necessary, Gaitskell was showing that Labour could be 'trusted' on defence, an approach that later led Tony Blair towards his nightmare in Iraq. As for another Labour leader, Harold Wilson concluded that following the deep internal tensions during the rest of the 1950s and early 1960s the party could only win when an expedient leader kept some form of unity. Wilson became an artist in pragmatism and won four elections.

Attlee had to make do with two. After the landslide in 1945, 1950 felt close to a defeat, although he stoically pointed out that a majority of one would have been enough. Navigating further economic crises that had echoes with those he had been forced to address in the late 1940s, with ministers ill, exhausted and in some cases dead, Attlee called another election in October 1951. This was an act of generosity towards his opponents. He had no need to call an election so soon after the previous one. The Conservatives won an overall majority even though Labour secured more votes. The UK's voting system brought down the change-makers of 1945.

Legacy

The Labour government established a new consensus rooted on the left. The Conservative governments of the 1950s did not seek to reverse many of the nationalizations and, having opposed its introduction, came to support the NHS. Even when in thrall to Thatcherism from 1979 they had to at least show enthusiasm for the NHS. Later when David Cameron's coalition in 2010 briefly challenged the basis on which the NHS was formed, a succession of his health secretaries wore NHS badges in their lapels to show their support. Meanwhile the Tory administrations of the 1950s also felt compelled to build homes, NHS spending went up and there was no significant change in fiscal policies. The government had changed the political weather in ways the Labour administrations that were to follow did not. But the unanswered questions in relation to a more active state in terms of who runs what, accountability, lines of responsibility, and appropriate levels of spending, meant that the turning point in 1945 was not as durable as it might have been.

Future Labour governments were ambiguous about the 1945 government's legacy. The Labour administrations in the 1960s closed significant sections of the nationalized railways, assuming the rise of the car rendered some train travel to be costly and unnecessary. As a result, British Rail was associated with decline even when it dared to be ambitious. From the early 1970s, Labour became immersed in an intense internal debate about the desirability of further extensive state ownership. From the left, Tony Benn campaigned on this theme to the extent that by the 1980 party conference he was calling for the banks to be nationalized. As with quite a lot of Benn's crusades this almost happened, after the financial crash of 2008. At the time his zeal triggered huge resistance from various besieged Labour Party leaders. This was the nature of the debate. To nationalize more extensively or not? The question bypassed a potentially more fruitful area of exploration. What are effective forms of public ownership and are there lessons from the successes and failures of the 1945 government? Ultimately Labour's divisions in the 1970s and 1980s cleared the space for Margaret Thatcher and others to privatize most of the industries that had been nationalized.

Nonetheless, the domestic reforms implemented from 1945 brought about a range of sweeping changes unmatched by any administration aside from the one led by Thatcher in 1979. Although there was much more continuity in foreign policy, there were still significant differences with what would have happened had Churchill won in 1945. Self-government for India was a project driven by Attlee with the same speed and focus that accompanied his agenda for the UK. In the 1930s Churchill had been a ferocious opponent of devolving power to India. He was equally critical of Attlee's more ambitious policy.

Meanwhile Attlee's highly contentious decision, made without the knowledge of his wider cabinet, to develop independent nuclear weapons was made with no sense of jingoistic grandeur. Attlee recognized that though the US was a pivotal ally it was not always a wholly reliable one. He concluded that the UK would need options as a power in its own right. In foreign policy there was a Churchillian edge, more from the foreign secretary, Ernest Bevin, than from Attlee himself, even if the two agreed with each other most of the time. With good cause, the former Labour minister Andrew Adonis called his biography of Bevin *Labour's Churchill*. Adonis meant this to be an unqualified compliment. But the Labour government was the first to struggle with the new ambiguities of the UK's place in the world in the post-war era, as it faced immense economic challenges while seeking to remain a global military power. Britain had seen off Hitler, but only with the intervention of the US. Subsequently the UK economy was dependent on loans from the US with stringent terms attached. Its currency was devalued four years after the war. Where did this leave Britain in the post-war world?

By the time Anthony Eden became prime minister in 1955 no leader had dared to attempt a precise answer. Arguably no leader has achieved one since. The Suez crisis in 1956 showed that even an incoming prime minister with a deep expertise in foreign policy could stumble fatally. Eden was not alone as a prime minister trying to discover where Britain stood. There were many dramatic prime-ministerial stumbles after him. But his fall from power was darkly spectacular.

2

THE SUEZ CRISIS

The Churchillian triumph glowed brightly in the immediate aftermath of the Second World War, even as he was slaughtered at the general election held in 1945. As time went on, his leadership quickly acquired a legendary sheen, to the point where his mighty presence hovered over future prime ministers whenever they came near to contemplating military action. After her victory in the Falklands War in 1982, Margaret Thatcher often referred to 'Winston', as if she had known him well – which she had not. The use of the first name implied that she was a natural heir. In fact, Anthony Eden was the immediate Conservative successor to Britain's heroic war leader, having waited impatiently for years to take over. He was so conscious of the Churchillian legend that at one desperate point in the Suez crisis, he invited the elderly figure to join his government as a form of endorsement. Churchill declined, privately scathing of Eden's handling of the debacle.

Following 1945, the UK's standing as a great power was already in decline, as it lurched from one economic crisis to another, dependent on US loans and wider US cooperation to keep afloat. Yet, in spite of all the pressures, successive governments continued to prioritize spending on defence and its imperial inheritance, although the purpose became confused and contentious. Aneurin Bevan and Harold Wilson resigned during the final phase of Attlee's government over the chancellor Hugh Gaitskell's plans to introduce prescription charges that would pay for increased spending on defence. Churchill won the 1951 election on a manifesto pledging that 'To foster commerce within the Empire we shall maintain Imperial Preference. In our home market the Empire producer will have a place second only to the home producer.'[1] Much of the western littoral of the Indian Ocean still belonged to the British Empire: from what is now the United Arab Emirates via Oman and Yemen to Somalia, Kenya and Tanzania. In Africa, it was still possible to travel by land from the Sahara to the Cape without leaving British colonies and dominions. The Empire still encompassed such colonies as Malaya (now Malaysia and Singapore), Ceylon (now Sri Lanka), Cyprus, Malta and Nigeria. Most colonies would only become independent in the 1960s.

As Britain clung to its overseas territories, the first moves were being made on the Continent towards what would become the European Union, with the foundation of the European Coal and Steel Community (ECSC) in 1951 and of the European Economic Community (EEC) in 1957. Britain looked on with indifference, not out of opposition, but on the casual assumption that this continental initiative was not something for oceanic, imperial Britain. 'Each time we must choose between Europe and the open sea, we shall always choose the open sea,'[2] was how Churchill put it to Charles de Gaulle on the eve of D-Day in 1944.

In Churchill's final phase as prime minister, he had a grand vision of mediating between the US and the Soviet Union while reinforcing the UK's status as an independent nuclear power. But Churchill was exhausted and distracted. When Eden finally succeeded him in 1955,

Britain's post-war role was unclear as the US and the Soviet Union emerged as the predominant global players and parts of Europe formed a new common market. Nor was Churchill qualified to look ahead. His assumptions and views were formed when Britain's global might was asserted and recognized without layers of qualifications.

The Suez crisis was the first significant event that highlighted Britain's new precarious position. President Nasser announced the nationalization of the Suez Canal in July 1956. Britain, France and Israel invaded in October and November that year, then withdrew after pressure from the United States. The seismic events would foster a deeper awareness among some in the British establishment of the UK's limitations as a global player. But the British exceptionalism that was challenged by Suez never completely dissipated. There were noisy echoes from the Suez era during the Falklands War in 1982 and the invasion of Iraq in 2003. The common factors that connect the Suez drama with those later crises include a tendency of prime ministers and others to look back to a partly mythologized past for guidance as they made their moves. The result is a complex cock-tail: the fickle responses of the media and public opinion in which 'British exceptionalism' could speedily move into nervy wariness; unreliable support from within government and parliament; Labour leaders sensing the need to appear 'strong' on defence; prime ministers having to twist and turn in an attempt to prevail; and, above all, dependence on the United States. Future prime ministers sought to learn the lessons of Suez but often found they were grappling with the same challenges as Eden.

Eden became prime minister in 1955 after a long wait during which Churchill showed a marked reluctance to step down. Like many prime ministers, Churchill could not let go, even though he had reassured Eden several times after his election defeat in 1945 that he would. On the whole, prime ministers are hopeless at recognizing that their time is up. Eden had become almost as fumingly impatient as Gordon Brown did later. Brown was tormented from 2001 onwards by Tony Blair's refusal to move on from Number 10. He finally made it in 2007.

Unlike Brown, Eden called a quick election soon after he became prime minister. Enjoying an early honeymoon with voters, he won and looked set to serve for several years at least. Eden was one of the more experienced figures to have led a British government and Labour was looking inwards, conducting another post-mortem over why it loses elections.

Unusually for a prime minister, Eden was already an expert in foreign affairs on arrival at Number 10. Since 1945, several incoming prime ministers had reflected only superficially on international issues, even though foreign policy would come nearly always to dominate their tenures. Eden had been a foreign affairs minister for four years from 1931, then served as foreign secretary until his resignation in 1938 in protest at Neville Chamberlain's policy of appeasement of Hitler and Mussolini. Nearly ten years in the Foreign Office during the dark storms of the 1930s was quite an apprenticeship for navigating foreign policy as prime minister. In addition, Eden was foreign secretary during the war and again when Churchill returned to power in 1951. Margaret Thatcher and Tony Blair, in contrast, went to war as prime ministers with no experience in foreign affairs before winning general elections as party leaders.

Yet Eden fell from office over his response to Nasser's nationalization of the Suez Canal. The master of foreign policy was brought down by foreign policy. The sequence from Nasser's intervention in

July 1956 to Eden's resignation in January 1957 was shatteringly intense, complex and full of warnings for future prime ministers about the challenges of navigating military conflicts. The warnings were largely unheeded.

The Suez Canal had been jointly owned by Britain and France and was seen by both countries as a vital conduit for the export of oil. This was one of many factors that triggered in Eden an instant fury when he heard the news of Nasser's nationalization. Ever since there has been some doubt as to the form of Eden's angry resolution. Evidently among the immediate options considered was a military strike to take the canal back from Egypt. Eden's press secretary, William Clark, recorded in his memoirs that Eden settled on force at the cabinet meeting that followed Nasser's intervention. While Clark's version of events is widely accepted by most historians of Suez, some argue that a 'dual-track' policy of applying diplomatic and economic pressure to induce Egypt to negotiate, coupled with the threat of force, was his more considered strategic plan in July 1956.[3]

This argument, which makes Eden less bellicose, is not as outlandish as it might seem. Once the threat of military action is made, as it was immediately in this case, events can take a course of their own. Troops assemble. The media and the public applaud the leader's strength in planning a military intervention. A leader cannot pull back. Diplomatic options can be deemed by the warrior leader not to have worked. What is undisputed is that from the moment he heard the news, Eden was at least ready to use force in order to retake control of the canal.

Whatever the possible equivocations in his own mind, Eden was well equipped to take command given his depth of experience. Indeed, a prime minister never appears more commanding than when they become determined war leaders, yet paradoxically, as moves are made towards war, they can quickly lose control. Military leaders, the cabinet, parliament, the media and theoretical allies become unpredictable. Soon prime ministers can lack command on all fronts. At the start of a possible military conflict, prime ministers are widely acclaimed for their 'boldness' when they are nowhere near as strong as they appear to be.

When prime ministers contemplate or decide on military action their calculations are many. Eden's uncharacteristic impulsiveness was partly explained by the fact that he loathed Nasser and had done for years. With the invasion of the canal Eden had been humiliated by a leader he saw as an upstart dictator and whom he had long wished to remove from office. This mingled with memories of the recent past. As the 1930s hovered over him, he wanted to show that those who broke the rules could not succeed.

There were also domestic calculations. Eden assumed the conflict would give momentum to a government that had quickly seemed to be running out of steam. The domestic reasons for a prime minister going to war are often overlooked. They seem puny in the context of military action. But prime ministers are human beings. The smart ones assess constantly where any move they make will leave them personally. The only alternative to Margaret Thatcher going to war over the Falklands in the spring of 1982 was her own resignation. She was not being 'brave' as a war leader; she was doing what she had to do in order to survive. This was by no means her only reason for seeking to regain the islands from the Argentinian junta, but questions over survival in office are ones that understandably concentrate prime-ministerial minds. At the very least, Tony Blair assumed that standing 'shoulder to shoulder' with President Bush over the invasion of Iraq in 2003 would be the least unpopular stance with the UK electorate and media. At times he dared to hope he would get what his team described at the time as a 'Baghdad bounce' in the polls. Again there were many other considerations that led him towards a war that proved to be another turning point for the UK's role in the world. The fate of his own leadership and the way he had positioned Labour as a governing party were two of them.[4]

Eden was the opposite of most new prime ministers. Having spent so much time in the Foreign Office he had given little thought to domestic policy. The Churchill government elected in 1951 lacked verve and even though Eden won an election during his prime-ministerial honeymoon, his domestic programme was also uninspiring. He left those matters to Rab Butler, his unofficial deputy, and Harold Macmillan, who replaced Butler as chancellor months after Eden won the 1955 election. Soon after Eden's election triumph, the Conservative-supporting *Daily Telegraph* published an editorial calling for 'the smack of firm government', a phrase that has been used regularly since to harass various prime ministers.[5] Deployed for the first time, the words tormented Eden, who was a sensitive and shy figure, characteristics that blended awkwardly with his stubbornness. As part of the mix he had the vanity and looks of a film star. He was a complex public figure, as most leaders are.

As a result of Nasser's intervention, Eden was suddenly presented with a mission that had the potential to electrify his leadership, to deliver the firmest smack of government. Here was something to excite *The Daily Telegraph*. Like his mighty predecessor he would go to war for a cause he assumed would command wide support in the UK and crucially in the US too. Perhaps in his desire to show his mettle, Eden had not reflected deeply on the possible consequences of his resolution.

Instead his assumptions were based on what had happened in the recent past. For leaders the future is hazy, an intimidating fog. Often they turn to the past for guidance, even though there is mountainous evidence that history is a wildly unreliable guide. At first, all the key players in the Suez crisis looked back to the 1930s. The Labour leader of the opposition, Hugh Gaitskell, was one of the first. He felt the need to adopt a hawkish tone without being precise about what he would do if he were prime minister. In a televised broadcast as the crisis erupted, Gaitskell declared: 'It's all very familiar. It's exactly the same as we encountered with Hitler and Mussolini before the war.'[6] Labour leaders often feel the need to appear as 'strong' on defence as their Conservative opponents, at least until public and media attention move to a different place. Eden also made the same parallel in a BBC broadcast on 8 August: 'The pattern is familiar to many of us. We all know this is how fascist governments behave . . . as we all remember only too well what the cost can be in giving into fascism.'[7]

That phrase 'we all remember only too well' was more revealing than Eden realized. Too often, leaders remember only too well and apply what happened in the past to a very different context. Neither Eden nor Gaitskell spelt it out, but the implication could not have been clearer. Hitler was removed by force and should not have been appeased for much of the 1930s. The same must apply to Nasser. The newspapers reflected and shaped public opinion, as they continue to do at times of international crisis. They were hugely influential in defining the political mood during the Suez crisis and future UK military ventures. At first in the summer of 1956 nearly all agreed with Eden and Gaitskell. The *Daily Herald*, no fan of Eden's government, was typical: 'No more Adolf Hitlers . . . There is no room for appeasement.'[8]

The dictators of the 1930s, the responses of Chamberlain and then of Churchill, were all on the minds of leaders, editors and indeed the voters when they voiced their first reactions to the nationalization of the canal. Yet the past does not recur. Egyptian nationalism in the 1950s took different forms to the Italian equivalent in the 1930s. Eden compared Nasser to Mussolini rather than Hitler, but the context and characters were not the same. Crucially that was the view at the time of senior figures in the United States' administration and the wider international community.

The UK and the US

The response of President Eisenhower determined the shape of the traumatic sequence that led to Eden's fall. Perhaps the slight evasiveness in the otherwise seemingly pugnacious early statements from Eden and Gaitskell suggested a part of them already sensed there might be trouble ahead. France wanted to strike immediately. Eden wanted to delay a little in order to build up wider international support, above all from the US. It was not forthcoming although in the early weeks he dared to hope it might be.

The delay in immediate military action led to a lack of clarity in Eden's messaging to the Commons, the media and the electorate. Like many prime ministers, Eden was obsessed with the media without really understanding how it worked. During the Suez crisis he wooed editors and senior broadcasters, but never understood the rhythms of news and comment. As with John Major in the 1990s, the evening newspapers, a first response from journalists to whatever was happening on any particular day, could occasionally drive Eden demented with fury. Similarly, Major's aides sought to hide the *London Evening Standard* from him in the 1990s as the newspaper proved to be a draining diversion whenever he managed to get hold of a copy.

After the initial flurry of jingoistic media support Eden struggled to convey his messages during the crisis. He was effortlessly telegenic yet lacked the gift of accessible persuasion and could not compete with Churchill's capacity for language. In the build-up to a potential war, messaging is as important as any logistical preparations. Eden agonized over how to highlight why he was taking military action during his TV broadcasts and in discussions with editors. Part of his problem was not to do with presentational gifts; he was unsure what his message should be.

There were many reasons why he wanted to take military action but he could not articulate them fully because he had to pretend a desire in the short term for a diplomatic solution. Blair, a much more polished communicator, also struggled, to his surprise, in the build-up to the war in Iraq. Among many challenges for both prime ministers, their messaging needed to be at one with the White House, tricky when Washington had different ideas about what should happen. Managing the relationship was difficult for Blair and he was seeking to follow the US administration. For Eden the challenge was a hundred times more difficult.

Relations with the US were central to the Suez crisis, as they were in all future conflicts involving the UK. Eden assumed that, at the very least, President Eisenhower would not oppose military action; a fatal mistake. From the beginning Eisenhower wanted all peaceful routes to be explored. He was not even willing to display reluctant acquiescence. At first he was lukewarm about the intentions of the UK and French governments and as Eden dared to hope he would move closer to his position Eisenhower became implacably opposed to military action.

Administration lawyers in the US, including Eisenhower's attorney general, Herbert Brownell, advised the president that Egypt had a legal right to nationalize the Suez Canal Company as long as it compensated the owners, which Nasser had promised to do. Eden and President Mollet in Paris had questioned Nasser's ability to operate the canal, but the Egyptian president had craftily pledged to keep it open, and traffic increased after Egyptian canal workers replaced Europeans. Nasser was outmanoeuvring Eden.

Eisenhower calculated that an invasion would be counterproductive and would probably result in the closure of the canal, at least temporarily. He also worried that invasion would be perceived as an act of Western imperialism that could drive much of the Middle East and Africa into the arms of the Soviet Union. America feared the Soviet Union would take advantage, which it did by invading Hungary in 1956, using the chaos of Suez as a cover. Eisenhower could not have been clearer from the beginning. He wrote to Eden at the end of July laying out his opposition to immediate military action and doubts about whether the US would become involved if other options failed to resolve the situation:

I have given you my personal conviction, as well as that of my associates, as to the unwisdom even of contemplating the use of military force at this moment. Assuming, however, that the whole situation continued to deteriorate to the point where such action would seem the only recourse, there are certain political facts to remember. As you realize, employment of United States forces is possible only through positive action on the part of the Congress, which is now adjourned but can be reconvened on my call for special reasons. If those reasons should involve the issue of employing United States military strength abroad, there would have to be a showing that every peaceful means of resolving the difficulty had previously been exhausted. Without such a showing, there would be a reaction that could very seriously affect our peoples' feeling toward our Western Allies. I do not want to exaggerate, but I assure you that this could grow to such an intensity as to have the most far-reaching consequences.[9]

These were all reasonable considerations. Eden was intelligent and experienced enough to recognize that Eisenhower might oppose the use of force. He did not think too much about the implications because he could not do so. He wanted to act and that was the end of it. If he had reflected too much on the possible barriers to military action he would not have raised the possibility in the first place. As a result he did not reflect until it was too late. Similarly Blair was intelligent enough to realize that invading Iraq might lead to civil war in the region and that the intelligence on Saddam's non-existent weapons of mass destruction might be wrong. He could not turn his mind to such challenging themes because he had agreed to go to war alongside the US. His sole priority, as with Eden, was to persuade the country it was 'the right thing to do', not to reflect on the reasons why it might be ill advised.

Eden was in relatively poor health at the start of the Suez crisis, but he had been well enough to win a general election the year before. Subtle contemplation in July 1956 might have rendered him impotent to do very much, fuelling the perception of a weak, lacklustre prime minister, but his poor health was not the cause of his conduct during the crisis. Rather, the unbearable pressures were a factor in his declining health.

For all his deep knowledge of foreign affairs Eden had stumbled upon a conundrum that he had chosen not to anticipate when he first heard about Nasser's intervention. He needed the US administration to be supportive, and yet the US could be an unreliable ally. Thatcher discovered the same when she turned to her close friend President Reagan as she went to war over the Falklands in 1982. Reagan was ambivalent at first, fearing that a rout of Argentinian forces in the south Atlantic would destabilize the region, damaging his battle against left-wing regimes in Latin America. Thatcher was taken aback to discover that she was a more devout believer in the 'special relationship' than Reagan was when she needed him most.

At one stage during the Falklands War, Reagan sought to persuade Thatcher to agree a ceasefire. The transcript of their exchange was later published. Reagan managed to make one point: 'I think an effort to show we're all still willing to seek a settlement . . . would undercut the effort of . . . the leftists in South America who are actively seeking to exploit the crisis. Now, I'm thinking about this plan . . .'

Reagan got no further. Thatcher stopped listening and interrupted him: 'This is democracy and our island, and the very worst thing for democracy would be if we failed now,' she stated.[10] Reagan did not press the matter or perhaps did not have the energy to resist the volcanic eruption on the other end of the line.

Eisenhower was much more assertive in 1956. In a reverse of the build-up to the war in Iraq it was Eisenhower who insisted that all options should be explored in the United Nations before military action was considered. In an early phase of the march towards Iraq, Blair persuaded Bush to go the UN. He did so on the basis that the UK would support the US in Iraq even if the UN did not support military intervention, informing Bush 'we'll be with you whatever'.[11] On such a basis Bush had little to lose. Blair needed the UN to deliver or he was trapped.

There are other parallels between Suez and Iraq. The choreography of the UK's awkward dance with the US was shaped by the limited timing in which military action was feasible. Meanwhile the feasibility of military action was determined by how the moves on the diplomatic dance floor were progressing.

In 1956, Eisenhower's call for diplomatic options to be explored had many consequences. One of them was a fear, as far as Eden was concerned, that Nasser could drag talks out over the winter, when conditions made military action much harder or practically impossible. After proclamations of defiant leadership in the summer of 1956, with its whiff of glamorous Churchillian resolution, Eden found the hard grind of delivering almost impossible to handle. He was not only dealing with the US. France was also working to a different timetable, having sought immediate military action in the Middle East. Eden assumed at first that he might have to put up with some futile diplomacy for two months but then military action would follow. The US had other ideas altogether.

As far as Iraq was concerned, Blair stressed or pretended to stress that war would only take place once diplomatic options had been fully explored. This was never going to be the case. Bush had his troops ready to go and wanted the invasion to happen in the early spring of 2003, before the summer heat. In effect Eden's misreading of the US destroyed his premiership. But Blair was also put under immense pressure by an unruly and divided US administration. At one point, trying to be helpful, Bush suggested that Blair withdraw from the planned invasion if the domestic political pressures became too much for him. The suggestion was implicitly humiliating. Bush was confident he would prevail in Iraq without the assistance of his eager prime-ministerial ally.

In the UK jingoistic support for war in the media and amongst voters has a limited time span. The sense of 'British exceptionalism' fuelled by the Second World War needs to be fed with military triumph. Thatcher was fortunate in that the flag-waving was followed immediately by the task force heading for the Falklands and victory. In the case of Suez the reaction in the US meant that Eden had at least to appear as if he were exploring a diplomatic solution. By early September, only a few weeks after Nasser had nationalized the canal, the political mood in the UK had changed. The media and the voters had become impatient.

Eden's Confused Message

The debates on Suez in the Commons from early autumn 1956 to the end of the year were more nerve-racking, intense and draining than those that would precede the war in Iraq. In 2003 the Conservative front bench supported Blair. In 1956 Gaitskell was moving from his early defiant support for military action towards critical opposition, partly because of the reaction from Eisenhower. From seeming like Churchill in July, Eden had to convince MPs untruthfully that he was exploring all options in early September. Blair was in a similar bind over Iraq, unable to declare that he and Bush were planning to invade Iraq even without the authority of the UN. In Eden's case it was pressure from the US that forced him to highlight non-military options.

One of the best sources for understanding Eden's agonized contortions is Hansard, the record of parliamentary debates. With a much smaller media in the 1950s, Eden's main forum for making his case was the Commons. He did so revealingly and often. On 12 September, he told MPs: 'The Government have done and are doing everything in their power to obtain a peaceful settlement which takes account of Egypt's legitimate interests and which adequately safeguards, as it must, the interests of the many nations vitally concerned in the Canal.'

This sentence is illuminating. Eden sought to argue that he wanted a peaceful settlement but one that safeguarded the interests of those nations dependent on the canal. Given that Nasser had no intention of addressing those interests by giving up his new control over the canal, Eden was being disingenuous, appearing to share Eisenhower's priorities while implying that they could not be met.

In the same speech he was smart in the way he made his broader case. Eden was facing some criticism for adopting an outdated imperialist swagger in his determination to regain control of the canal. To counter such largely unfair claims, he portrayed himself as being an internationalist. On this he was being sincere. Or at least he had convinced himself that there was no lofty backward-looking imperialism in his approach:

'Nationalisation' is, indeed, a wholly inappropriate word to apply to Colonel Nasser's action. I suggest that the word 'seizure' would be more accurate, but if that should offend anybody—and I do not want to offend anybody—we shall have to coin a new and hideous word, the accuracy of which cannot, I think, be challenged. What Colonel Nasser has done is to 'de-internationalise' the Canal.

In other words, Eden was nobly acting on behalf of all who were internationalist and against self-interested parochialism, or that was what he sought to imply and perhaps believed. When trapped, prime ministers often come to believe contrived arguments framed for their own convenience. He concluded with another reference to the 1930s while blaming Nasser for rejecting diplomatic initiatives:

I should like to finish, if I may, on this personal note. In these last weeks I have had constantly in mind the closeness of the parallel of these events with those of the years before the war. Once again, we are faced with what is, in fact, an act of force which, if it is not resisted, if it is not checked, will lead to others. There is no doubt about that. If Egypt continues to reject every effort to secure a peaceful solution, a situation of the utmost gravity will arise.[12]

Eden was still defiant and yet he had no choice but to also become more defensive about his intentions. Gaitskell was one of those now putting him on the defensive by highlighting his view that UN support was essential. Gaitskell's speeches in the Commons over the autumn were also illuminating. They showed how quickly an opposition can move when media and public opinion have already done so. In the build-up to possible conflicts, oppositions tend to follow rather than lead:

I must, however, remind the House that we are members of the United Nations, that we are signatories to the United Nations Charter, and that for many years in British policy we have steadfastly avoided any international action which would be in breach of international law or, indeed, contrary to the public opinion of the world. We must not, therefore, allow ourselves to get into a position where we might be denounced in the Security Council as aggressors, or where the majority of the Assembly were against us.[13]

Gaitskell was echoing Eisenhower and reflecting an impatient wariness apparent in parts of the media. Eden was becoming increasingly trapped. With the US failing to support him he needed an irrefutable argument to justify military action. This is when prime ministers who are widely recognized as figures of integrity get themselves into deep trouble. Blair contrived disingenuously over Iraq in an attempt to escape his forms of incarceration. Eden did the same in relation to Suez.

His most desperate contrivance involved Israel. In October, a secret meeting took place outside Paris in which Britain and France enlisted Israeli support for an alliance against Egypt accompanied by a plan of clunky deviousness. The parties agreed that Israel would invade the Sinai. Britain and France would then intervene, purportedly to separate the warring Israeli and Egyptian forces, instructing both to withdraw to a distance of sixteen kilometres from either side of the canal. Eden, who had been wary of Israel's involvement, now colluded in the scheme. In the light of this subterfuge, stirred by Britain and France, Eden hoped to argue that Egypt's control of such an important route was too tenuous, and that it needed to be placed under Anglo-French management.

Blair was similarly awkward when getting UN resolutions to back the invasion of Iraq and in the aftermath of his failure to do so. In their different ways both Eden and Blair were decent public figures and for much of their careers were gripped by the need to secure the 'trust' of voters. The UK's ambiguous place in the world, defined by a contradictory mix of deep insecurity and a soaring sense of British 'exceptionalism' along with their own half-formed interpretations of that ambiguity, gave them no choice but to twist and turn when they undertook military action.

Eden twisted most desperately when he made another statement to the Commons at the end of October, by which time a large body of MPs had become doubtful about what he was up to. Eden was at his most devious:

> The United Kingdom and French Governments have now addressed urgent communications to the Governments of Egypt and Israel. In these we have called upon both sides to stop all warlike action by land, sea and air forthwith and to withdraw their military forces to a distance of 10 miles from the Canal. Further, in order to separate the belligerents and to guarantee freedom of transit through the Canal by the ships of all nations, we have asked the Egyptian Government to agree that Anglo-French forces should move temporarily—I repeat, temporarily—into key positions at Port Said, Ismailia and Suez.
>
> The Governments of Egypt and Israel have been asked to answer this communication within 12 hours. It has been made clear to them that, if at the expiration of that time one or both have not undertaken to comply with these requirements, British and French forces will intervene in whatever strength may be necessary to secure compliance.[14]

Eden did not add that the UK and French governments had agreed to the Israeli intervention to give them a fresh reason to take military action. By then, Eden was targeting a huge audience of sceptics. They included some of his cabinet and wider parliamentary party, the British media, the electorate and above all the US. He failed on all counts. On 1 November, the UN agreed a motion calling for a ceasefire in the region, the precise opposite of what Eden had hoped would happen. The UN did so with the active support of the US administration.

Eden was in a huge mess. He could not state the UK was on a war footing in the Middle East because there was no support in the White House and the wider international community for such a stance. Yet the UK and France were intervening in order, supposedly, to break up the conflict between Egypt and Israel.

In the Commons, Gaitskell tormented Eden over the lack of clarity. Eden had moved from a Churchillian war leader in July to an evasive, defensive prime minister by November. Again the intense exchanges in the Commons are the most vivid way of chronicling Eden's darkening nightmare. There were ironic echoes with the final debates at the end of Neville Chamberlain's premiership. Having resigned as Chamberlain's foreign secretary, Eden was one of the tormentors then. Now he was the struggling prime minister facing the apparently principled critics. Asked for an explanation of what was happening, he declared with an all too obvious evasiveness: 'We are in an armed conflict; that is the phrase I have used. There has been no declaration of war.'[15]

What did he mean by an 'armed conflict'? Wisely Eden avoided precise definition. Following the UN resolution calling for a ceasefire, the Commons met on a Saturday to debate the situation. The staging in itself was highly charged. Saturday sittings are rare in parliament. One was held after the Argentinian invasion of the

Falklands in 1982 and again when Boris Johnson brought back his Brexit 'deal' in 2019. The rarity in itself heightens emotions, the historic sense of significance.

By then Gaitskell was on a roll. He had accused Eden of betraying his country in exchanges earlier in the week. Now he went for him on the grounds of competence and judgement, the themes that brought about the fall of Chamberlain:

The Suez Canal is now blocked and that the consequence of the intervention by Her Majesty's Government, far from facilitating the passage of ships through the Canal, has had precisely the opposite effect.

Is the Prime Minister further aware that the Israeli Government have announced that the fighting in the Sinai Desert area is virtually at an end, and that, therefore, the original situation, from that point of view, has substantially changed?

The Canal is blocked, there has been no rescue operation for British ships, no British lives have been saved, and all that has happened is that the intervention of Her Majesty's Government on behalf—or, rather, against Egypt—has no doubt prematurely brought the operations in the Sinai Desert to a close . . . What Her Majesty's Government have undoubtedly done, of course, is to intervene against Egypt, which was clearly attacked by Israel. I do not know whether they regard that as a matter of which they should be proud. I do not know whether they regard that as separating the combatants. I do not know whether they regard that as settling hostilities. What they have done is to bomb a number of civilians as well as military installations in Egypt. What they have done is to destroy all faith in collective security. What they have done now, by refusing to accept the

United Nations Resolution, is virtually to destroy that institution, which the Prime Minister once described as the hope of mankind.[16]

Again there are several parallels with Iraq and one huge difference. Blair was under immense pressure from a significant section of his party at least to secure UN support in relation to Iraq, but he was siding with the US and the Conservative leadership was unbothered about the UN route. Yet at times Blair looked pale and ill with stress. Eden was under much greater strain with the US against his position along with the Labour leadership at Westminster. In the Lords, the archbishop of Canterbury argued the military operation might be illegal. Later archbishops were to become fairly persistent critics of Conservative prime ministers but an onslaught in 1956 was unusual. As often happens, the internal political pressures fed on themselves. Eden's Foreign Office minister, Anthony Nutting, resigned a few days after the Saturday Commons sitting. Another junior minister, Edward Boyle, stood down shortly afterwards.

Military Action and Fickle Support

A prime minister can survive the resignation of two junior ministers. Much more decisive, Eden also faced the more formidable challenge of dealing with the multi-layered calculations of the two ministerial heavyweights below him, his chancellor, Harold Macmillan, and his unofficial deputy and leader of the house, Rab Butler. Both wanted to be prime minister. For prime ministers there is nothing unusual in managing ministers aching with such ambition. A decade later around a third of Harold Wilson's cabinet hoped to succeed him.

But the stakes become much higher when a prime minister is in deep trouble. Eden made many calculations when Nasser nationalized the canal. So did Macmillan and Butler.

At first both were supportive with qualifications. Their qualifications multiplied speedily. They could see what was happening in front of their eyes. On the day of the Saturday Commons debate on 3 November, Eden delivered a TV broadcast. Although the most telegenic of politicians he was not at ease when speaking direct to camera for several minutes. The most famous section of his broadcast highlighted the degree to which the focus had shifted since the summer. In July Eden had taken some satisfaction in being like Churchill in his desire to rid the world of a 1930s-style dictator. Now he pleaded with his audience that he was not a casual warmonger but a figure that had always sought to avoid conflict whenever possible: 'All my life I've been a man of peace . . . a League of Nations man . . . a United Nations man . . .'[17]

The grainy recording of his address on YouTube has a ghostly quality, a retrospective symbolism, as if Eden was already becoming a fading public figure. In reality he was fighting for his political life, speaking a partial truth. Eden had been committed to the League of Nations and the UN, but he had also responded impulsively to Nasser's nationalization of the canal. The next day there was a big protest at Trafalgar Square against military action. This was another of Eden's minor worries, but like the much bigger demonstration on the eve of the war in Iraq in 2003, protests are unnerving for prime ministers. Demonstrations provide a visceral reminder of opposition anger in a way that opinion polls do not. At a cabinet meeting on the same day, Eden sought to lock his ministers into backing the military operation. He partially succeeded. But after tentative military action from Britain and France as part of the 'plan' to separate Israeli and

Egyptian forces, including a UK parachute drop on 5 November, the US sought a UN resolution to impose sanctions on the two European countries. Eden had no choice but to call off the operation. After this, the views and positioning of his senior ministers moved to the centre of the political stage.

As chancellor, Macmillan was inevitably aware of the economic damage that would arise from US opposition to the UK's military intervention. He genuinely believed that the consequences for the UK economy would be severe, but his economic brief was also a protective shield. It enabled him to accomplish a deft, political, convenient U-turn from support for Suez to calling for a ceasefire. At first he had been more gung-ho than Butler. By the autumn, following discussions with his counterparts in the US, he could see where this misjudged venture was heading.

The past had determined the early assumptions of all the key players, distorting their judgement, as it would with future leaders in military interventions. Butler's approach to Suez was framed by the 1930s, but for different reasons to those of Eden and others. Back then, Butler had been a strong supporter of appeasement, placing him in a wholly different position to Churchill, Eden and Macmillan, who had all famously opposed Neville Chamberlain's foreign policy. Partly because of his personal history, Butler felt the need to at least partially back Eden and be seen to do so. He had been a dove in the 1930s. Now he must be a little more hawkish. In the early weeks of the crisis, Butler tried to restrain Eden, but to little or no effect. His typically subtle approach alienated both sides. In arguing for a more restrained response he infuriated the early supporters of military action, while his failure to restrain the prime minister earned him the opprobrium of the plan's opponents.

Arguably, Butler's attitude was more consistent than that of his rival. In July, Macmillan was all for the use of force. He did not advise Eden to move cautiously. Then he made a leap to the other side of the argument when it proved expedient. Publicly, Butler defended Eden and Suez, while privately he was more critical. Of course, the nuanced approach rarely works when the UK is involved in military action: some cabinet ministers and Tory backbenchers regarded Butler as a figure they could not wholly trust, the supporter of appeasement now almost supporting military action but not quite doing so.

Macmillan was more skilled at being devious. The art of deviousness is an important qualification for leadership and difficult to pull off. It must pass largely undetected. A politician cannot succeed in their manipulative moves if everyone suspects them of being a schemer. Later Harold Wilson became famous for being devious, which meant he could not have been as devious as his colleagues widely assumed. In his response to Suez, Macmillan was more of an artist than Butler. Macmillan had more space to equivocate, both as chancellor and because he'd opposed appeasement and therefore had no need to prove his muscularity.

Macmillan's support for Eden's policy at first was sincere. Yet when the fragility of the enterprise was becoming clear, he discreetly questioned the strategy of the chiefs of staff and argued as chancellor that no risks should be taken until the US gave its full support. He made the case on the grounds of the economic situation. Butler was now leader of the house, no longer in the Treasury, and had no such ministerial cover for a shift towards overt scepticism – and he lacked the suppleness to find a protective shield.

When a cabinet turns over military action a prime minister is doomed. Blair knew he could manipulate most of his cabinet to stay on board over Iraq, but worried intensely what his ambitious chancellor, Gordon Brown, might do. If Brown had opposed military action Blair would have become as fragile as Eden. Brown did not do so. Deep down, for all sorts of reasons, Blair knew a split between the two of them over Iraq was unlikely. The leader of the house and former foreign secretary, Robin Cook, resigned on the eve of the Iraq war, but no other cabinet minister did so. Eden was under much greater internal pressure with his two heavyweight colleagues getting restless.

By November 1956 he was too ill to continue as leader and took a break in Jamaica. Butler deputized for him, as he had done for Churchill. As Eden's stand-in he had no choice but to be even more overtly loyal. Both Butler and Macmillan addressed the powerful 1922 Committee of backbench MPs later that month. Butler made clear his concerns about Suez but was in effect acting prime minister, and he struggled to be both loyal and disloyal simultaneously – again part of the artistry required of potential leaders. Macmillan was less constrained and used his limited space ruthlessly, highlighting the economic risks of a failed military venture or indeed any military action opposed by the US. Sometimes events and circumstances conspire to place cabinet ministers in a position where only one route is available to them. This was the case with Butler as Eden moved towards his doom. The obstacles on the route prevented Butler from becoming prime minister. The road was much clearer for Macmillan, the chancellor able to cite his concerns for the British economy as he challenged subtly the increasingly besieged Eden.

Eden never returned to lead. In January 1957, his doctors advised him to stand down on health grounds. This left Butler and Macmillan as the only two possible successors. Unusually for him, Butler was more confident than he had cause to be. Normally he was a perceptive reader of the political rhythms and possessed a well-developed sense of where he was placed at any given time on the crowded political stage. This time he misread it badly. In his overconfidence, Butler even went as far as preparing a statement that would form his televised prime-ministerial address to the nation. He was acting prime minister, after all, and after the traumas of Suez, he dared to anticipate the smoothest transition to him becoming the prime minister permanently.

In reality, he never stood a chance. Macmillan was a more textured politician who had managed his rise to the top with a greater sense of self-interest. He was the better Commons speaker, witty and combative, who'd made his mark as a successful housing minister, which was then a post of cabinet rank, and later as a stabilizing chancellor. Conservative leaders were still selected rather than elected when Eden fell. Senior party figures trusted Macmillan over Butler.

When Eden resigned in January 1957, citing ill health, there had been no equivalent prime-ministerial fall. Arguably that is still the case. In 2022 Liz Truss served as prime minister for only four weeks, but she had not won an election. In July 1956 Eden was enjoying heady acclaim for his 'strong' response to Nasser. The response made him fatally weak. Eden had suffered from poor health for several years and yet after his resignation he lived until January 1977, dying aged seventy-nine. It was the Suez crisis that had led to his fall. There was no way through for him. He had wanted to go to war, without defining the military operation in such terms, and discovered slowly over several months that he could not do so. His authority within his government, the Commons and the media was fatally undermined.

Eden, Suez and Consequences

The fall of Eden had an inevitable impact on his prime-ministerial successors. Although there was debate about the degree to which Suez signalled a more constrained role for the UK in world affairs, there was consensus on one point. The UK could not act without the support of the US. No future prime minister would risk a military venture without US acquiescence at the very least. They knew what happened to Eden. The sense of British 'exceptionalism' faded until the Falklands War in 1982 when it erupted with intensity on such a scale that it conveyed its own strange type of continuing fragility. After the 2016 Brexit referendum, 'exceptionalism' took a dramatic new form with much talk of the UK being 'world-beating' on many different fronts, as it chose to go it alone outside the European Union. But what would happen when the UK was exposed as relatively isolated in the second half of 1956 without overtly choosing to be so?

After Suez, the opposite dynamic was in play compared with the Brexit referendum in 2016 and beyond. In the most immediate manifestation of a post-Suez turning point, Macmillan sought to join the Common Market. He realized that the UK would be stronger as part of the European project than as an isolated power unsure of quite how strong it was, militarily or economically. Edward Heath had been chief whip during Suez, observing at first hand Conservative MPs changing their minds or intensifying initial doubts about Eden's plans. Macmillan appointed Heath as one of his main negotiators with the Common Market. The talks got nowhere, a failure that highlighted further Britain's vulnerable place in the world following the fall of Eden. In 1963 President De Gaulle opposed the country's application on the grounds that it was a land of traders not farmers, 'insular, maritime and linked by her exchanges, her markets and her supply routes to the most diverse and often the farthest-flung nations'.[18] De Gaulle had a point.

Macmillan's successor, Harold Wilson, also made a failed attempt to join, but De Gaulle cast a second veto in 1967, the year when Wilson was forced to devalue the pound. When Heath won the 1970 election his driving mission was to join the Common Market. He pulled it off in 1973, although in doing so he pulled the pin of a hand grenade, in terms of its explosive impact on British politics for decades to come.

Only Harold Wilson in the 1960s dared to defy a US president, by refusing to support militarily the war in Vietnam. Wilson's policy was an attempt at balance, giving the US moral support while resisting pressure to send troops. A rising star in the Labour Party at the time, Shirley Williams noted that 'Wilson was put under huge pressure by Lyndon Johnson who was very rude and very mean.' Another future cabinet minister, Peter Shore, noted approvingly that it was 'hard to imagine any other Labour leader resisting such strong American pressure so successfully.'[19] Later Tony Blair was to prove his point.

But in some respects Wilson was acting as weakly as Blair in relation to Iraq. Both were making domestic calculations even if their conclusions led them to move in opposite directions. Wilson worried with good cause about holding the Labour Party together if he backed the US by sending in troops, as well as the economic costs of doing so. Blair was concerned about what he considered to be his coalition of support that spanned Middle England, seats in the north of England that were to defect to the Tories in December 2019, and the backing of Murdoch's newspapers. Blair went with the US assuming that this was what was expected of different types of

Labour leader. Wilson went the other way in order to keep his party together. But both agonized about the UK's relations with the US, as they were doomed to do after Suez.

The Suez crisis began a period of muddled British foreign policy, half in and half out of Europe, hailing the special relationship with the US and yet with unresolved questions about whether the UK was a subservient partner or a force in its own right.

The ambiguity of the UK's place in the world led to the fall of many prime ministers after Eden. Suez was only the beginning. Thatcher, Major, Cameron and May all lost their jobs largely because of internal rows about the UK and Europe. Although he won another election, Blair's authority was never the same again after Iraq, in which he opted to back the US from the beginning. Boris Johnson sought to become Churchill-like in his support for Ukraine. He quoted his hero when speaking to the Ukrainian parliament and apparently also in his phone calls with the Ukrainian president. Some Brexit supporters argued that Johnson's assertiveness in relation to Ukraine highlighted a new UK muscularity outside the EU. But Johnson left office with the war in Ukraine ongoing and with layers of blurred lines that raised further questions.

With Eden as his foreign secretary, Churchill knew what to do in 1940 when he became prime minister. The challenge was mountainous but clear. By 1956 there was no clarity regarding the UK on the international stage. There has been no clarity since.

In spite of the Suez crisis, the Conservatives won another election in 1959, their third successive victory. Eden was punished for Suez but his party thrived electorally under Harold Macmillan, a prime minister who learnt the art of projection more speedily than Eden. Harold Wilson broke the pattern in 1964 by leading

Labour to victory with a small overall majority and in 1966 he won a landslide.

Wilson's leadership in the 1960s was more noteworthy than immediate history suggested. In their memoirs Wilson's ministerial colleagues tended to suggest that he largely wasted his years in power, especially considering his large overall majority. Wilson did lose confidence after the trauma of devaluation in 1967. All prime ministers who endure a major sterling crisis are never the same again. Yet the establishment of the Open University, the new Race Relations Act, the Equal Pay Act (implemented in 1975 but passed in 1970), an impressive social housing building programme (more striking given the lack of building from the 1980s onwards) and significant investment in public services all brought about substantial change. The social reforms implemented by the Wilson government in the 1960s marked a profound turning point, one that changed many people's lives for the better. For all the noisy protestations at the time and since, there has been no subsequent attempt to reverse the reforms. It is to this period that we now turn.

3

THE 1967 ABORTION ACT AND
A CIVILIZED SOCIETY

Some historic reforms are easier to implement than others. Indeed there is a pattern that suggests what type of change is relatively straightforward to bring about and what is so intimidatingly daunting that even the attempt to reform can weaken a prime minister considerably. The 1960s provide a template.

The social reforms, the most enduring laws introduced by Harold Wilson's government from that era, made their way onto the statute book without causing too many prime-ministerial jitters let alone an implosion within a cabinet capable of getting worked up about other matters. They generated a huge amount of highly charged and emotive resistance at the time, but have remained in place largely unrevised and have never been dominantly contentious themes in general elections since. They mark one of the most significant turning points in post-war Britain and yet were the political equivalent of pushing at an open door.

The contrast between the relatively smooth passage of the Abortion Bill that became law in 1967 and the doomed attempt to reform the trade unions in the final phase of the same Labour government casts light on what is possible and what is not in British politics. The

Abortion Act placed the UK well ahead of much of the world in its approach to the issue. The plans to reform the trade unions began with a white paper, 'In Place of Strife', launched in 1969. The proposals got nowhere, facing insurmountable obstacles within seconds of their publication. In the UK, seeking to recalibrate industrial or economic policy is far more challenging, particularly for Labour governments, than changing people's lives with the implementation of humane social reforms.

The pattern extends well beyond the late 1960s. After his 1997 landslide victory Tony Blair did not dare to challenge elements of his Thatcherite inheritance, out of an expediency that conveniently became for him a passionate conviction. Blair calculated the fallout of any policy initiative by what reaction it might provoke from Rupert Murdoch's newspapers and to some extent, in his early years, on the line that the *Daily Mail* might take. He felt their middle-England readers were his constituency. Yet with some initial wariness he became genuinely bold in the pursuit of social reforms, the most significant of which was civil partnerships for gay couples, as life-changing for some as the Abortion Act. The Civil Partnership Act was passed shortly before the 2005 general election which Blair went on to win. The supposedly contentious policy did not feature in the campaign.

Among those who had voted in favour were David Cameron and George Osborne, two Conservative MPs who took over the party's leadership in December 2005. Social reforms tend to attract cross-party support, making them easier and politically safer for cautious Labour leaders to contemplate.

They played a vital role also for Cameron and Osborne, who found it impossible to stick to their early tonal approach in relation to complex economic and environmental policies. In his first few years as leader Cameron's main slogan was 'Vote blue, go green' in order to symbolize a party that had changed and was moving to what is imprecisely defined as the 'centre ground'. But as Prime Minister, Cameron could be heard despairing about the 'green crap' being imposed on him by his Liberal Democrat partners in the coalition that was formed in 2010. The green crap was proving to be expensive in terms of public spending and living standards, and with some of his MPs. The historian A. J. P. Taylor once described himself as having 'strong opinions weakly held'. Cameron was similar. He lost interest when a slogan had to become complex policy. Having declared that his main priority as leader could be summed up in three letters, 'NHS', he authorized his health secretary to produce a mountainous white paper that proposed the breaking up of the health service. He ended up sacking the health secretary and struggled to improve the NHS.

More widely, at first, Cameron declared a belief in the value of higher public spending but quickly retreated to the comfort zone of turbo-charged Thatcherism after the financial crash in 2008. Cameron and Osborne were the only leaders of a supposedly mainstream party in the Western world advocating real spending cuts. Even President George W. Bush sanctioned a fiscal stimulus, as did the highly cautious Angela Merkel in Germany. The British duo wanted to be on the so-called centre ground but could not find their way towards it when contemplating economic policy and public-service reform.

But on social change Cameron and Osborne discovered they could be progressive reformers. Their coalition government legalized gay marriage, causing an inevitable rumpus in parts of the Conservative Party. Nevertheless, the internal furore didn't last and it wasn't long before some of the party's prominent opponents admitted they were wrong. For Cameron the radical reform worked on every level. He wore it like a protective shield as he claimed he was on the centre ground, when his other policies were to the right of Margaret Thatcher's. He managed to convince parts of the BBC, *The Guardian*, *The Independent*, the *Financial Times* and a considerable section of the Blairite wing in the Labour Party that he was a 'modernizing centrist', largely on the basis of his social reforms. Oddly in a country with a strong conservative streak, social reforms tend to last the course, coming without too many political dangers and often with considerable political benefits.

The path towards the Abortion Act shows why. By the mid-1960s the war and its challenging aftermath seemed like a distant epoch. The Beatles were at their intoxicating peak, the contraceptive pill was in use and the minidress was in fashion. After the austerity of the post-war years parts of the UK were 'cool'. There was much talk of 'Swinging London' and the 'Swinging Sixties', more enduring slogans than 'Cool Britannia', a description applied for a brief moment in the heady summer of 1997.

For those living in 1965, there had been twenty years of peace and growing affluence. National Service had ended in 1960, the use of the death penalty became more limited in 1957. Commenting sixty years later on the Beatles' first single, 'Love Me Do', released in 1962, the writer Peter Paphides noted: 'It sounds like the first young people with money in their pockets, walking into the void created by post-war affluence and the end of conscription. In this void, you can scream and cry and dance and lose your mind.'[1]

The Profumo scandal that erupted in 1963, during the dying days of the Conservative government, drew back the curtains on a more decadent hedonism: if politicians and glamorous models were having risky affairs in 1945, the curtains remained firmly closed. These developments were part of the backdrop to the implementation of the Abortion Act and the other social reforms in the mid to late 1960s. Almost accidentally they became the greatest legislative achievements of the Labour government that ruled from 1964.

They were accidental in the sense that they were not the consequence of a great political plan drawn up by the Labour leadership as it prepared for power. The major social reforms, the Abortion Act, the law decriminalizing homosexuality, the ending of strict theatre censorship, the Divorce Act that made divorces easier to secure, had not featured in any of the main parties' manifestos. As is usually the case in UK elections the main political focus and divide in the early 1960s had been over economic and industrial policy, along with debates about the provision of decent public services. Yet for much of the 1960s, economic and industrial policy tottered along erratically. The social reforms were the great leap forward.

The Abortion Act, which finally passed in 1967, would not have happened when it did without three contrasting men at various stages of their careers. They were all elected politicians and together showed the power of politics to bring about profound change. At the very least all three emerged unscathed from the experience. In the eyes of many, their reputations were greatly enhanced.

One was the youthful Liberal backbencher David Steel. The second was the ambitious and defiantly liberal Labour home secretary, Roy Jenkins. The third was the socially conservative prime minister, Harold Wilson. They were not acting alone. The legislation ultimately passed was based on decades of campaigning by women's groups and pro-abortion organizations. There had already been several unsuccessful abortion bills. However, by 1965, polls suggested that more than seven out of ten people supported some sort of reform, a relatively benevolent background for a major change of policy.[2] Prime ministers analysed opinion polls as obsessively then as they do now, although focus groups had yet to become another source of paralysing prime-ministerial fear. Nonetheless the failure of previous attempts showed that in spite of the public mood, determined political focus was required.

The carefully calibrated proposal to make abortions legal and available up to twenty-four weeks in a pregnancy originated in a private member's bill introduced by the twenty-nine-year-old Steel. Usually such bills are doomed. This one was not. Steel never became a minister, but later he was a leader of his party, the Liberals. Yet this single piece of legislation places Steel as one of the change-makers in the second half of the twentieth century, although his bill could not have got close to the statute book without the determined cooperation of senior ministers.

Steel was also lucky, as he acknowledged modestly in his memoir.[3] But good fortune tends to arise only when the political tides are moving in the direction of the politician's cause. Steel was elected in a closely fought by-election six months after the 1964 general election. If he had lost there would have been no legislation forthcoming in the politically convenient form that it took, a private member's bill that allowed the Labour government to be one step removed, a useful place to be when emotive issues are under consideration. On entering the Commons, Steel put his name forward in the ballot for members' bills and came third, giving him a rare chance. He described the ballot as an 'annual raffle' for backbenchers.[4] He was one of the lucky winners. The device is usually an opportunity for an MP to highlight briefly a concern or passion and then everyone moves on, including the MP espousing the cause. In this case, senior ministers had different ideas.

Steel's next bit of serendipity related to the pivotal issue of timing. The ballot took place after the election in 1966, which unusually had been held in March – most general elections take place in the summer or autumn. The early poll meant there was an exceptionally long parliamentary session, starting in the spring of 1966 and going all the way through to the summer and early autumn of the following year. Steel's bill did not become law until October 1967. He needed the time for it to progress and he got it, partly because the parliamentary session lasted eighteen months. According to Steel, 'we needed every week of that to get the bill through'.[5]

Steel suggests with good cause that his next crucial element of good fortune was that all the key Labour ministers were actively supportive. The Home Office minister, Dick Taverne, a close friend and ally of Jenkins, contacted Steel on the day his bill was selected to express his backing. The health minister, Kenneth Robinson, had been the author of one of the six previous attempts to legislate on the issue of abortion. None of them found sufficient parliamentary time. Steel was also working with a minister of health who was 'openly committed to this cause'.[6] Meanwhile the father of Labour's chief whip John Silkin had been promoting an abortion bill in the Lords which Steel had in effect inherited as the basis for his. Lastly, Douglas Houghton, the chairman of the parliamentary Labour Party, was married to the then chair of the Abortion Law Reform Association. Unusually for an ambitious plan, the political forces were aligned neatly.

The Abortion Law Reform Association played a significant role in guiding Steel towards this issue as he decided what cause to adopt for his bill. Formed in 1936 the pressure group was assiduous in engaging not only with MPs but also parliamentary candidates. During various elections in which he had stood, Steel had filled in a questionnaire from ALRA stating that he was in favour of changes to the abortion laws.

ALRA was a small but astute pressure group, knowing where to focus most of its efforts. From the 1950s, ALRA increasingly turned its attention to the House of Commons. No major party was willing to consider abortion law reform as party policy, so in the 1950s and early 1960s ALRA worked on converting individual MPs, mostly from the Labour Party, to the cause. After Labour's big election win in 1966, there were a lot of new and youngish MPs in the Commons to target.

Steel's biggest piece of luck was that Roy Jenkins was home secretary. Jenkins became the star of the 1960s Labour government, with his huge appetite for work and fun. He wore expensive suits, drank vintage claret, spent weekends playing tennis and sometimes having affairs with women from more lavish backgrounds than his own. Yet he was nowhere near as stuffy or precious as he could appear to be. He had an intense interest in other people, and a desire to engage that was fairly egalitarian, extending to the views of local voters when out on the campaign trail. He had curiosity and was a good listener.

Jenkins was widely seen, and to some extent saw himself, as a Labour liberal, at ease with the Liberal Party at a time when his senior colleagues tended to view the party with patronizing indifference. His liberal instincts were also to play a part in his final rise and fall in the 1980s as he renewed his partnership with Steel for a much wider political project, the creation of the SDP/Liberal alliance. Jenkins's reforms as home secretary defined the 'permissiveness' of the late 1960s as much as any feted rock group or libertarian celebrity from that decade. Indeed, his mastery of legislative change shows why politics matters more than some voters dare to concede. He gave Steel the time required for his bill to take legislative form and also spoke in its favour. In his memoir he noted that 'while members of the cabinet would be free to vote against, I would be free to speak in favour from the despatch box.'[7] He did so with energy and verve. There were several all-night sittings in the Commons during July 1967 before the bill became an act the following October.

Jenkins's tenure at the Home Office had a consistent theme, a commitment to social liberalism that extended well beyond his support for the abortion bill. This tendency is highly unusual in this particular cabinet post and framing a recognizable narrative at the Home Office is not easy. Most home secretaries stagger from one unforeseen crisis to another without leaving a distinct legacy to accompany their hyperactivity. Jenkins had a resolute sense of mission that transcended the unpredictable eruptions of events. As well as Steel's bill he supported the Labour MP Leo Abse and his bill that sought to decriminalize homosexuality, a proposal he described as an 'important and civilizing measure'. More widely he abolished the use of flogging in prisons and supported measures aimed at ending censorship in the theatre. He also announced that he would introduce legislation banning racial discrimination in employment, which took legal form in the Race Relations Act, passed once he had moved to the Treasury. As one senior Home Office official, Philip Allen, noted later: 'They would never have become law without him'.[8]

Part of Jenkins's artistry, at least in this stage of his political career, was an ability to find the right language to make a contentious case. In a speech made in 1969 he argued that the social reforms made 'us a more civilized society'.[9] He often deployed the term 'civilized', which is deeply reassuring. The phrase 'permissive society' was one he never used. It was deployed more by his critics. The evangelical social conservative Mary Whitehouse, a celebrity campaigner in the

1970s, spat out the two words to show her contempt, harder to do when referring to a 'civilized' act.

Jenkins and Steel proved to be a formidable partnership. The home secretary facilitated and put the broad case. Steel was a details man, subtly forensic, showing some early signs of the guile that played its part in the formation of the SDP/Liberal alliance in 1981. He framed his bill with the assistance of the Labour MP Alex Eadie and the Conservative peer Lord Lambton, cooperation that illustrated cross-party support. The Commons' chamber is built to be tribal, two sides screaming at each other. The political intensity inevitably falls when the disputes are not wholly defined by party affiliation. Given that social reforms are not often determined by party loyalty, the political mood is much calmer in parliament. A government's opponents are unable to claim that its plans will wreck the country when some of the advocates are sitting beside them on the same benches.

Steel liaised openly with the Labour whips in the Commons but also worked with what he described as an 'unofficial Conservative whips' operation'. In his words, 'there were a lot of Conservative MPs who wanted the bill to succeed'.[10] Outside parliament he had the continued support of the Abortion Law Reform Association. The British Medical Association and the Royal College of General Practitioners Association were also active backers, mainly owing to the number of women who went through the trauma of illegal back-street abortion. The bill was carefully framed to counter overblown claims that Steel was seeking indiscriminate access to abortions.

As a biographer himself, Jenkins was an accomplished observer of political figures and he was impressed with Steel: 'He must have been under considerable pressure. I think that as a young member of the house with a marginal constituency and without a great party machine behind him, he has shown exceptional courage.'[11]

Neither Jenkins nor Steel could have prevailed without the tacit support of the Prime Minister, Harold Wilson. He had different governing priorities to Jenkins and was as distant in temperament from the 'Swinging Sixties' as some of the Conservative MPs opposed to legalizing abortion, even if he did arrange craftily to be photographed with the Beatles on several occasions. As a mighty prime minister re-elected by a landslide in 1966, he could have stopped the social reforms from being implemented if he had wanted: he would have had the backing of other senior ministers including the politically muscular chancellor and fellow social conservative James Callaghan. But he did not.

Wilson was a sharp reader of the political rhythms. He noted the opinion polls showing a majority of voters supported the reforms and he knew his landslide victory had led to a much bigger and younger parliamentary Labour Party, ready to accept or to actively support abortion. According to Jenkins, 'a substantial majority of ministers' were in favour of reforms in relation to abortion and homosexuality. In his memoir, Jenkins suggests that Wilson gave him more political opportunities than his close friend Hugh Gaitskell would have done had he lived.[12]

Inevitably Wilson had some doubts about Jenkins's liberalizing agenda. He was particularly worked up about the lifting of theatre censorship, specifically because he was worried about a forthcoming play about his wife Mary. But he wisely decided that this was not a strong enough reason to block the legislation. By choosing not to be a prime-ministerial barrier, Wilson played his part in all the significant social reforms of the mid to late 1960s. The 1968 Theatres Act followed the pattern of the abortion legislation in that Jenkins was a passionately sincere advocate in lifting outdated censorship rules. Wilson noted that popular opinion on the whole backed his home secretary, including prominent writers, actors and directors. Wilson had made 'modernization' his theme from the early 1960s. He did not have social reforms in mind at the time but he noted the anachronism of the centuries-old practice in which censorship of the British stage was conducted through the office of the lord chamberlain. Censorship in this form and any other was scrapped in 1968. Productions became more experimental and daring. They would not have been to Wilson's taste but they would not have happened had he wanted to block the change.

Similarly without enthusiasm Wilson sought no prime-ministerial veto in relation to abortion. The key battle was being fought out in the Commons, and the parliamentary opposition in 1966 and 1967 lacked the leadership of the pro-abortion MPs. They assumed that their best weapon would be lack of parliamentary time for the proposals to reach the statute book, underestimating the determination of Labour ministers to ensure the bill became law. The Conservative MP Norman St John-Stevas and his fellow opponents tested the bill line by line during the committee stage, partly as a wrecking tactic. In response the government gave it more time; and as Steel pointed out, he was pursuing a cause in the longest possible parliamentary session. At its final third reading the bill was passed with 167 in favour and only 83 against. The opponents had run out of steam.

Their arguments had been relatively easy for supporters of the bill to dissect and discredit. Early on, the anti-choice campaigners and parliamentarians recognized that their moral and religious arguments would not prevail with the majority of MPs or indeed the wider electorate. They constantly changed their ground, moving away from the principle to the apparent practical implications, claiming that abortion was a dangerous operation that posed great risks to women and therefore that by opposing legal abortion they were doing women a good turn and saving them from harm. When opponents regularly change their arguments, the other side tends to be winning.

After the legislation had been implemented statistics showed that abortion in the hands of the medical profession was safe. The opponents of a liberal abortion law moved their ground again by claiming there were adverse mental effects and psychological harm. The act endured partly because anti-abortion campaigners continually shifted their case. Supporters of the act never felt at risk politically or worried about the substance of their case on the basis of the onslaught from the anti-abortion lobby.

A later outburst in 1975 from the sometimes intimidatingly fluent writer and broadcaster Malcolm Muggeridge was typical. He denounced the act as 'a transgression against the very basis of our mortal existence and symptomatic of all that has gone wrong with Britain'.[13] A stylishly accessible writer, Muggeridge could frame arguments if he chose to do so, but opted for the cathartic scream in ways that left the act undisturbed.

In 1989, the Commons staged one of its regular debates on the Abortion Act. This was two years after Margaret Thatcher's third landslide election victory and her parliamentary party was not packed with progressive liberals. Nonetheless opponents of the Abortion Act had to put up with a debate staged at five o'clock in the morning. The chamber was virtually empty. One of the speakers was the Conservative MP Ken Hargreaves, who claimed to note a more propitious context for opponents of the legislation:

At the end of a parliamentary Session which has seen the pro-life movement inside and outside Parliament at its most active, it is appropriate that we should debate the administration of the Abortion Act, although some of us would have preferred the debate to take place at a more civilised time.[14]

His argument in some senses was that the Abortion Act had not been effective enough:

It was said at that time that the Act would reduce the rate of illegitimacy. Now, over 21 years later, it is running at 15 per cent and rising. We were assured in 1967 that the Act would mean that every child would be a wanted child. Today, every time we pick up a newspaper we read of yet more cases of sexual or physical child abuse. In 1967, women were assured that the Abortion Act would make them free. Today, there is a dramatic increase in requests for post-abortion counselling.

The Labour MP Jo Richardson put the case for the act. She sounded like a lofty minister rather than an MP who had been on the opposition benches for a decade. On this she was speaking with the prevailing mood.

I remind the House that there have been 14 Commons attempts by anti-abortion people to try to change the Abortion Act and two Lords Bills on the subject. All 16 attempts were introduced over the past 20 years. I have not been involved in all of them, but I have been involved in a good many—I am not an unfeeling person, contrary to what some hon. Members might think—and I have watched carefully and I have heard the same arguments, and I am not at all convinced that there is any need to do more than improve the Abortion Act by going a little further.

I have added up the time that has been spent over the past few years on debating abortion Bills and private Members' Bills and added on the time spent on private Members' motions about private Members' Bills on abortion, and ten-minute Bills and Adjournment debates. Parliament has spent more than 350 hours on the issue. Those 350 hours could have been more practically spent.

The 350 hours of debate changed nothing, while the impact of the Abortion Act was immediate. The rate of legal abortions rose sharply. While 2,800 legal terminations were reported in the whole of 1962, almost 10,000 were performed in the fourth quarter of 1968 alone. Numbers continued to increase rapidly over subsequent years, reaching 167,149 in 1973 for England and Wales alone, before declining slightly over subsequent years. Britain was at the international vanguard of liberalizing legislation. For all the attempts in parliament to neuter the act, it was amended only once, when the time limit for an abortion was reduced from twenty-eight weeks to twenty-four in 1990.

Almost precisely the same pattern followed in relation to the Sexual Offences Act, passed in 1967, legislation that legalized consensual homosexual acts in private and over the age of twenty-one. As in the abortion campaign, the recent past played an important role in framing opinion. In the 1950s, there was an increase of prosecutions against homosexual men and several well-known figures were convicted. The government set up a committee led by John Wolfenden to consider the laws on homosexuality. In 1957, the committee published the Wolfenden report, which recommended the decriminalization of homosexual activity between men above the age of twenty-one. The report sought to establish a 'realm of private that is . . . not the law's business'.[15] Wolfenden and his committee members took three years to reach this relatively daring conclusion. They were still premature in their considered reflections. The then prime minister, Harold Macmillan, did not act due to fear of a public backlash. But Wolfenden framed arguments that would come into play only a few years later under a different government. In 1965, during the first term of Wilson's administration, several politicians sponsored a sexual offences bill, another private member's bill, that drew heavily on the Wolfenden report. The key sponsors were Humphry Berkeley, a Conservative MP, Leo Abse, a Labour MP, and Lord Arran, a Conservative peer. As with the abortion legislation, cross-party support helped to create a relatively safe political context. This was not a Labour government putting its neck on the line. At the same time opinion polls were suggesting that most voters did not believe that homosexuality should be a crime. By 1965, a majority of MPs appeared to be in favour of changing the law. Berkeley's bill passed a second reading by a decent margin. This was when Harold Wilson was leading with a tiny overall majority.

Its passage was interrupted by the 1966 general election, but the changed political context helped the cause. Labour's landslide victory increased the number of MPs who were likely to support the bill. Abse re-introduced the bill with the active support of Jenkins and the acquiescence of Wilson. The proposal legalized acts that met the conditions of two consenting adults in private as proposed by Wolfenden. It did not apply to Scotland and Northern Ireland. Both the bigger parties permitted a free vote. Labour and Liberal members were mostly in favour, while Conservative members were largely opposed. But there were significant divisions within the Tory parliamentary party. Margaret Thatcher and Enoch Powell were among the Conservative MPs voting in favour. They did so largely on the grounds that it was not the business of the state to interfere with what adults did in private, a small state stance that shows how those on the Conservative right can be part of a coalition in favour of social freedoms.

Consequences

The success of abortion reform in the 1960s and its subsequent support did not mean that governments were quick to recognize that the limited empowerment of women should lead to more women exerting power. The Abortion Act was passed by a House of Commons that was largely male. Nearly a quarter of a century later in November 1990, when the relatively liberal John Major became prime minister, he selected an all-male cabinet, adding Gillian Shephard in a last-minute panic when an adviser noticed that there was not a single woman in his top ministerial team.

The decision of Labour to support positive discrimination in selecting female candidates for the 1997 election was revolutionary in terms of political representation. Following the imposition of all-women shortlists, 101 female Labour MPs were elected to the Commons. As its former deputy leader Harriet Harman pointed out on the twentieth anniversary of the 1997 election, the numbers were a huge leap from when she entered the Commons: 'When I was elected in 1982, only 3% of MPs were women and I was one of only 10 female Labour MPs. Women's voices were not heard in parliament and women in the country could not see their concerns reflected on the political agenda.'[16]

Margaret Thatcher was not remotely interested in female representation in her cabinet, in the Commons or anywhere else. She was excited by economic reforms rather than social change. Yet she made only one attempt to counter the wider social reforms of the late 1960s. In 1988, her government passed an act that outlawed 'the promotion of homosexuality'. Not a single prosecution was ever brought, unsurprisingly given the imprecision of the term 'promotion'. It was repealed in 2003 by a Labour government that was instinctively cautious about being out of step with the right-wing newspapers. Even so, there was barely a squeal. Instead the government got the bonus of the Conservative MP Shaun Woodward defecting to Labour, partly out of protest at the Tories' support for the 1988 law.[17] Legislating against historic social reforms is more politically challenging than implementing them in the first place.

Civil partnerships became law in 2004 under the Blair government towards the end of its second term. Conservative MPs at the time were divided on the issue and the party leadership did not impose a three-line whip mandating them to take a particular stance on the bill. Blair was uneasy at times when he faced the opposition of a united Conservative Party over some contentious policies. He was more at ease instigating significant change when he had the support of some Conservative MPs. The internal divisions in the Conservative Party over social reforms made the implementation of civil partnerships more politically straightforward than, say, the tax rise to pay for increased NHS spending that the Conservatives were united in opposing.

David Cameron also made much of being a 'social liberal' after the bill legalizing same-sex marriage was passed in 2013. According to Sir Craig Oliver, Cameron's press secretary at the time, the seeds were sown from a characteristically informal discussion on the topic.

> We went for dinner in Davos one year . . . we went to a res-
> taurant and the menus weren't appetizing . . . we worked out
> that everything on the menu was horsemeat . . . and there was
> some banter about this was a bit strange going to a restaurant
> where everything was horsemeat . . . then David Cameron said,
> as he often would, let's talk about a subject . . . I want to hear
> both sides. He liked people debating in front of him [and]
> he chose same-sex marriage as the subject. One aide said it's
> not worth the candle – you're going to spend a huge amount
> of political capital and then [Cameron] turned to me. I said
> you're asking the WRONG person: my brother's gay and he
> had a tough time at comprehensive school. It seems extra-
> ordinary to me that the state can deny two people who love
> each other that they can marry. And he said I think you're right
> Craig. It would be mean not to do the right thing in those
> circumstances . . .[18]

The historic reform was not wholly dependent on an exchange over horsemeat. The Liberal Democrat minister Lynne Featherstone launched a consultation in March 2012 on how to introduce civil marriage for same-sex couples in England and Wales. By the end of the year, the coalition had resolved to put forward legislation within the lifetime of the parliament. MPs in all the main parties were given a free vote, as was so often the case with social reforms. Cameron had to rely on cross-party support to secure a majority of 366 to 161. But his act of defiance caused him little subsequent difficulty with his party. Instead some of the prominent internal opponents soon admitted they had been wrong. The former cabinet minister Nicky Morgan was one who soon repented: 'I voted the wrong way . . . if it was put now there would be a wholly different response from the Conservative Party'.[19]

When Cameron called a general election in 2015, gay marriage was not a contentious issue. Indeed, it was not an issue at all. Cameron won an overall majority, to his surprise, although his fears that he would not had nothing to do with gay marriage.

Compare and Contrast

The social reforms in the late 1960s began the pattern of seemingly controversial social policies becoming legislation without too much bother. What a contrast between the Abortion Act and the failure of the attempt to place the trade unions within a new legal framework, proposals that did not even get beyond the white paper. The different outcomes help to explain why the UK is socially progressive compared with most equivalent countries and yet has poorer public services and is much less economically productive.

The policies were proposed by the dazzling, restlessly impatient employment secretary Barbara Castle as part of the white paper 'In Place of Strife'. Her report proposed an Industrial Board with significant powers to enforce agreed settlements in industrial disputes, and the creation of a new statutory body, absorbing the powers and responsibilities of the National Board for Prices and Incomes, that 'would be concerned with the whole range of problems involved in the public accountability for economic performance of private industry and the public sector'.[20] Castle was a true heir of the 1945 Labour government, albeit less effective in implementing change.

She was a planner, believing in an active state helping to deliver economic growth and higher living standards, but with unions accepting responsibilities as part of a new legal framework. She had long supported prices and incomes policies as means of planning an economy. The new proposals included compulsory balloting by unions before calling a strike, should the secretary of state for employment order them to. The change, combined with the report's suggestions to end the 'closed shop' industries where membership of a trade union was compulsory for employment, was an imaginative attempt at trade-union reform that might have pre-empted those of Edward Heath and Margaret Thatcher. It got nowhere.

Her plans were being prepared as the bulk of Jenkins's social reforms had reached the statute book. After having been a successful home secretary, Jenkins was promoted to chancellor, wondering with increasing frequency whether he might be prime minister soon. In contrast, Castle's (admittedly remote) chances of becoming Labour leader and prime minister were destroyed by her attempt at a major reform to industrial relations. In her biography, Anne Perkins opens the relevant chapter with a striking sentence: 'The decision to legislate on industrial relations destroyed Barbara's career.'[21] Reviewing Perkins's book, the then foreign secretary, Jack Straw, reached a similar conclusion: 'Barbara fell, and never properly recovered, as a result of the humiliating failure of her greatest project – reforming the trade unions.'[22] Straw had been Castle's special adviser and succeeded her as the MP for Blackburn. He knew a thing or two about stormy internal disputes. He was writing his review when foreign secretary at the height of the Iraq crisis in 2003.

Castle's approach to trade unions, fair and constructive but not sentimental, was ahead of its time. Her attempts in the late 1960s to establish a new framework were doomed from the start. She never had enough support at the beginning of her tempestuous journey and certainly not by the end. Revealingly, she did have the enthusiastic backing of Wilson. That should have been enough. Jenkins could not have made his successful legislative moves without Wilson's support. In this case Wilson's backing made no difference.

Castle's failure to see that all paths towards reform were blocked was a consequence of what could be her brittle and sometimes misplaced self-confidence. She would be often too ambitious in her objectives and her means of achieving them. Unlike Rab Butler and Roy Jenkins, she was not a patient incrementalist. She enjoyed the drama of the big political move, whether it was setting up a new cabinet department or publishing a transport bill, another far-sighted set of plans which was too contentiously weighty to stand much of a chance.

Castle had cause to act in relation to the unions. In 1968, the year before her proposals were formally published, 4.6 million days had been lost through disputes. Her confidence to act was based partly on a distorting sense from her recent past. As with foreign affairs, in domestic politics, the recent past is a dangerous guide to the immediate future. Castle calculated that she could achieve consensus around her plans partly on the basis of her relative success in dealing with unions when she was transport secretary. In this respect and others, her trauma with the unions was a preview of what was to happen to Edward Heath in the early 1970s. Heath had been a successful minister for labour under Harold Macmillan, forming constructive relations with the unions. As a result, he acquired a fatal sense that he could work with them in the transformed circumstances of the 1970s. Castle's experience in the late 1960s should have been a warning. Callaghan should have taken note too. Mistakenly he assumed when he became prime minister in 1976 that he would be able to work with his friends in the unions. But they would give him a more hellish time than that experienced by Heath and Castle.

Union leaders did not see any virtue in Castle's plans whatsoever. Instead they were opposed to them and were outraged that one of the cabinet's left-wingers was taking them on. Partly taking their cue from the unions, most of the cabinet opposed the proposals without reflecting on them for more than a moment or two. Callaghan's authority had been hugely undermined by the devaluation crisis that took place in 1967. Few chancellors have recovered from a devaluation when they have been at the helm. Callaghan did, at least in terms of his standing within the Labour Party. He did so partly as a result of his unswerving opposition to the white paper, a stance that was both sincere and calculating. Without the support of the cabinet, much of the parliamentary party and the trade unions, Wilson had no choice but to drop 'In Place of Strife'. Neither he nor Castle had the authority to impose their will.

The internal coalition opposed to their plans was vast. Callaghan and his wing were not alone. On the other side of Labour's 'broad church', Castle's old friend Michael Foot noted the 'clamours for a Labour government to drink the poison that would kill it.'[23] At this point, Foot's politics were miles away from Callaghan's but the two men were united in their opposition to 'In Place of Strife'. When Labour returned to power in 1974, after the Heath government, Wilson made Foot his employment secretary. Foot was close to the big union leaders and sought to remain that way. Even though industrial relations became much worse than in the late 1960s no minister dared mention 'In Place of Strife'. Wilson regarded Foot as one of the big successes of his 1974 government, regularly singling him out for praise. Foot did not reciprocate. He and his wife, Jill

Craigie, remained stern critics of Wilson for the rest of their lives, unlike Benn and Jenkins who changed their views retrospectively and Castle who always remained a supporter.

Returning to the late 1960s, Castle had acted impulsively before seeking wider support. She was like Theresa May announcing as prime minister her detailed plan to leave the European Union in 2017 without having ensured that there would be widespread support within her cabinet, her parliamentary party or the European Union. May pressed on only to find impossible resistance. Castle persisted for a little bit but was never going to prevail.

Change without Big Political Risks

Why is it much easier for prime ministers as diverse as Harold Wilson, Tony Blair and David Cameron to implement social reforms than it is for most governments, especially Labour administrations, to make changes on a similar scale in other policy areas? Why did more socially conservative prime ministers such as Margaret Thatcher not make much attempt to scrap or significantly revise the changes?

The answer is that social reforms are nowhere near as contentious as they appear to be at the time. All of the significant changes that became law from the 1960s onwards commanded support from across the parties. The political stakes are much less intense when party is not pitted against party. The changes are also relatively straightforward to put in place. Once abortions were legalized within specified limits they became available legally rather than taking place in back-street clinics. When gay marriages were legal it was straightforward for same-sex couples to arrange a ceremony. But how to reform trade unions amidst industrial strife in the late 1960s when a Labour cabinet regarded sensible propositions as an act of reckless betrayal? How to make privatized public services more efficient and effective in the late 1990s and the early twenty-first century when discussions about new forms of state ownership had become almost taboo? How to improve services in a country that seeks US levels of taxation and European standards of public provision? How to move on from Thatcherism under David Cameron and George Osborne when their instincts guided them towards rebooting the Iron Lady's economic policies? There were no easy answers, and in some cases no answer at all.

The UK still has some of the most socially progressive laws in the Western world. It has also struggled persistently with low productivity along with fragmented, unaccountable and underfunded public services. In order to find out why it is a model in one policy area and so poor in rising to other complex challenges, follow the smooth legislative paths of the social reforms and the haphazard attempts of various governments to make the UK a more productive country with a higher quality of public life.

The intense rows over issues relating to gender identity in the early 2020s might appear to challenge this thesis. Arguably the resignation of Nicola Sturgeon as first minister in Scotland in 2023 was caused partly by her support for trans rights. The Labour leader Keir Starmer struggled with questions that seemed straightforward about defining a woman and a man. Some Conservative strategists hoped to start a 'culture war' in which trans issues were a part in the hope of discomfiting their opponents. But these were the early skirmishes of complex and highly emotional themes. On the basis of the recent past the social liberal will prevail in the end. There was enough noise around homosexuality in 1957 to deter the relatively liberal Harold Macmillan from implementing the Wolfenden report. A few years later a cross-party consensus surfaced that was broadly in favour of the proposals. In the early 2020s there was confusion about the trans issue between parties and within them. This applied to the Conservatives as much as the other parties. The first MP to come out as trans was a Conservative. Jamie Wallis was commended for his bravery by the then prime minister, Boris Johnson. At the same time Johnson attacked Starmer as a 'lefty lawyer' who did not know who a woman was. When a prime minister can both praise a trans MP and condemn another party leader for seeking to be tolerant of trans people, we know we are at an early stage of a debate that will rage and then settle without great electoral consequences, like the rows that raged when Jenkins and many others made their moves in the 1960s.

As well as implementing the famously enduring social reforms, Wilson's widely underestimated 1960s governments made several other historic innovations. Wilson took a direct interest in the launch of the Open University, a new institution that gave adults the chance to get a degree by part-time study. Wilson was a strong advocate of lifelong learning, seeing the OU as part of his vaguely defined modernization agenda. Indeed, he was much keener on the OU as a modernizing emblem than he was with regards to the social reforms themselves. The education minister Jennie Lee, wife of Nye Bevan, established a model for the OU based on the idea of widening access to the highest standards of scholarship in tertiary education, and set up a planning committee consisting of university vice-chancellors, educationalists and television broadcasters.

In 1970, Wilson's government passed the Equal Pay Act, although it did not take effect until 1975 under the next Labour government. These were significant changes, but Wilson's government of the

1960s also had to navigate its way through market and industrial turmoil that the doomed 'In Place of Strife' sought to address. As it turned out, its struggles were minor compared with those that erupted around Edward Heath after the 1970 election. Economic fragility was a theme of the post-war era in the UK. Governments were more or less coping until a turning point in 1973: the quadrupling of oil prices, after which the fragility deepened dramatically.

4

THE PRICE OF OIL QUADRUPLES

Sometimes a prime minister faces a dilemma and discovers there is no solution. In the relatively benevolent context of his first term in power, Tony Blair put it succinctly. In the summer of 1997, twenty points ahead in the polls and with a landslide majority, he noted that most days he faced nightmarish decisions that came down to whether he should 'cut my throat or slit my wrists'.[1] Edward Heath would have given much to face Blair's problems during the heady, intoxicating era of 'Cool Britannia'. In 1973, the newish Conservative prime minister, Edward Heath, was confronted with a conundrum that made the rest of his leadership in Number 10 a form of hell and brought about his dramatic fall.

Suddenly the era of cheap imported energy came crashing to an end. Characteristically, Britain was wholly unprepared for the consequences. On 6 October 1973 Egypt and Syria launched a surprise attack against Israel on the Jewish holy day of Yom Kippur. Eleven days later, on 17 October, the Arab oil-producing countries deployed a lever that was aimed largely at the US but caused even deeper problems for the much more economically fragile UK. OPEC declared it would be reducing oil production by 5 per cent while suspending oil supply to the US. The reduction in the amount of oil produced, combined with the embargo, triggered a quadrupling of oil prices in the UK.

The United States, Israel's main ally, might have been the main target but the economic superpower could cope more or less with the punishment. President Richard Nixon implemented a limited rationing programme aimed at safeguarding American oil supplies and at ensuring continued low prices. There were shortages at petrol stations in the US, unsurprising given that the price of a barrel of oil had surged from $2.59 to a staggering $11.65. But the impact in the US was the equivalent of a minor storm compared with the tornado that hit the UK.

The wild increase in energy costs could not have come at a worse time for the Conservative government. To the surprise of many, Edward Heath had won the general election in June 1970. Heath had been an awkward campaigner and an irritable communicator. His party had been slaughtered under his leadership at the 1966 general election. Yet voters had turned to the Conservatives in 1970.

As a new prime minister, Heath had a self-confidence in his abilities to lead and rule that was largely unjustified. He had been a distinctively successful minister in the late 1950s and early 1960s and had a strong sense of what he wanted to do in power. If his leadership from the 1970 election until the oil price shock was erratic it was because his sense of prime-ministerial duty outstripped any coherent visionary zeal. Expediently he did what he felt was right even if his actions were at odds with previously declared commitments such as his famous declaration that his government would not support 'lame duck' industries and other evocations of a swashbuckling 'laissez faire' approach. He had become an interventionist in government because he felt with good cause he had no choice but to intervene.

By the early autumn of 1973 Heath had already navigated many crises and dared to hope that he might be rewarded with another election victory perhaps in the summer or autumn of the following year, merely for hanging on. In his opening years as prime minister there had been states of emergency, power cuts, strikes and policy U-turns. Yet the latest polls in the summer of 1973 showed that the government was only a couple of percentage points behind Labour. At least Heath appeared to have solutions even if they were haphazard and often contradicted his earlier plans: Labour appeared to be split on all the key issues and without clear direction. For all his moodiness Heath was an optimist. He had been one of the minority at the top of his party and in the media who thought he would win in 1970. In the summer of 1973 he was likewise hopeful about the next election. Perhaps the economy would be growing faster by then, inflation might have been cowed and he could start planning for a calmer second full term. Neither he nor anyone else had a developed sense prior to the oil price rise that he would not even have another full year as prime minister.

The OPEC decision on oil dashed any hope he might have had. Britain was hit hard because it relied on imported oil for 50 per cent of its energy needs. Heath was not the first prime minister who had failed to plan for an energy crisis and he would not be the last. When Russia invaded Ukraine in the spring of 2022, Germany, far more dependent on Russian gas than the UK, nevertheless had far more energy in reserve compared with the UK. Contingency planning was not part of the UK's political culture with its focus on the short term and in its wariness of planning ahead.

Heath faced a huge increase in energy costs just as he was seeking to enforce the latest phase of his over-complicated incomes policy. Oil quadrupled in price at a supremely sensitive point when he was desperate to avoid another clash with the National Union of Mineworkers. The NUM had every intention of securing a pay deal well above the limits of Heath's recently imposed legislative framework and the freakish rise in oil had given it the economic might to do so. With oil so expensive the UK became more dependent on coal.

This was the dilemma without a solution. Overnight Heath had become trapped by the OPEC decision. Suddenly he was much weakened in his negotiations with the miners even if he was slow to recognize the degree to which the dynamics had changed. His dogged stubbornness made him a poor reader of the political scene, not least when seismic change was taking place. There was a dutiful rigidity about Heath. He wanted to do what he considered to be fair and decent but sometimes he could not see what was in front of his eyes. In effect the miners were worth a lot more, but Heath feared the inflationary consequences of paying them rates that broke his incomes policy.

The seeds of the crisis were sown long before OPEC dealt its deadly blow, within months of Heath becoming prime minister. Strikes by dockers and power workers forced him to introduce two states of emergency by the end of 1970. In December of that election-winning year heating and lighting were rationed. The restrictions in the depths of winter led to a rush on candles, a more rational form of panic buying than the frenzied dash for toilet rolls at the start of the Covid pandemic in 2020.

Rooms lit by candles became a discordant symbol of the Heath era. He had hoped to be a modernizing prime minister, shaking up government to make it more responsive to contemporary demands, and yet a primitive darkness was a feature of his short period in charge. Power cuts punctuated people's lives during this early phase of the Conservative government although they became wrongly associated with his final days in Number 10 when other equally dramatic measures, such as the 'three-day week', meant there was no need for sudden and unexpected cuts in the power supply. The shortage of energy was managed differently in the winter of 1973 but with familiar constraints.

A pattern of pay demands took shape from the beginning of Heath's leadership. In response to industrial action from power workers soon after he took office the government commissioned an independent inquiry led by Lord Wilberforce. In February 1971 it recommended that the power workers receive a 15 per cent pay rise, close to what their union had asked for in the first place. The subsequent deal triggered other pay bids on a similar scale. Here was the deadly sequence. A union made a pay demand. Heath resisted. There were strikes as a result. An independent body came down more or less on the side of the union's demands. Heath was left in the worst of all worlds, dealing with strikes and then implicitly rebuked by independent pay reviews.

His original plan was to introduce a new legal framework for unions, much tougher than Barbara Castle's doomed plans in the late 1960s. For Heath new laws for unions were much easier to contemplate than to implement. He should have had a clearer path towards establishing a new legal framework for unions than Castle. There were no members of his cabinet with deep-rooted connections to the unions as there were in Wilson's government. Instead there was consensus in Heath's administration that unions must face new legal constraints. In this case though the Conservative government made a different error to Wilson's. Heath and his ministers framed their plans in a way that seemed punitive rather than part of a modern state in which the rights of unions were recognized as well as their responsibilities.

Heath blew his reforms as spectacularly as Wilson and Castle had done but this time only once they had been passed in parliament. In 1972 his government introduced the Industrial Relations Act, which sought to define 'unfair industrial practices', and introduce secret ballots before strikes and a 'cooling off' period in advance of industrial action so that further attempts at negotiation could be made. The idea behind the act was based on the small-state philosophy that continued to thrive in the Conservative Party for years from David Cameron's 'big society' and on to Liz Truss's fleeting libertarian populism. In this case Heath sought to depoliticize the industrial turmoil by establishing a legal framework and leaving it to the courts to decide whether unions were acting illegally or not. The idea was that he and his government would take a step back. It did not work in the early 1970s or subsequently. In the end governments are responsible for the smooth running of a country and feel compelled to intervene in some form or another. Heath was more dutiful than some of his successors and would not have found stepping back particularly easy. As it turned out he became directly involved with the negotiations with miners and some other unions.

His willingness to do so suggests he was never wholly convinced by the Industrial Relations Act. Whatever he thought of it, the unions found an easy way to scupper the plans. Only thirty-two unions registered with the newly established National Industrial Relations Court and the Industrial Relations Commission, the bodies formed to take control of industrial conflict. Within six months the government had abandoned the act, a second attempt to bring trade unions within a legal framework failing within four years. From then on Heath followed his own stronger instincts for direct personal involvement. He would become the chief negotiator with the most formidable unions, especially when the NUM flexed its muscles.

The economic backdrop reinforced Heath's (and his government's) tendency towards direct intervention. In 1971 there was a steady rise in unemployment. As for Wilson and Callaghan, Heath's formative political years were the 1930s. The three prime ministers regarded unemployment as a social evil and an economic calamity. As the number of those out of work rose towards a million, Heath's government became more active. It rescued Rolls-Royce in January 1971 and the Upper Clyde shipbuilders in June. The following year an industry bill gave the government more powers to assist companies.

Heath's boldest attempt to revive the economy was his government's budget in 1972, a set of proposals that became known as the 'dash for growth', a dash that proved to be disastrously counter-productive. Heath was an unlucky prime minister and his biggest bit of bad luck before the oil rise was the sudden death of his chancellor, Iain Macleod, weeks after the 1970 election. Macleod was the perfect foil to Heath: self-confident, with an awareness that communication in the media was part of the art of governing. Above all Heath trusted Macleod's judgement and was content to suspend his instinct for control-freakery in relation to his newly appointed chancellor.

His decision to replace Macleod with the inexperienced Anthony Barber showed that Heath had every intention of taking full control of economic policy. Barber was not formidable enough to challenge the prime minister who had elevated him suddenly to the Treasury in the midst of an economic crisis. Barber became known for the 1972 budget, but it was Heath's programme as much as his. Heath would and could have stopped him if he had disapproved. In the 'Barber boom' budget the novice chancellor pumped an additional £2.5 billion into the economy in order to increase pensions and benefits along with tax reductions including a cut in income tax and incentives for businesses to retain jobs. The injection of cash was to be paid for by increased borrowing. He also announced he was lifting constraints on spending. At the time of the budget inflation was around 7 per cent. With a flourish Barber forecast UK growth would be at 10 per cent within two years.

What followed triggered comparisons many years later with Kwasi Kwarteng's mini-budget in September 2022 when he borrowed to finance tax cuts in another 'dash for growth'. Unlike Kwarteng and his boss, Liz Truss, Barber and Heath survived what followed but the 1972 budget contributed to the turmoil rather than alleviated it in any way. In fact, a year later Barber was forced to deliver a budget that dashed in the opposite direction. When inflation soared, oil quadrupled in price and the miners struck, he imposed steep spending cuts. His dash for growth had failed spectacularly, increasing inflation in a way that impaired his attempts to expand the economy. When Liz Truss and Kwasi Kwarteng unveiled their calamitous mini-budget of unfunded tax cuts, there were many references in the critical commentaries to Barber's budget as a previous example of reckless borrowing. But there were significant differences. Truss and Kwarteng borrowed to deliver tax cuts for the wealthiest. Heath and Barber planned to put more money in the pockets of the less well-off and to invest in public services. But there were also gloomy parallels. Both fiscal events propelled the UK economy closer towards the cliff's edge. In both cases the policies were humiliatingly reversed.

A Perfect Storm

During the autumn of 1973 the crises of inflation, miners' strikes and the oil price rise were all unavoidably interconnected, feeding off each other to trigger yet another state of emergency: under Heath, emergencies had become normal. Heath's close ally Douglas Hurd noted that after OPEC made its announcement, the 'earth began to move under the government's feet'.[2] The immediate context was Heath's efforts to impose a pay and incomes policy. Heath was not a great strategist. He calculated in a reasoned manner and worked on the assumption that others would respond in a similar way. Although gripped by politics from an early age he was not especially political, or did not understand the art of persuasion and the importance of thinking several moves ahead when framing policies. He saw that something needed to be done, and then did it, without thinking through the subtleties.

As we have already seen, leaders look to the past for guidance even though the challenges they face are distinct and new. The future is hazy. Leaders cast their nervy eyes ahead and see little or nothing. They are drawn to the past because there appears to be a route map of sorts even if it is of little relevance to the new dilemmas they face. The past may even lead them towards their doom and yet they cannot help but reach for it as their fickle guide.

This was especially the case in the 1970s when three prime ministers turned to an incomes policy as a means to get them into calmer waters. Such an approach is the ultimate form of state intervention, a government determining the legally acceptable level of pay rise. In each case the approach of the three prime ministers brought about their fall, even if for one of the trio the fall was voluntary. The 1970s were an intimidating decade for prime ministers. They never felt in control as disruptive strikes were called and inflation soared. Yet each of the prime ministers, Heath, Harold Wilson and James Callaghan, tried to pull levers in an attempt to regain the initiative. Through their incomes policies, they ceded even more control.

Legally enforced incomes policies were not necessarily fatal for those who chose to deploy them. In the 1970s they were developed successfully in Scandinavia, West Germany and the Netherlands. But in those cases, they were part of a wider framework in which unions, employers and government agreed a range of responsibilities and rights in carefully thought-through arrangements. An incomes policy only works as part of a bigger enterprise in countries where governments plan ahead as a matter of course. In the UK, they were introduced haphazardly and then either petered out or collapsed amidst ruinous industrial conflict. By the start of the 1970s they had been tried in the UK several times. The Labour chancellor Stafford Cripps imposed a wage freeze from 1948 until the 1950 general election. The Conservative chancellor Selwyn Lloyd announced a 'pay pause' in 1961. The pause did not last for very long. Harold Wilson tried out a pay freeze from 1966 for three years. By the end, he had become convinced the measure caused more problems than it solved.

In each case the policy was rushed and implemented in near panic. In other European countries the policy was carefully considered and arose from a wide political consensus. In the UK, the main opposition party, Labour or Conservative, stridently opposed the latest version of an incomes policy introduced by their political rivals. With a dark irony the shadow chancellor, James Callaghan, forensically tore apart Selwyn Lloyd's 'pay pause' in 1961, proposing an alternative policy:

[T]his House deplores the handling by Her Majesty's Government of the Pay Pause, which has undermined the well-established machinery for freely negotiating wage settlements, is grossly unfair in operation, and provides no long term solution to the problem of inflation; and further regrets the failure of Her Majesty's Government to propose measures that will increase productivity and remove the underlying weaknesses in the national economy.[3]

As prime minister, Callaghan introduced his own incomes policy that similarly prevented 'freely negotiating wage settlements'.

When he was a relatively new leader of the opposition, Edward Heath opposed Wilson's pay freeze in 1966. He had cause to do so. *The Observer*, still broadly supportive of Wilson at this stage in his leadership, noted 'the pedigree of the Government's . . . policy is suspect: it is by haste out of desperation. And it has been introduced in the most unfavourable circumstances imaginable: in an atmosphere of confusion and bitterness'.[4] Once again, Heath would later succumb to the same temptation.

In the 1970s, Heath, Wilson and Callaghan all adopted British-style incomes policies, separate from any wider governing project and with the main opposition party unwilling to support what the government was doing. In each case they turned to this form of complex intervention for an honourable reason: they were alarmed about the impact of double-digit inflation and high unemployment. But they also acted in a terrifyingly new context: a turning point.

The year before the oil price rise, Heath announced an incomes policy that would be implemented in three stages. One of the many problems with this phased approach was that each new stage provided a fresh focus for Heath's opponents to renew and revise their onslaught. Stage one in 1972 took the form of a ninety-day freeze on wages and prices. This was due to expire at the end of February 1973. On 17 January 1973, in his last full year in power, Heath announced stage two would permit pay rises to be limited to a basic £1 a week plus 4 per cent. He also announced a new pay board would be established to preside over the limited variations permitted within stage two. These first two stages were reasonably successful. Stage three was the fatal part of the sequence, coming into effect at around the same time oil prices soared.

The stage three package was far more complicated partly because it had to appease the miners without making them become known as a 'special case'. There was the option of a flat-rate pay rise or an increase of 7 per cent. In addition, there was leeway for productivity bonuses and further rewards for unsocial hours. There was also a commitment to make further progress towards equal pay between men and women but this was nowhere near as robust as the proposals of the outgoing Labour government in 1970 that finally became legislation in 1975 when they resumed power.

Stage three was more Heath-like than stages one and two: reasoned, logical, quite generous but also contorted and vague, an attempt to pacify wild waves by insisting that they must become calm. A few months earlier, in July at their annual conference, the miners had voted to back a pay bid of 35 per cent. Heath was desperate to avoid another conflict by finding a compromise acceptable to them without leading to similar pay demands from other unions. He took personal control of the pay negotiations with the NUM president, Joe Gormley. Here was an unlikely duo propelled together by fast-moving events. Gormley had been a miner from the age of fourteen and was a pragmatic leader of his union surrounded by more militant figures on the NUM executive. He was gruff and autocratic, and he could act with guile when he needed to. Heath was similarly autocratic and blunt. But both lacked the space to be assertive. Gormley required the backing of his executive. Heath was trapped by economic constraints and a growing sense of political fragility. In the early autumn of 1973, Heath and Gormley met secretly to explore options. Gormley liked Heath. Indeed, he trusted him more than he did the Labour leader, Harold Wilson. Naively Heath thought he had secured a deal with the NUM leader in which the miners received higher wages through the stage three reference to 'unsocial hours' working. The National Coal Board made an offer of 7 per cent, the maximum allowed under the pay policy, plus another 4 per cent for working unsocial hours. Gormley took the offer back to his executive hoping to argue that the miners had been treated as a special case. But in his usual clunky manner Heath felt the need to stress that this was emphatically not the case. The pay offer was within the limits of stage three. Heath had assumed that Gormley wielded the power of an autocrat. He did not. The NUM executive rejected the pay offer. They were in a position to do so after the OPEC price rise. As Hurd noted in his diary: 'The government had to burn oil to save coal . . . now they had to burn coal to save oil . . . we were being manoeuvred once again towards the same fatal field, still littered with relics of the last defeat.'[5]

Heath decided to bypass the National Coal Board, becoming more personally involved in the dispute. The NCB had been established partly to put distance between ministers and issues relating to miners' pay and working conditions. Inevitably in an economic crisis there could be no such distance, not least when Heath still felt he was well equipped to find a resolution. Yet there was no room for a deal when he was committed to maintaining his pay policy and the miners were equally determined to get a deal that reflected their new muscularity. A hugely disruptive overtime ban began in November 1973, instigated by the National Union of Miners. Shift work and safety procedure meant the ban cut production much more proportionately than the number of hours lost. Almost immediately output fell by 40 per cent. The government announced yet another state of emergency, the fifth since 1970.

The new constraints were some of the most severe since 1970 as the days got shorter and the temperatures fell. There was a ban on the use of energy for advertising, restrictions on heating of offices, shops and schools and a warning that petrol rationing might be necessary. Heath continued to engage with the NUM, again in ways that Gormley could not help but admire. But the admiration did not extend to finding a consensus between the two of them. At the end of November the entire NUM executive met at Number 10. During the discussions one junior member played the miners' ace: 'Why can't you pay us for coal what you're willing to pay the Arabs for oil?'[6]

The government had no satisfactory answer and the NUM executive voted to continue the overtime ban indefinitely. Heath was trapped, convinced that stage three could not be broken without bringing down his government. Yet without conceding substantial ground to the miners he risked a crisis that would also destroy his relatively short-lived administration. Heath was inflexible as a leader, and yet there was a reason for his refusal to give more ground. If he did so, other unions would also seek to bust stage three, further fuelling the inflation that his pay policy was designed to prevent.

Early in December 1973, Heath appointed the diligent conciliator Willie Whitelaw as his new employment secretary, hoping that he could find a way through. But Whitelaw was not Houdini. If the miners were not treated as a special case the strikes would continue. If the miners were treated as a special case, other unions would demand to be similarly viewed. If not an escapologist, Whitelaw did try to wave a wand in a meeting with Gormley. Within the confines of stage three Whitelaw proposed that 'waiting and bathing times', the necessary additions to their working day, could be the excuse for a higher pay rise for miners. This proposal went nowhere. Harold Wilson heard about the still secret discussions and made the suggestion himself. Exhausted ministers could not be seen dancing to Labour's tunes and in any case the NUM executive was not in any mood to agree. For some on the executive, the dispute was not only about the pay deal, but being seen to break Heath's pay policy and therefore to bring down his government.

As Christmas approached, Heath announced further restrictions on heating and street lighting. The most vivid new rule was his instruction that TV channels must shut down at 10.30 p.m. This was the era of three UK channels in which individual programmes were watched by many millions. There were no video recorders, let alone Sky+. Behaviour therefore tended to revolve around TV schedules. If a favourite programme was missed it was gone forever, or at least until a repeat was on offer. A TV scheduler determined a viewer's routine. Now Heath had become a scheduler. Suddenly *Match of the Day* was broadcast much earlier on a Saturday night. The Michael Parkinson chat show that normally followed the football at a late hour was switched to Friday evenings in a slot before the 10.30 deadline. Each change to the viewers' routines was a reminder of the deepening crisis that Heath was struggling to resolve.

On 13 December Heath made his most dramatic announcement in a competitive field. He declared that there would be a three-day working week in order to preserve energy. Unable to disguise his exhaustion, in a televised broadcast that same evening he acknowledged this would be the 'hardest Christmas since the war'.[7] This is not exactly the message a prime minister would hope to deliver in what was in effect the build-up to a general election. In the recording still available on YouTube, Heath looks as tired as Eden when he made a TV address at the height of the Suez crisis. Eden fell within weeks. So did Heath.

There was a bleak irony about Heath's final days in power. The three-day week was an example of shrewd planning, a tough decision made amidst nerve-shredding chaos. There was not a big drop in productivity and there was no need for sudden power cuts as energy was being used more sparingly. Nonetheless this dark dance between the government and the NUM could not last for much longer. Something had to give.

In the end, and with some reluctance, Heath saw only one way out of the trap. After some doubts he decided to call a general election for the end of February 1974, a rare winter poll. Prime ministers are not irrational most of the time. If they announce an election, one of the biggest decisions they have to make, there are good reasons. The Conservatives were ahead in the polls. Labour was divided and Harold Wilson seemed tired and detached. As is usually the case most newspapers were backing the Conservatives, turning their bullying might on Wilson in particular and Labour more widely. On this basis, Heath calculated he would win. No prime minister calls an election on the assumption they will lose. He assumed wrongly that he had a powerful argument over the question 'who governs?'. Famously this was his framing of the campaign. Above all he had concluded that only a renewed mandate would give him the space to defeat the miners and provide a protective shield for his pay policy.

Even so Heath was taking a huge risk. It was one that he failed to pull off. He was still a wooden campaigner. Having rightly warned of a bleak Christmas a few weeks earlier it was a tough pitch to make. In effect he was stating, 'Your Christmas was the worst since the war . . . nothing has got better since . . . vote Conservative'. Heath had also not fully realized that there was support for the miners amongst many voters. During the campaign, an independent body published a review that broadly backed the miners' demands.

The Conservative MP Enoch Powell unexpectedly did not stand in the election. Powell and Heath loathed each other. Powell had already caused trouble by supporting the miners' demands on the basis of market principles, arguing with steely logic that more expensive oil made miners bigger players in the energy market. In the election campaign, he stirred the pot even more mischievously. Powell urged voters to back Labour because it was offering a referendum on the UK's membership of the Common Market. Wilson was still more agile than Heath, pledging to end the miners' strike and the threat of wider industrial action and to reduce some food prices. As a bonus he had secured the support of Powell.

It was a strange, ghostly election campaign. Wilson's front-bench colleagues thought he was going to lose and would resign as party leader immediately after. Wilson planned to hide from the media if Labour had lost. Both Heath and Wilson looked exhausted partly because they were, two leaders in their fifties looking considerably older. By far the liveliest leader was the Liberal Party leader, Jeremy Thorpe, largely based in his North Devon constituency, elegantly leaping over fences to greet voters, holding press conferences in London via a televised link, witty and charming.

At a point when Heath had implied Britain had become ungovernable, the result made it much harder for any single party to rule. Labour won five more seats than the Conservatives, but did so with fewer votes. The Liberals won significant support but only fourteen seats. The UK had elected a hung parliament, a rare occurrence under a voting system designed to allow one party to win an overall majority.

Harold Wilson Turns to Face the Turning Point

Heath tried to cling on but failed to secure a deal with Thorpe. He had lost the art of making deals with unions or party leaders. Of course, a coalition with Thorpe would have been unlikely to be stable in the light of what would happen to him. Soon Thorpe would be in court accused of conspiracy to murder. But that prospect was not an obstacle in the aftermath of the election. And Thorpe's party would not allow him to keep the Conservatives in power as Heath would not contemplate electoral reform, the persistent issue for Liberals. On the Monday evening, partly to his own surprise, Harold Wilson became prime minister again.

In March 1974 Wilson was far more politically deft than Heath or his successor, James Callaghan. Almost accidentally he tried to move the British debate about unions, pay and social justice slightly closer to the Continental model. But because he was doing so in Britain, a country wary of planning, and as leader of a Labour Party that had rejected Barbara Castle's 'In Place of Strife' a few years earlier, he could not be precise about his intentions. There was another reason. Wilson was not wholly sure what form his plan would take. At the February 1974 election and beyond he proclaimed a new 'social contract', vaguely defined because any policy burdened by precision tended to cause big trouble, as Heath had discovered.

Once safely installed as prime minister with a small overall majority, having won another election in October of the same year, Wilson delivered a degree of clarification at the party's shorter-than-usual annual conference in November.

It is a contract between Government and people. All the people. It is a contract under which this Government has pledged itself, as no other Government in British history has pledged itself, to the promotion of social and economic justice in Britain. Social and economic justice between the people and between the regions of our country.

It is a policy for social and economic equality. But it is a policy with obligations, with responsibilities as well as rewards. You cannot pick and choose. It is not a policy from which you can extract the parts you like and reject the parts you do not.[8]

But the trade unions were in a mood to pick and choose. They regarded higher pay rises to keep up with price increases to be a pivotal form of social and economic justice. What did Wilson mean by the 'responsibilities' that would come with 'rewards'? Presumably he was referring to pay restraint but if he had specified such a topic, all hell would have broken loose. Like Heath, Wilson was trapped – but in a different way. He had opposed a statutory incomes policy in both the 1974 election campaigns, partly to expose the flaws of Heath's leadership. Therefore he had to make the social contract work as a voluntary arrangement, but how could he do so when unions regarded their pay demands as a necessary route towards social justice?

Wilson's employment secretary, Michael Foot, had settled the miners' strike and was inclined to be similarly generous to other unions. This was not because he was a soft touch. He sincerely saw the validity of their various demands. Wilson regarded Foot as one of his most successful appointments during this phase of his rule, recognizing that his new cabinet minister was also seeking some degree of balance between the rights of unions and their responsibilities under the social contract. However no balance was struck. By the summer of 1975 inflation was soaring to new heights, at one point reaching nearly 25 per cent.

Unlike Heath, Wilson almost managed to escape from his trap. Here was his incarceration: how to introduce an incomes policy when you are supposed to be against it? In July 1975, he announced a 'voluntary' pay policy. In reality it was another attempt at enforcing pay limits. Private employers who agreed to high wage demands would not be allowed to increase prices to pay for them. Therefore they were in no position to pay wages they would be unable to afford. Subsidies to local authorities would also be withdrawn if they negotiated inflationary pay demands. Nationalized industries would likewise lose subsidies if they agreed inflation-busting deals. This was the nearest any of the three prime ministers in the 1970s came to navigating a way through the obstacles. Wilson placed the onus on employers to address the crisis of wage inflation and he gave them no choice but to do so. A combination of conceding to pay demands in the aftermath of the February 1974 election and the imposition of punitive sanctions from the summer of 1975 meant that there were no significant strikes under Wilson after his return to power.

But he was papering over the cracks. There had been no formal deal with the unions and the pay policy declared as 'voluntary' was in effect compulsory. The economy was still in crisis. The day before Wilson resigned in March 1976 his government lost a vote in the Commons on proposed spending cuts aimed at stabilizing the pound and reassuring the markets. During his resignation interviews, Wilson admitted that the same problems kept on recurring and it needed fresh minds to address them. He had long planned to step back when he reached sixty in the spring of 1976, but like Heath he had been made weary by his attempts to escape the traps only to find there were new forms of imprisonment. The challenges of the 1970s, made much worse by the end of cheap energy, had laid low two prime ministers.

James Callaghan's Turn

James Callaghan fared even worse. In the early 1970s he had mocked the idea of a pay policy, partly to torment Heath's government, as he had done in the early 1960s when the Conservatives had tried to impose their 'pay pause'. Soon Callaghan turned to the same solution too, even though he knew at some level that such enforced constraint would hasten his terrible fall. When he became prime minister, Callaghan assumed he would be better able to deal with the unions. He had formerly been a full-time trade union official. He spoke for the unions when Barbara Castle had proposed a new legal framework, ensuring her ideas never got off the ground. He soon discovered he had no grounds for his self-confidence on this front.

A few months into Callaghan's leadership, sterling was under huge pressure. In an attempt to appease the markets the chancellor, Denis Healey, proposed spending cuts of a billion pounds, a move opposed by a section of the cabinet and a significant portion of the parliamentary Labour Party. But the government was running out of options and needed to borrow from the International Monetary Fund. The IMF's condition for a loan was spending restraint. This was another turning point related to the oil price rise that had deepened the UK's economic crisis. The loan was a humiliation for the government and voters did not forget the summer of 1976 and the subsequent dramas for a long time. A potent line of attack from the Conservatives at the time and for many years was that the government had been 'bailed out' by the IMF and that Labour could not be trusted to run the economy.

Within the Labour Party, the role of the IMF fuelled a debate about accountability and democracy. The then energy secretary, Tony Benn, seized on the intervention of the IMF to argue that democratically elected governments were no longer in control of their own economic policies, a theme he was to develop in ways that gripped the left of his party. More immediately Benn was the most prominent member of the cabinet to argue against the spending cuts proposed by Healey. He was not alone in the cabinet, but with considerable tenacity Callaghan backed his chancellor and prevailed.

In his memoir Healey acknowledged the Treasury's forecasts were far too pessimistic, a reminder that in an economic crisis, the tendency of the Treasury is to overcorrect. Many years later, in 2010, the Treasury moved as one with its chancellor, George Osborne, as he instigated real-terms spending cuts that delayed rather than speeded up economic recovery. Rishi Sunak and his chancellor Jeremy Hunt did the same in the autumn of 2022. Here was Healey's retrospective verdict on what happened in the summer of 1976:

By this time the Conservative press was screaming for public spending cuts. Its frenzy was not discouraged by the Treasury's own misleading statement that public spending was taking 60 per cent of GDP, and by the official Treasury forecasts which overestimated that year's public sector borrowing requirement by over £2 billion . . . it was all I had to go on and it was worrying the markets.[9]

Forecasts were often unreliable whether made by the Treasury or later the independent Office for Budget Responsibility. But the unreliability was irrelevant if the markets detected reckless fragility. The early autumn 1976 Labour Party conference in Blackpool was far from thrilled about the planned spending cuts, with a future leader, Neil Kinnock, leading the cries opposing them. At the last minute, Healey decided to turn back from a planned trip to an IMF conference abroad in order to address his party's conference. With a dramatic flourish, his hair looking as if it was struggling with gale force winds, he declared that he had 'come from the battlefront'. With some in the conference hall jeering and others cheering, he put the case for spending constraints and his deal with the IMF.

At the same conference, his first as prime minister, Callaghan was inadvertently helping Margaret Thatcher on her way by clearing the ideological ground. Callaghan was no monetarist but he made it a little easier for Thatcher to put her case:

We used to think that you could spend your way out of recession and increase employment by cutting taxes and boosting spending. I tell you in all candour that option no longer exists and that as far as it ever did exist, it only worked on each occasion since the war by injecting a bigger dose of inflation into the economy, followed by a higher level of unemployment.[10]

The view of both Callaghan and Healey that tight spending controls were required placed further constraints on public-sector pay. With inflation still extremely high there were similar pressures on the private sector. Callaghan became the third successive prime minister in the 1970s to be wary of incomes policies and then adopt one, out of desperation and in a short-term attempt to plan for order rather than chaos.

In July 1978, Callaghan announced a new pay norm of 5 per cent. The evening before, on ITV, he argued that the limit was 'not harsh', the same view Heath had taken of his staged incomes policy that Callaghan had opposed. As with Heath, the unions took a different view. Callaghan's old friends and allies in the unions wanted to secure higher deals.

In the winter of 1978/9, with a general election looming, strikes erupted on a wider scale than earlier in the decade. Industrial action by workers at Ford in late 1978 was settled with a pay increase of 17 per cent, well above the 5 per cent limit the government was seeking to impose on public-sector workers, on the assumption that private companies would follow suit. At the end of 1978, a road hauliers' strike began. Many public workers took similar action, including an unofficial strike by gravediggers and strikes by refuse collectors, leaving uncollected rubbish on some streets and in prominent public spaces, including London's Leicester Square. Additionally, NHS ancillary workers formed picket lines to blockade hospital entrances with the result that many hospitals were reduced to taking only emergency patients. The images of rubbish mounting, the dead unburied and blocked-off hospitals became part of 'the winter of discontent'. There were many reasons why Labour lost four successive general elections from 1979. The 'winter of discontent', or the way the saga was portrayed, was one of them.

A Path Clears for Margaret Thatcher

During the 1992 election, the Conservative television broadcasts were punctuated with images of piling rubbish from the cold January of 1979. Labour MP Nick Thomas-Symonds, a biographer of Harold Wilson, believes that the final series of strikes under the Labour government explains why Wilson and Callaghan became ghostly figures soon after they left power.[11] Labour wanted to show that it was moving on and rarely referred to the duo. The media broadly accepted Tony Blair's narrative that he led 'New Labour' while Wilson and Callaghan had been 'old'. There was no 'Wilsonism' or 'Heathism' as there was soon to be 'Thatcherism' and 'Blairism'. The prime ministers of the 1970s were condemned as failures struggling to make sense of raging inflation while keeping unemployment at a level that they found more or less acceptable. For their successors it was safer for them to be consigned to history.

Almost immediately after the 1979 election, and for decades to come, there was little acknowledgement of the context in which the three prime ministers had struggled to stay afloat. As Margaret Thatcher pursued her economic experiment with her implicit rebuke of all that Heath had come to represent, she did not reflect on what she would have done in 1973 when oil became impossibly expensive and the UK became far more dependent on coal. She had been education secretary at the time and had kept her head down in cabinet as Heath, Willie Whitelaw and others struggled with the dilemmas posed by the end of cheap energy. She made no contribution. Later she conveyed disapproval of Heath's interventionism by proclaiming that 'the Lady is not for turning'[12] in relation to economic policy. (However, she never voiced her disapproval explicitly;

it is only some Labour leaders who feel the need to overtly turn on their predecessors.)

Thatcher was lucky. Instead of facing a nightmarish energy dilemma, her premiership coincided with North Sea oil becoming available in bountiful quantities. By the mid-1980s, North Sea oil was delivering the Treasury 10 per cent of its revenues. Thatcher spent the proceeds to prop up her economic experiment. The oil paid for tax cuts and welfare benefits. She did not consider whether there should be a long-term plan for oil revenues. Once again planning was not part of the UK's political culture and was emphatically not part of her mindset. She needed the money and spent it. Other countries such as Norway used their tax on oil to modernize infrastructure and industry, establishing a sovereign wealth fund as a protective barrier against future economic crises. There was none of that in the UK. Instead the Treasury spent every penny on current expenditure, leaving nothing for capital projects or future emergencies. In the mid-1980s, one cabinet minister boasted to *The Observer* columnist William Keegan, 'we've spent the North Sea oil financing the unemployed'.[13]

The oil boom was rarely cited when Thatcher's admirers recited her apparent triumphs. On the day she died, the BBC's *World at One* devoted an hour to analysis of her leadership. There was no mention of North Sea oil being a key factor in the economics and politics of the 1980s.[14] Thatcher herself never cited the oil boom when looking back on 'Thatcherism'. She had no motive to do so. She saw herself – and sought to project herself – as the crusading pioneer, not a leader buttressed by the good fortune bubbling out of the North Sea. Nor did she dare to imagine what might have happened if Heath, Wilson and Callaghan had had the oil available to them. Their prospects would have been considerably strengthened and the quadrupling of international oil prices would not have been so disruptive.

Instead their hands were tied. They were so constrained that the OPEC price hike was both a turning point and for a time part of a continuing pattern. The prime ministers sought to take back some control through pay policies. In doing so they almost knowingly chose to lose ultimate control.

Also unknowingly, they were moving towards the biggest turning point since 1945, the election of Margaret Thatcher. With an impulsive radicalism she swept aside the assumptions of the 1945 Labour government and a substantial portion of the policies that arose from them. She moved on also from the corporatist instincts of the administrations that ruled in the 1960s and 1970s.

In doing so Thatcher led the most significant post-war turning point partly because her policies endured for so long. Thatcher was prime minister for more than eleven years and the Conservatives were in power for a total of eighteen. Attlee's Labour governments were out of power after six years. Thatcher continued to cast a spell long after she was removed from power. Her instinctive radicalism and the shrewdest political instincts of any leader in modern times combined to transform her country and her party.

5

1979

The election of Margaret Thatcher, first as party leader in 1975 and then as prime minister following her victory in May 1979, triggered multiple turning points. She changed her party and she transformed her country. The one-nation Conservative Party, known for its flexible pragmatism, became a different political force fizzing with ideas on the radical right, loyal to conviction rather than to leaders. At her peak Thatcher had full control over her party, but after her time in power the Conservatives became almost impossible to lead. In many respects the country was changed beyond recognition too, from one that was staggering out of the so-called 'winter of discontent' in 1979 to a different, though still troubled, land in 1990.

Remarkably, Thatcher continued to mesmerize for decades to come, long after she left office and indeed following her death. For her party and the Conservative-supporting newspapers she became a constant reference point. Who was she backing in subsequent Conservative leadership contests? The candidate she backed always won. Had she been alive how would she have voted in the Brexit referendum? Successive Conservative prime ministers and chancellors turned to her policies in the 1980s as a guide for what they should do in different eras. Tony Blair paid homage, praising many of the changes introduced in the 1980s. When Gordon Brown became prime minister she was an early visitor to Number 10. In the 2022 Tory leadership contest candidates sought approval with party members by claiming to be the most devoted disciple of Thatcher and Thatcherism. Attlee and his government changed Britain in many ways. Thatcher's counter-revolution went wider and deeper.

The brilliance of the Attlee government was to make the most of the political space that had opened up after the war, but any administration would have moved to some extent in the direction that Labour strode determinedly. The past also played a part in the rise of Thatcherism, but in a different way. Her path was not as inevitable as the one that Attlee took. The traumas of the 1970s were the immediate context, the equivalent for Thatcher of what the war had been for Attlee. The corporatist approach of Heath, Wilson and Callaghan had failed to bring about stability let alone a robust economy. Their governments intervened to the point where cabinet ministers were not only deciding pay levels but also the price of bread on any given day of the year. When inefficient industries were in trouble the state often stepped in to save them rather than face what the three prime ministers in the 1970s regarded as unacceptably high levels of unemployment. As a result, the inefficient industries stumbled on. When some unions flexed their muscles, governments resisted at first and then either succumbed or faced tumultuous strike action. In the 1970s inflation reached 23 per cent, the unions were assertive and prime ministers appeared to be weak, struggling with the management of their parties as well as the country.

Thatcher was one counter to the dark chaos. She would not be an interventionist in the same way as they were. Instead she was content to let unemployment soar and allow prices to be determined by the market. Before long, even those ministers from the late 1970s who had intervened to decide prices found it preposterous that they had done so. In the 1980s there were new assumptions about what was required or not required from government. When inefficient industries moved towards bankruptcy they would close. Inflation would be addressed by strict controls on the printing of money. The state had proved inept at running services so Thatcher's government would privatize them. Councils were profligate so she would take away the money they wasted and reduce their powers. If unions were stroppy she would take action to limit what they could do and challenge them when she knew she could win. This counter-revolution, not only to the 1970s but to the orthodoxies in place since 1945, became known as Thatcherism. No previous prime minister had been flattered with an 'ism', not even Churchill.

Famously Thatcher claimed there was 'no alternative' to her revolution, and her dominance in policy-making for more than a decade seemed to bear her out.[1] She prevailed over all internal and external opponents, an extraordinary triumph of will. But her revolution was not an inevitable consequence arising from the failures of previous decades. It was far from the case that there was 'no alternative' as she suggested. By 1979 the UK had reached the end of the road. It could not go on as it had been doing. But was Thatcherism the only option available to arrest deep decline?

In the late 1970s and early 1980s, the senior Conservatives who disapproved of her were almost as scathing of her as those internal critics who were alarmed by the rise of Liz Truss in 2022. Ian Gilmour, a cabinet colleague until Thatcher sacked him in 1981, would go on to publish, in 1992, the most damning book on her leadership that has yet to be written.[2] At one point in *Dancing with Dogma*, Gilmour described Thatcher as the 'mistress of the irrelevant detail' and noted how in meetings she would cling to one unimportant fact from which she could not be prised. Much later Michael Heseltine made a similar point, 'she would talk about a policy or an idea based on a farmer she met or what tenants she met did with their council house . . . and this wasn't intellectually appealing.'[3] Seeing her at close hand, they did not see an intellectual titan, but a leader clinging to prejudices spurred on by radical impulses.

They were two of her critics, but their view of her has almost been drowned out by the subsequent adulation that intensified over the years. Following her long leadership, not least when a series of shallow Conservative prime ministers led from 2010, Thatcher acquired an even greater reputation for depth and being a forensic master of detail. Gilmour and Heseltine paint a more nuanced picture of Thatcher's capacity for deep thinking.

In *Dancing with Dogma*, Gilmour argued that the economy grew less quickly than under Thatcher's predecessors, that insofar as people did unusually well in the period this was a result of redistribution of wealth from the poor to the more affluent, that her policies were directly responsible for the devastation of the manufacturing industry, that the constitution had suffered severe damage from her authoritarianism, and that her foreign and defence policies were based largely on illusion.

Gilmour was one of Thatcher's early cabinet ministers whom she dismissed as 'wets'. There were quite a few of them in senior positions after 1979, including Gilmour. They had a clear view that the medicine of Thatcherism would kill the patient before any revival became possible. Their 'one-nation' Toryism was one of several options that might have taken hold after 1979. It consisted in a recognition that judicious public spending could be an investment rather than a waste and lead to economic growth; some decisions were better made at a

local level even if a few councils were reckless; and a more concili-
atory view of working with other agencies would be better than the
warrior's approach preferred by Thatcher.

But the 'wets' were useless at politics. They were soon on the backbenches protesting impotently as Thatcher won landslides. Partly,
they were identified with the failures of the past; they were either
supporters of Edward Heath, or Thatcher and her allies made sure to
push that association. But they only had themselves to blame. They
did not organize in a way that might have given Thatcher more of
a challenge internally. A few of them gave coded speeches at fringe
meetings during party conferences. They then returned to their ministerial posts and kept their heads down. None of them resigned,
but instead chose to press on until Thatcher was in a strong enough
position to sack or demote them. She did so in a cabinet reshuffle
conducted in September 1981 when she had acres of political space.
Earlier in that year there had been a formal schism in the Labour
Party with the formation of the SDP. She knew then that Labour
could not win the next election and that meant only she could. Gilmour was sacked in the reshuffle. Jim Prior was moved to Northern
Ireland, arguably more of a punishment than being removed from the
cabinet altogether given that he had held a key post. He had been an
increasingly uncomfortable employment secretary as unemployment
soared. In the same reshuffle, Thatcher promoted her ally, Norman
Tebbit. It was the most significant post-war reshuffle, as Thatcher
began to define more clearly her distinct view of what form her revolution would take.

Thatcher's external opponents were even more pathetic than her
internal ones. After losing in 1979, the Labour Party turned in on
itself. James Callaghan clung on as leader until the autumn of the
following year, uninterested in engaging with the battle of ideas that

Thatcher had essentially unleashed. He had his own battles to fight with the left of his party, but irrespective of internal opponents, Callaghan was a dream opponent for Thatcher. She was excited by ideological debates. Callaghan had never been one to engage in a battle of ideas and was far too busy defending the record of the last Labour government that was being attacked with as much intensity from the left as it was from the Thatcherite right. She had the stage to herself without having to try particularly hard.

Hidden amid the chaos of her external opponents, there was an abundance of ideas and policies that might have taken the UK in different directions. From the left of the Labour Party, Tony Benn was a counter to Thatcher with his evangelical focus on extensive state ownership, import controls, sweeping new powers for trade unions, support for unilateral nuclear disarmament and opposition to Britain's membership of the Common Market. Benn admired Thatcher as a 'teacher' from the right and she came to respect him too, as their views merged on Europe, accountability and the sovereignty of the Westminster parliament. But Benn's views did not prevail for long in the Labour Party, let alone the wider country. His framing was also parochial: he focused on the betrayal of previous Labour leaders and the need for the party membership to hold the leadership to account. He fought and nearly won the deputy leadership in 1981, but Denis Healey held on by less than 1 per cent. As Thatcher noted that autumn mischievously, 'They're fighting each other when they should be fighting me'.[4] The SDP also sought a different course to the one that Thatcher pursued. Its founders, the so-called Gang of Four, all of whom had served in the Labour cabinet that lost the 1979 election, were social democrats. Their 1983 election manifesto, agreed with the Liberal Party, outlined a role for the state that showed there was yet another active state alternative to Thatcher, alongside

Benn's agenda: 'There is no need for hopelessness. By giving a moderate and well-directed stimulus to the economy, accompanied by a firm and fair incomes policy, we can change the trend and begin to get people back to work.'[5]

But the SDP/Liberal alliance never stood a chance. Labour was too strong in Scotland and the north of England to be replaced. At the same time, Labour was too weak to win. This was the political context in which Thatcher made her revolutionary leaps. Her internal opponents were sidelined to the point of irrelevance. Labour had decided to leave the main political stage for several years and to turn in on itself.

With much of the media fully on board with the Thatcher revolution, there was no grown-up conversation in the UK after the trauma of the 1970s about whether a modern state might have an important role to play and what form it should take. Were there lessons from West Germany as its economy grew more robustly than that of the UK? Could there be a genuine social contract, a common feature in northern European states, rather than the vague contrivance proposed by Harold Wilson in the mid-1970s? What about models in northern Europe that combined high levels of investment in public services with greater productivity and fewer strikes? There were plenty of potentially fruitful turning points in 1979. For various reasons, including her own political brilliance and the ineptitude of opponents, Thatcher had the stage to herself and chose the direction that the UK would take.

As Gilmour and Heseltine implied, Thatcher could be simplistic in her approach to ideas and the policies that arose from them. In her wariness of the state, she did not delve much more deeply into alternatives than Liz Truss, the prime minister who was removed from office after four weeks in the early autumn of 2022.

In contrast, Thatcher was prime minster for more than eleven years. Her durability is more connected to her astute reading of politics than the potency of her ideas. That was the difference with Truss. The shortest-serving Conservative prime minister was a poor politician. But Thatcher knew how to win elections and to prevail in any policy dispute, while also recognizing the importance of timing and patience, so that her often half-thought-through impulses nearly always took meaty legislative form.

The clue as to how she pulled it off when Truss failed spectacularly was in the opening words of the Conservatives' 1979 manifesto. Thatcher wrote the foreword to the document and placed her credo at the heart of her party's pitch. Here she is, her political voice fully developed shortly before she moved into Number 10:

> For me the heart of politics is not political theory, it is people and how they want to live their lives.
>
> No one who has lived in this country during the last five years can fail to be aware of how the balance of our society has been increasingly tilted in favour of the State at the expense of individual freedom.
>
> This election may be the last chance we have to reverse that process, to restore the balance of power in favour of the people. It is therefore the most crucial election since the war.[6]

There is a book to be written on her opening sentence alone. Thatcher was being craftily candid. She was not especially interested in political theory, or indeed economic theory. Most voters were not either. In her candour she was placing herself at one with the electorate. She had political friends and allies in right-wing think-tanks who were immersed in ideological theories of one kind or another. Her role was to appropriate their ideas and adapt them to her strongly felt prejudices. Her concern was for 'people and how they want to live their lives'. Her father, Alfred Roberts, ran a grocer's shop and made ends meet by hard work and balancing the books. He did not need the state as far as she saw it. As a Conservative leader she was married to the wealthy Denis. He was not especially dependent on the state and nor was she. As far as they had to deal with the state, it tended to get in the way.

But her concern for 'people' was narrow. She gave little thought in the years that followed her 1979 victory to the 'people' whose lives were brutally disrupted by her policies, the job losses, the fracturing of communities, the decline in public services. Yet part of her political strength came from the sincerity of her assertion. She believed wholeheartedly that she was freeing 'the people' from the tyranny of the state.

In the next sentence, she suggested that the state was the enemy of 'individual freedom'. At the very least this was a selective interpretation of freedom. There were laws that some people disapproved of and felt constrained by. There always are. Equally, even in the stormy 1970s, the state gave many people more freedom than they would have had without forms of active government: the freedom to continue working, the freedom to negotiate equal pay between men and women and all the rest of the priorities of the tottering Heath/ Wilson/Callaghan administrations. Freedom is a complex term, but one that she seized and defined in her own terms, a talent that has usually eluded Labour prime ministers.

She wanted to restore the balance of power in 'favour of the people'. Which voter would disapprove of such a proposition when expressed in such a generalized form? Even the BBC would struggle to balance one of their banal 'vox pops' if voters in a shopping centre were questioned about 'freedom'. However hard a desperate reporter searched, he or she would not find a single voter declaring 'what I want is less freedom'. As a result Thatcher formed a bond with voters as Boris Johnson did later when he and others in the Brexit referendum urged them to 'take back control'. Who is against acquiring more control over their life?

This simple assertion that opened the 1979 manifesto was the seed that produced many other radical but limited ideas. Thatcher's transformation of the UK and her party took many different forms that were to some extent sequential. One big change naturally followed on from another.

She began with monetarism, the ideological underpinning of her early attempts to address the wild inflationary pressures that wreaked havoc during the 1970s. One of the guides leading her towards a rigid form of monetarism was Sir Keith Joseph. Her political friend was a deeper and more tortured thinker than her. Although not as self-confident as she appeared to be, Thatcher was never greatly troubled by doubt. Joseph often was. Nonetheless after the Conservatives were removed from power in February 1974 he became a passionate evangelist for controlling the monetary supply irrespective of the consequences in terms of unemployment. For Joseph if the money supply grew at a faster rate than the economy's ability to produce goods and services, then inflation would follow and that was the end of the matter. In a speech during the October 1974 election campaign Joseph delivered what became a seminal text for the early period of the Thatcher government elected five years later. Given the wide postwar consensus on the need to avoid high levels of unemployment, the speech laid the foundations for the first major turning point after 1979. Unemployment became a price worth paying.

To us, as to all post-war governments, sound money may have seemed out of date: we were dominated by the fear of unemployment. It was this which made us turn our back against our own better judgement and try to spend out of unemployment.[7]

The speech was a political event. *The Times* published it verbatim. Seemingly Joseph was tearing up the sacred Beveridge text on which post-war economic policy had been based. In his Stockton Lecture two years later, Joseph expanded on the policy implications that would accompany the revival of 'sound money':

Monetary contraction in a mixed economy strangles the private sector unless the state sector contracts with it and reduces its take from the national income. Public expenditure must be cut therefore and all the taxes. A climate of entrepreneurship has to be created and restrictive practices broken down . . . we are over-governed, over-spent, over-taxed, over-borrowed and over-manned.[8]

Thatcher agreed with every word, and after she became leader spent much time with Joseph and assorted right-wing think-tanks that shared his views. Inflation was a monetary phenomenon and the way to deal with it was to reduce the degree of monetary growth accompanied by much tougher constraints on public spending. Another key figure for the monetarist revolutionaries was Thatcher's first chancellor, Sir Geoffrey Howe. As Truss and her chancellor Kwasi Kwarteng demonstrated, while it may be fun to agree with leading right-wing thinkers over a glass or two of wine at a safe distance from economic policy-making, the hard grind of being in government is much more challenging. Howe was up for the hard grind, a dogged believer. Unlike Thatcher he was not interested in theatrical flourish to accompany his evangelism.

Yet the monetarism as espoused by Thatcher, Howe, Joseph and other true believers was never applied with the purity they sometimes claimed. The turning point in economic policy was an acceptance of high unemployment and the pursuit of income tax cuts while constraining public spending. But the ruthlessness of the pursuit was eased by the proceeds from North Sea oil and the cash raised from the sale of publicly owned assets to the private sector. Indeed privatization was to become the more enduring revolution.

Their attempts to kill off inflation were initially a failure. The story of a supposedly purist attachment to monetarism can be told following Howe's first three budgets. In a budget a chancellor not only delivers policies but seeks to frame arguments that explain and justify his or her programme. In this early phase Howe and Thatcher worked well together, even if she already found him irritating and he quickly became frustrated that she alone was seen as the economic pioneer.

Howe had a reputation for being dull. Denis Healey, then in the shadow cabinet, famously described facing him in the Commons as like being 'savaged by a dead sheep'. *Private Eye* suggested the definition of a bad party was one in which on arrival a guest heard the words 'Sir Geoffrey is in good form tonight.' His apparent dullness annoyed Thatcher, who was much more of a performer and who preferred male colleagues who displayed a hint of flirtatious exuberance. As is usually the case when politicians are stereotyped, the caricature of Howe was wide of the mark. He was politically bold to the point of stubbornness and had a curiosity about politics across the political spectrum. His favourite newspaper was *The Independent* in its early classy phase, not a supporter of the government's economic policies, although by then Nigel Lawson had replaced him at the Treasury. He enjoyed debating with opponents within his party and beyond and was as much of a pioneer as Thatcher. He was the one who had to come up with the detailed policies, even if his early budgets were a revealing chronicle of failure.

In his first budget speech in June 1979, weeks after the election, Howe outlined his dire economic inheritance as he saw it.

Consumer spending rose last year, in percentage terms, by seven times as much as manufacturing output. We actually manufactured 4 per cent less goods in 1978 than in 1973. But the volume of manufactured imports went up by 13.5 per cent. Though demand was rising strongly, and unemployment remained high, the economy was almost unable to increase supply. The current account of the balance of payments was barely in surplus last year, despite a massive contribution of £3½ billion from North Sea oil and gas. And well before the last Administration left office, inflation was back on a rising trend. Although many price increases had been held back behind the general election dam, the rate of inflation in the six months to April—excluding seasonal foods—was running at no less than 12.3 per cent at an annual rate.

On that form and on the policies which brought it about, there is little reason to expect any improvement in the future. Productivity is rising less than half as fast as in the early 1970s. There is no sign of any change for the better there. Last year's growth in demand could never have been sustained, because, as the trade figures make clear, it was largely met from imports. That was the main reason why the recent fall in unemployment was, in any event, likely to be reversed.[9]

His assessment was rather like the verdict of the hotel inspector who listed all the faults in *Fawlty Towers*. At the end, Basil asks, 'Apart from that is everything else all right?' The difference was that the hotel inspector's demands did lead to the infamous hotel improving even if there was a rat on the loose. Howe's solution to economic malaise was monetarism combined with the actions suggested by Joseph five years earlier. In the short term, at least, his plans made matters worse. Here were his proposed remedies:

> We need to squeeze inflation out of the system. It is crucially important to re-establish sound money. We intend to achieve this through firm monetary discipline and fiscal policies consistent with that, including strict control over public expenditure.
> . . . We are committed to the progressive reduction of the rate of growth of the money supply.[10]

The new chancellor announced a VAT rise, incremental income tax cuts with promises of more to come, along with tough new constraints on public spending. The government was no longer going to print money to keep the economy afloat, thereby in the view of Thatcher and Howe killing off inflation. Instead the UK economy was in recession by the time he delivered his second budget in 1980. There was more than the equivalent of a rat on the loose. In the era before the Office for Budget Responsibility, the Treasury issued its own forecasts. They were as grim as those delivered by any independent analyst: 'The Treasury projections published today suggest that output may fall in 1980 by up to 2.5 per cent.'[11]

But Howe insisted that there would be no turning back whatever the short-term pressures to do so:

Relaxed monetary and budgetary policies might bring higher output—even higher living standards—in the very short run, though even that is questionable, but in reality they would simply fuel fresh inflation. Such policies would inevitably undermine the confidence of financial markets, industry, and consumers. The action that would then be necessary to deal with the ensuing crisis would, equally certainly, destroy jobs and cut living standards still further.

Restraint of the growth of money and credit is, then, essential, and it needs to be maintained over a considerable period of time in order to defeat inflation.[12]

The supposedly dull chancellor was taking huge risks. He proposed increases in prescription charges and indirect taxes along with even tougher constraints on public spending for most services. The leader of the opposition, James Callaghan, responded by describing it as the 'meanest budget since 1931'.[13]

By the time of the 1981 budget, productivity was projected to fall by another 1 per cent and unemployment to reach three million and stay there for the rest of the parliament. Confronted by relatively high wage increases in 1979 and 1980, it was an article of monetarist faith that this would not cause inflation unless the government printed money. The monetary posture necessitated high interest rates that helped to force up the exchange rate which in turn greatly weakened industry. Public borrowing was going through the roof. Inflation was heading towards 20 per cent. Howe had presided over the largest one-year drop in industrial output since 1921. And unemployment had risen by more than a million, to a previously unimaginable 2.5 million. The government hadn't even managed to control the money supply – its number-one stated objective.

In order to bring down interest rates and to devalue the pound, the 1981 budget combined a relaxation of monetary policy with a fierce fiscal squeeze. Margaret Thatcher's economics adviser, Alan Walters, put it bluntly: 'In spite of rapidly increasing unemployment and falling output the government introduced the toughest peacetime budget in memory'.[14]

Howe announced in his most famous budget that he was going to raise taxes substantially, in the middle of a recession. To do so he used a 'stealth tax' that has been deployed many times since then, called in the technical jargon 'fiscal drag': he didn't raise income tax thresholds to take account of inflation. But with inflation running at 16 per cent in those days, it was not very stealthy. In the spring of 2023 the chancellor, Jeremy Hunt, did the same in relation to thresholds as inflation rose. The move became part of a narrative about the 'cost-of-living crisis'. It was not very stealthy then either. In 1981 there was also a windfall tax on oil and bank profits that would not look out of place in a budget from Gordon Brown.

Headline-writers and commentators were incensed. Economists were, for once, almost united. Three hundred and sixty-four of them later signed a letter to *The Times*, claiming that monetarist policies had no basis in economic theory, would deepen the recession and should be abandoned. Everyone who was anyone, it seemed, had signed, including two past and future Nobel laureates (James Meade and Amartya Sen) and several Blair advisers-to-be (including Julian Le Grand and Anthony Giddens).

Despite the uproar, all the economists agreed that the 1981 budget was a turning point in one important respect: it marked the first time when inflation had been placed irrevocably at the top of the list of government economic priorities, ahead of employment. That shift had begun in the final years of the Callaghan government, but the 1981 budget made it irreversible. The economists who signed the letter thought that it would be impossible for any government to survive unemployment of three million. Margaret Thatcher proved them wrong.

The UK economy did start growing soon after the 1981 budget, although unemployment reached three million as had been forecast and the quality of most public services declined, partly as a result of spending constraints. Quite soon, the 1981 budget became mythologized, triggering a new fashionable orthodoxy in the UK. Public spending was largely seen as wasteful and new arguments opened up that services could be improved by 'reform' alone, reforms that included a much greater role for the private sector.

The orthodoxy endured for decades. When the global financial crisis of 2008 erupted, the shadow chancellor, George Osborne, turned to Thatcher's two chancellors, Howe and Lawson, for guidance. The changed assumption after 1979 was that a smaller state boosted the economy and if that also meant high unemployment, so be it. When Jeremy Hunt became chancellor amidst economic turmoil in the autumn of 2022, he turned to Osborne and his former senior aides for advice. The models that influenced them all were the opening budgets after the 1979 election. Indeed 'sources' close to Hunt told the *Daily Mail* that the 1981 budget was his precise inspiration.[15]

Of the prominent ministers in the 1980s, only Michael Heseltine made the case for an active state, even daring to write directly to Thatcher asking for some additional funding to help his plans to revive inner cities, most specifically Liverpool. Heseltine's energetic activism did help to revive Liverpool, the East End of London and a few other inner cities. Yet few within the governing party or the influential and dominant Conservative newspapers sought to draw wider lessons from the resurgence of these troubled urban areas. Howe was even opposed to what Heseltine was seeking to do, urging him to let 'market forces' determine the fate of Liverpool and other rapidly declining cities.

In the Conservative newspapers, the constant demand was for more tax cuts to be financed by spending cuts. Their urging was both strident and parochial. The mighty editors did not look abroad to learn lessons about the constructive role a modern state could play. As Heseltine was to declare at the Conservative Party conference in 1992, as president of the Board of Trade, he planned to intervene to help businesses 'before breakfast, dinner and tea'. He pointed out that this was what the Japanese government did with its powerful industrial strategy. The German government had the same goal but used different means as did powerful regional governments in less centralized states in Europe. Heseltine was ebullient on the conference stage but he might as well have been speaking Latin. There was little enthusiasm after the applause had faded. His departmental budget had been cut drastically, leaving him with little room to intervene constructively as other governments did in comparable countries. Those early budgets from 1979 had transformed thinking in the UK media and political establishment about what makes an economy successful. The essence of the new ideology was that the more government kept out of the way the better it would be, the precise opposite of the 1945 revolution.

There was, however, a twist. Thatcher regarded much of local government as profligate. To her frustration, the big metropolitan authorities were all Labour-controlled. In London, Ken Livingstone's Greater London Council was both a radical counter to Thatcherism and popular according to opinion polls, at least when the Conservative government announced its abolition along with the other metropolitan authorities. There were many noisy controversies during Livingstone's leadership of the GLC, but one was emblematic. Livingstone introduced a 'Fares Fair' policy in 1982, subsidizing fares on public transport that were some of the highest in Europe.

The subsidy was paid for by boroughs across London in the same way tax is raised throughout the UK for programmes that will not always benefit every taxpayer. However this principle was challenged by the Conservative-controlled Bromley Council in south London. It argued that most of its (wealthy) local taxpayers would not benefit from the lower fares and that the entire project was unlawful. The council won the case and in March 1982 fares on London's buses and tubes doubled. For a brief period, the capital had come to life with cheaper fares and less traffic congestion. But by then, Thatcher was winning the argument about spending being a 'waste'. London's much-read newspaper the *Evening Standard* hailed the council's victory and there were no great protests. Those dependent on public transport paid up even though in some cases the fares were a significant proportion of their salary. Similarly Thatcher abolished the GLC and other metropolitan councils without a great deal of fuss and with considerable support from the Conservative newspapers. But it did mean that the small-state prime minister was becoming a keen centralizer in spite of herself.

Central government quangos became responsible for the provision of services, including public transport in London. They were accountable only to ministers. London had no elected authority. Central government had seized control without thinking through the implications. Obscure quangos became responsible for increasingly unreliable services in London. In other parts of the UK, deregulated buses also became more expensive, if they ran at all. Non-profit-making services were cut. Voters could not punish local councils as they were not directly responsible. With the decline of public transport, they were being left behind.

The Miners are Defeated and the City Gets a Big Bang

The acceptance of high unemployment severely limited the power of the unions. Thatcher refused to intervene to support ailing industries even if the problems that afflicted them were in some cases temporary. The shipyards, the steelworks and the mines closed, along with British car manufacturers that could no longer hold their own. From the start of her period in office, she held no meetings with trade union leaders and yet she moved carefully in seeking to challenge them directly. On this, she displayed a subtle patience, conceding to high pay demands at first and avoiding an early confrontation with the miners. It was not until after her 1983 landslide victory and when coal stocks were high that she was ready to confront the miners over pits that she regarded as uneconomic to keep open.

There was a cinematic sequence in the mid-1980s, involving a kaleidoscope of turning points for the UK. Thatcher 'defeated' the miners after a long strike that drained all those involved of any energy. Pits were closed, miners lost their jobs, the president of the NUM, Arthur Scargill, faded from influence. The newish Labour leader, Neil Kinnock, aged speedily and had no honeymoon with the voters because of his barely concealed torment over a strike held without a ballot of union members. Simultaneously, there was a sweeping deregulation of the City of London in 1986, known appropriately as the 'big bang', built on the earlier decision taken in 1979 to abolish exchange controls. The 'big bang' was a momentous modernizing event in the history of the Square Mile, introducing electronic screen-based trading, breaking up old 'closed shops', sweeping away the cosy old-boys' network of British-owned banks and opening up the City to international banks. All this contributed to the astronomical growth of UK financial services. Meanwhile mines closed and communities shrank. There was no attempt by government to revitalize towns and villages dependent on mining after the pits had closed. A number became as ghostly as the City of London became fizzed with an around-the-clock energy.

Brutally but effectively Thatcher had resolved the issue that had brought about the fall of Heath, Wilson and Callaghan. In 1979, 29.4 million working days were lost to strikes. By 1990 when Thatcher left office there were less than two million.[16] As the old manufacturing sectors declined, there was a curious reverse-imperialism where the UK gratefully accepted companies from abroad moving to the UK, training and employing UK workers in new modern ways and more widely assisting in the revival of the economy. On 8 September 1986, Thatcher opened the Nissan plant in Sunderland with the hope that it would 'provide a steadily grow-ing number of jobs in an area which really needs them' and 'show in the clearest possible way how such areas can help to recover their prosperity and self-esteem'.[17] Toyota and Honda soon followed. (Of course, Nissan later became totemic after the Brexit referendum in 2016, when ministers went out of their way to ensure that the com-pany remained in the UK.) Ambiguity and confusion about the role of foreigners in the UK economy became more intense under Thatcher than before 1979. Foreign companies such as Nissan were welcomed unequivocally, as were star footballers from around the world. Yet later, those that came from Eastern Europe as a result of the UK's membership of the EU were seen as a threat by some voters, even those who arrived because of demand for their skills.

Thatcher reflected and fuelled ambiguity and confusion. She was exuberant when companies moved to the UK from other countries, but became increasingly angry with the EU while never contemplating withdrawal and while also relishing the benefits of the single market that she had helped to create. Thatcher had campaigned for the UK's continued membership in the 1975 referendum, held two years after the UK had formally joined under Edward Heath. To Heath's fury she was never an enthusiast as prime minister and by the end of her time in power noisily hostile. After 1979, the UK became paradoxically both more closed-minded and far more open to global players to arrive and flourish on its insular stage.

On Thatcher's most extensive project, there was no ambiguity. She became more obsessed by the issue of ownership than the Labour government of 1945 or the left of the Labour Party in the 1980s. Her party and the media followed. Ultimately the leadership of the Labour Party paid homage too. The Attlee government had nationalized extensively. She became an evangelist for privatization.

A Change of Ownership

The scale of the change Thatcher brought about in public ownership was immense. The switch from state to private ownership was the biggest turning point after 1979. By the time Thatcher left office in November 1990, over 50 per cent of the public sector had been transferred to the private sector and 650,000 workers had switched. Around 1,250,000 council houses had been sold, most to sitting tenants under the 'right-to-buy' provisions. Similarly, contracting out was well-established in the NHS and the local authority sector.[18]

A testimony to her conquering will was the attitude of the first

Labour government after her leadership ended. By the time of the 1997 election her main opponents did not dare to challenge her views on ownership even though she had left Number 10 nearly seven years earlier. Indeed, Tony Blair and Gordon Brown promised more privatization. They dismissed any defence of state ownership as 'old Labour' or 'hard left'. Her dominance over the issue was her biggest ideological victory by far, though by no means the only one. Such was the scale of her victory that when Blair espoused similar ideas to hers about the virtues of privatization he was regarded as being on the 'centre ground', battling it out with the left of the Labour Party that dared to advocate new forms of state ownership. A big leap to the right soon became part of a 'centrist' consensus, an epic political achievement for Thatcher not least when many of the privatizations were implemented with poor results in terms of public-service delivery. The outcomes were overlooked.

Her ideological conquest was based on her own assertiveness and largely selective reporting of what she was doing. If the Labour government of 1945 was flawed in its failure to establish a compelling thought-through framework for nationalization then the privatization of the Thatcher era was far more erratic and haphazard.

The most striking switch from public to private in her first term was the sale of council houses, with local authority tenants becoming property owners at a time when house prices were rising. Housing illustrated most vividly Thatcher's preoccupation with ownership. The sale of council homes involved building little new housing stock, which would have been a more arduous project. Instead the transfer from public to private was Thatcher's first populist crusade. The term 'right to buy' was a clever slogan, echoing the opening sentence of her 1979 manifesto. Here was a celebration of her version of 'freedom'. Tenants lived in council-owned homes. They should have more than the 'freedom' to buy them. They should have the 'right' to do so. The liberation became part of an early Thatcherite crusade to create the ultimate property-owning democracy. As a bonus for her, the government received a one-off financial windfall from the sale of homes in the public sector. The numbers were not as juicy as North Sea oil, but nevertheless substantial, totalling nearly £2 billion in 1982–3, the year of her election landslide victory.

Although these sums were substantial they were nowhere near the actual value of the properties that were sold off at considerable discounts. Thatcher was not as thrifty as she thought she was. 'Right to buy' was an early example of what the former Conservative prime minister Harold Macmillan went on to identify as 'selling off the family silver', a powerful if outdated metaphor. In a speech to the Tory Reform Group at the Carlton Club in November 1984, Macmillan noted provocatively: 'First the Georgian silver goes . . . and then all the nice furniture that used to be in the saloon. Then the Canalettos go.'[19]

Macmillan had always deployed wit as a political weapon and with considerable impact. The clip of the speech is on YouTube and the audience can be heard laughing along with him. But he was making a serious point. Thatcher had a reputation for Calvinistic prudence, one that she had earnestly cultivated and believed to be a true reflection of her 'sound money' approach to the economy. But her preoccupation with the transfer of ownership was financially reckless. State assets were sold off cheaply, making it almost impossibly expensive for governments to buy them back again if they wanted to explore modern forms of state ownership. It was the equivalent of selling a house at a reduced price to raise some quick cash, and for the parting owners to realize they would never be able to move back in again even if they wished to do so. Here was the formal break with one-nation Conservatism as represented by Macmillan. The break arose over ownership and privatization.

One of Thatcher's best biographers, John Campbell, argued that Macmillan's intervention was harmful to her: 'The image of ministers like a lot of dodgy asset strippers knocking down the nation's heirlooms at a cost well below their true worth subtly undermined Mrs Thatcher's carefully created reputation for thrifty housekeeping . . .'[20]

The subtlety was lost on most voters. In some respects, Macmillan inadvertently assisted Thatcher. He was old, from another era when prime ministers owned much family silver. Although persistently highlighting her attachment to 'Victorian values', part of her electoral appeal was an appearance of modernity, being part of a new zeitgeist. The has-been Macmillan was admonishing the restlessly impatient change-maker. Much of the media and quite a lot of voters were by then with the change-maker.

Nonetheless, Macmillan was right. Thatcher's crusading support for private ownership had many consequences. Her environment secretary during the first term, Michael Heseltine, was alert to the long-term dangers of 'right to buy' as well as the immediate benefits. At first, he successfully argued that councils should be allowed to keep three-quarters of the income from sales, in order to replace the homes sold. But speedily, the share of the income from sales that went to councils was eroded. Far fewer affordable rented homes were built in the 1980s and 1990s compared with the 1970s, the decade of economic storms. Thatcher was not interested in the hard, unglamorous grind of affordable housebuilding. The switch in ownership was what excited her.

After Thatcher's landslide victory in 1987, her favourite cabinet minister, Nicholas Ridley, the latest environment secretary, announced a 'housing revolution'. Ridley was an ideological soulmate, a privately charming chain-smoker, who like his prime-ministerial admirer pursued policies that had not been properly thought through. His housing revolution consisted of the introduction of housing action trusts, new bodies that would be responsible for improving estates and accountable to central government. In addition, private landlords would be given new rights to buy publicly owned housing. Once again, the focus was on ownership, another switch from public to private or from local government to the centre. Ridley's housing revolution involved the building of no new housing.

The shortage of new affordable homes led to soaring housing benefit bills as those on low incomes could only find accommodation in the increasingly expensive private rented sector. Government indifference to the shortage of affordable rented housing was as big a turning point after 1979 as the sale of council homes.

It was in the second and third terms that Thatcher's appetite for transfers of ownership greatly increased, to the wary concern of Macmillan. Yet for a leader supposedly driven by ideas, a conviction politician, Thatcher never set out coherently why she had become such a fervent advocate of privatization. Indeed the lack of a coherent explanation from her has triggered speculation ever since as to what the purpose was. Were the industries privatized to make them more efficient? Was it to raise money for a government desperately in need of cash? Above all, did Thatcher want to reduce government involvement in industry? Did she want to bear down on public-sector pay by weakening the unions? Was she keen to widen share ownership? At different times all these factors came into play and with results far more mixed than mythology suggests, or suggested by the 1990s, when the Labour leadership felt compelled to worship at the same altar.

Thatcher's authorized biographer, Charles Moore, highlighted her abiding hatred of the nationalized industries because of the amount of time and government money they consumed. She argued persistently that private ownership is 'often more efficient because people know they're on their own whereas if they're nationalised they think "oh well we can turn round and the taxpayer has got to subside us." '[21] The flaw in this argument was that the new privately owned companies could not be allowed to fail either and the government would still be forced to intervene.

On the whole, inefficient state monopolies were replaced by even more inefficient and expensive private monopolies. In place of competition a state regulator was established for each industry. The agencies included OFTEL, OFGAS, OFWAT, and many others similarly titled. They struggled to achieve the required balance of ensuring good value for consumers while giving the private providers space to deliver services profitably. Regulators often lacked specialist expertise and the power to intervene. At best, they had influence which they exercised through a process of negotiation and consultation with the privatized company. The relative success of OFTEL owed a great deal to the fact that in the telecommunications sector, some level of competition was possible. Gas, water and the other utilities struggled to create the equivalent of robust competition through regulation.

The same applied to the fashion for 'contracting out' services previously overseen by councils or the NHS. Before the Thatcher revolution, cleaners were as much part of a hospital as the doctors and nurses. When private companies were brought in to clean hospitals, those who worked for them were detached from the wider purpose of a hospital while the companies they worked for were unaccountable to patients and the wider electorate.

Similarly, ruling parties of local councils could be removed at an election. The companies awarded long contracts to clean the streets could operate impervious to voters' verdicts on their services; even if one of the local electorate's concerns was the cleanliness of streets, they could safely be ignored. Thatcher was not bothered if voters could not hold street-cleaning companies and many others to account. A study by the authoritative *Public Administration* journal on contracting out, conducted shortly after Thatcher left office, concluded: 'Contracting out has reduced costs but at the expense of the quality of services . . .'[22]

In spite of the negative evidence, contracting out and privatization remained hugely popular with Conservative leaders and to some extent within parts of the Labour Party too. Tory-run Barnet Council in north London took the experiment to its ideological conclusion. In 2005, fifteen years after Thatcher had left the political stage, the council leadership viewed the idea of a small council in the same way that Thatcherites had championed the small state.[23] The basic idea was to drastically shrink Barnet's council, mostly by handing an array of local services – highways, planning, regeneration, phone helplines, even cemeteries and crematoriums – to the outsourcing company Capita. The council signed two decade-long contracts with Capita – worth about £500m to the company. The arrangements began to unravel expensively. In 2018, a handful of council services, including finance and human resources, were brought back into the public sector. Two years later the council ditched Capita as the administrator of its pensions scheme, and another five council services came back in-house. Then, in May 2022, Labour regained control of the council – taking sixteen seats from the Tories for a total of forty-one – and swiftly announced that Barnet's era of outsourcing had come to an end. By then the council had paid £229m more than the original contracts had set out, for poorer public services.

On the national stage, by the third decade of the twenty-first century, even the Conservative Party began to question the privatization programme. As private water companies poured sewage into the seas, it became apparent that there was no competition and the 'market' was not working. Water privatization had been instigated after the 1987 election by Nicholas Ridley at the same time as his 'housing revolution' without new houses and the introduction of the poll tax – a flat-rate local tax, one of the few turning points that did not endure.

Similarly, the energy 'market' proved to have long-term problems. In effect companies gambled on the price of natural gas. There were no long-term plans to store it in case of sudden shortages and soaring prices. In order to widen the market, the government encouraged smaller firms to challenge the larger established companies. But when prices leapt, as they did when Russia invaded Ukraine in 2022, a lot of the newer companies were threatened with bankruptcy. The government had to intervene in the way it would have done in the previous era of state ownership. The government bailout of the once fashionable company Bulb cost several billion pounds. In the topsy-turvy world of British politics, some of the Conservative newspapers were furious about the outlay but it was a consequence of the privatization they had called for.

The same contradictory emotions were aroused by the railways. They were privatized after Thatcher left office but the measure was implemented partly to appease her followers, who were beginning to stir against her successor, John Major. What followed was familiar. Whenever there was serious disruption in the railways, a regular occurrence, the Conservative-supporting newspapers turned on the government, but the government was no longer responsible. Except that ultimately, it was responsible. An economy depends on the smooth running of the railways. A government cannot sit back if a train company goes bankrupt or fails to deliver. The government holds all the risk when a service goes wrong; a private company gets the profits for shareholders when it manages to meet the modest requirements laid out by the government to secure a contract. Layers of mediating agencies were required to make the complex system remotely viable. There was little clarity about who was responsible for what, not least when there was chaos on the railways.

A Special Relationship

As the domestic revolution of the 1980s and 1990s took hold, the UK's place in the world became more distinctive, personified by Thatcher's restless leadership. The long-serving prime minister became more confident and assertive as she formed close ties with presidents in their pomp. The foundation of her foreign policy was her close relationship with President Reagan. In some respects they were incomparably different in outlook and personality. She set out as a stern monetarist. He borrowed indiscriminately to fund tax cuts. He was effortlessly charming in a way that put people at their ease. Her charisma was more dependent on a strident and intimidating ebullience. But they both shared a disdain for the state and were hawkish in relation to foreign policy, at least until both concluded that Gorbachev was a Soviet leader they could work with.

Thatcher also won a war, which marked in a somewhat pitiful manner a turning point in the way a significant number of voters saw their country after the humiliations of the 1970s. They had become used to decline. Now they were led by a winner. After victory in the

Falklands in the summer of 1982, some changed their view of Thatcher too. The Iron Lady had become a victorious war leader. Yet victory in the Falklands was another ambiguous turning point. Before the invasion, the Argentinian government, a fascist junta, noted much talk in the British administration about cutting back on the resources required to defend the islands. The war itself was yet another consequence of the endless search to discover how much less government could do, in this case in relation to defence spending. Detecting weakness or indifference, the Argentinians made their move. Thatcher's response was widely regarded as an act of Churchillian leadership, not least by her. But the decision to send the task force was not courageous. She had no choice. The only alternative would have been to resign and she had no intention of doing that. She followed the only course available to her and the events that followed gave parts of the country a new patriotic pride. She made sure she was the most prominent figure at the victory parades and her poll ratings started to soar.

There is a widespread theory that her success in the Falklands led to her landslide election win in 1983, a year later. This is not the case. The schism in the Labour Party of 1981 meant that neither Labour nor the SDP could have won the election. The anti-Tory vote was inevitably split. That meant there was only going to be one winner from 1981 onwards. Thatcher would have won big even if the Falklands had not been liberated.

Compared with the warmth of her relationship with Reagan, she could be cold or ferocious with other members of the European Union. Yet she was at her most creative in relation to Europe. The single market was largely her initiative and no country benefited more than the UK. She had crude anti-German instincts largely based on the Second World War and was uneasy with the French. She shared with the left-wing Labour MP Tony Benn a fear that the EU was increasingly a threat to the sovereignty of the Westminster parliament. But unlike Benn she never advocated leaving or proposed a referendum on the UK's membership while she was prime minister. There is no evidence such moves even crossed her mind when she was in office. Her senior adviser in Number 10, Charles Powell, does not believe she would have been a supporter of Brexit. Yet her hostility to the EU by the end of her leadership sowed the seeds for Brexit, giving permission to Conservative MPs to become ideological insurrectionaries in her mould.

An Enduring Turning Point

By the time Thatcher was forced out of office, much of the UK was in thrall to the private sector and private ownership, public spending was viewed with wariness, tax cuts were worthy of euphoric celebration, forms of medium- to long-term planning by government were seen as dated and market forces were viewed widely as the benevolent driving engine to sustain and revive the economy. This was all in vivid contrast to the 1970s and the orthodoxies that shaped the 1945 government when centralized planning defined what followed.

'Thatcherism' became a mighty creed. To challenge the shaky foundations on which her beliefs were based became almost impossible, even for political opponents. In terms of party politics, she changed the Labour Party, at least under the leadership of Tony Blair. Above all, she transformed the Conservative Party. Given that she was driven by ideas and ideological verve it is unsurprising that over time her parliamentary party came to move closer to her restless personality. Conservative MPs made life hellish for John Major, her successor, in the 1990s. Their cause was opposition to the Maastricht Treaty. With her encouragement, a significant section of the parliamentary party rebelled in key votes. Major had to go through painful contortions merely to stagger on, holding votes of confidence, standing down as party leader in order to fight a leadership contest in 1995. When the party next returned to power, insurrectionary Conservative MPs removed Theresa May, Boris Johnson and Liz Truss from office. They revelled in their rebelliousness, almost enjoying themselves.

From the autumn of 2022, Rishi Sunak led with a big majority inherited from the party's previous election victory, but he was in effect leading a minority government. On most issues he could not be guaranteed the support of one faction or another. In the party created by Thatcher, principle trumped loyalty. The Conservatives became harder to lead than the Labour Party, a mind-boggling reversal of roles.

Thatcherism in its early form arose from her instinctive reading of how to win an election following the troubled leadership of Edward Heath. Her strong leadership when her party was in opposition was not because she felt especially robust. She did not. In her shadow cabinets and early cabinets she recognized the need to appoint internal opponents to senior positions. But she sensed that an appearance of determined assertiveness would be popular when the Labour prime minister, James Callaghan, seemed so weak. While Callaghan was forced to chair cabinet meetings that sometimes lasted several days, Thatcher declared to the annoyance of some colleagues that she would have no time for such dissent.

Having won an authority-enhancing general election, she framed her entire project around 'freedom'. Even if many did not feel 'freer', voters gave their backing to the cascade of turning points in the 1980s. Thatcherism began as a governing force soon after the so-called 'winter of discontent'. Those images of chaos helped to suggest that Thatcher had succeeded in imposing a new order on a country that had become ungovernable. With a largely doting media there was much talk of an 'economic miracle' taking place, the unions docile and the economy growing (though never more than by around 2 per cent and there were two recessions during her leadership). After the disruption of the 1970s, voters responded to homilies about making ends meet even if her frugality was accompanied by an impatient recklessness in relation to the use of funds from North Sea oil and the fire sale of state-owned assets.

The context was the key to her durability. The 1970s had been such a chaotic mess her messianic sense of purpose came as a relief to a significant proportion of the electorate. Although her privatizations were in some cases costly and inefficient, few looked back with affection to the state-owned British Rail or the nationalized telephones. In the absence of a properly mediated debate about how to run a modern efficient state, the UK was left with a rushed move from public to private ownership and a curiously passive acceptance that this was how it had to be in one of the wealthiest economies in the world. People would travel to Europe and note cleaner streets, better transport provision and, if they fell ill, more efficient health care. They returned to the UK and navigated as best they could the gap between growing private affluence for some and the public squalor. There were few protests and voters in England continued to vote for Conservative governments until Labour's landslide in 1997.

Thatcher's continuing hold over fashionable orthodoxy was remarkable and unique amongst twentieth-century prime ministers. The more measured and reflective John Major, her immediate successor, felt obliged to privatize the railways almost to prove his

Thatcherite credentials when they were being called into question. As a new chancellor in 1997, Gordon Brown, on other matters to the left of Tony Blair, introduced an absurdly convoluted public–private partnership for the London Underground that was expensive and quickly became unworkable. Thatcher would have been proud of him and perhaps was. She described Blair as her ultimate achievement, a leader closer to her in some respects than he was to his Labour predecessors.[24]

David Cameron's vision of a 'big society' was all about rebooting Thatcherism with his view that there was such a thing as society but it was not the same as the state. George Osborne's economic policies, specifically his approach to public spending, went further than she did, but she was the model. In the Conservatives' 2022 leadership contest the final two candidates, Sunak and Truss, competed to prove who was more like Thatcher. Sunak went as far as travelling with his wife to Grantham, Thatcher's hometown, to be photographed next to her statue. Truss went further, photographed in a tank as Thatcher had been and later wearing clothes that mirrored Thatcher's favourite outfits.

Given this context, it is easy to lose sight of the fact that more voters in total backed Labour and the SDP/Liberal alliance in 1983 and 1987 than Thatcher's Conservative Party. Those parties made proposals to the left of New Labour. The UK was not as right wing as it appeared to be. But with the opposition suffering a rare formal split the election victories of the Conservatives led to much talk of a Thatcherite zeitgeist sweeping the land.

Attlee and the 1945 Labour government were widely revered long after their relatively short rule came to an end. But their turning points did not endure in the same way. In the 2020s the UK was still Thatcher's country.

6

LABOUR WINS THREE
ELECTIONS IN A ROW

By the time of the 1997 general election the Conservatives had
ruled for eighteen years. The election therefore marked a clear turning point in one obvious sense: there was a change of government.
Britain was not used to this. Under the leadership of Tony Blair and
Gordon Brown, Labour had not only won but had done so by the
biggest landslide since the war. Blair, Brown and a relatively small
group of senior figures around them had learned how to win an
election from opposition. To some extent, New Labour was a project
about securing election victories in what its leadership considered to
be a conservative country.

For Labour, winning was rare. By 1997, only Harold Wilson
had managed it as a Labour leader in opposition. Wilson won an
overall majority in 1964 and though he did win again in February
1974, it was by such a narrow margin that he could only form a
fragile minority government. Given that elections in the UK often
do not lead to a change of governing party, those that do at least
mark a political turning point. From 1951 to 1964 the Conservatives won three elections in a row. From 1979, they won four in a
row. The natural dynamic in the UK was for the Conservatives to

reinvent themselves in power and Labour to spend the seemingly endless opposition years rowing about how to win and govern. So 1997 was a dramatic reversal of this dynamic. Suddenly it was the Conservatives' turn to analyse powerlessly what they had done wrong and how they needed to change. Labour had the rare space to act in government. The election victories in 2001 and 2005 reinforced the scale of the changed dynamic. It had always been Harold Wilson's aim to make Labour the 'natural party of government'. For many years Blair appeared to have achieved the objective. During this long period of rule, one author, Geoffrey Wheatcroft, went as far as writing a book with the dramatic title *The Strange Death of Tory England*. But within five years of the book's publication in 2005, a Conservative was prime minister once more.

The name of Blair's party was central to the mission. New Labour was defined by the party's past and was an overt rejection of it. Blair, Brown and their small entourages claimed to be 'new' and therefore dismissed the party's past as 'old'. On one level this was a clever juxtaposition. The internal tensions in a party notorious for division had suddenly become tamely chronological, in the sense that everything that had happened was old, and everything that was happening now and in the future was new. Although some in the party's leadership were to regret the degree to which they rejected the past, and became resentful as they became the 'old', there was a potency about the party's rechristening, a symbolism of fresh vivacity in that adjective 'new'.

The lessons that Blair and Brown learnt about how to win arose from crushing defeats. They had both become MPs for the first time in the 1983 election, when Labour had been slaughtered in Margaret Thatcher's first landslide win. As they rose through the party, Labour lost again and again. The most vivid lessons for them came from the 1992 campaign, an election that many, both within Labour and beyond, expected the party to win. Instead the Conservatives won an overall majority for the fourth time.

At the heart of that election was the familiar British debate around the theme of tax and spend. At the start of the election the shadow chancellor, John Smith, had published an alternative budget that outlined detailed proposals for tax rises and tax reductions. The idea was partly to show that Labour was ready for government. Smith was described as 'Labour's chancellor' at the launch and other events. The 'shadow' had been dropped. Smith also hoped to prove that most voters would be better off under a Labour government. The publication had the opposite impact. Most voters do not read the details of a budget, let alone an alternative budget. They might read headlines and pick up a sense of the way proposals and ideas are being played out. Smith's plans became part of an onslaught from the Conservatives and the media from the moment they were loftily unveiled. Noisily and repeatedly, the media claimed that 'Labour's sums don't add up', and that therefore there were hidden 'tax bombshells' still to explode. The shadow budget, instead of being a win for Labour, became a powerful weapon for the Conservatives.

At the end of that campaign, after Labour had lost again, the party's focus group guru Philip Gould presented a bleak picture to the National Executive Committee. Gould concluded that the main reason why Labour had been defeated was that the party was not trusted when it came to taxes or public spending, the most fundamental responsibilities of government.

The 1992 election post-mortem was the immediate backdrop to the formation of New Labour. When Tony Blair acquired the leadership in July 1994 after the sudden death of John Smith, he and Gordon Brown addressed the daunting context of 1992 in the most overt way they could. Gordon Brown had already begun work on restoring 'trust' in relation to economic policy, having become shadow chancellor in 1992. From the summer of 1994, Blair and Brown pursued ruthlessly a strategy that killed off the pre-election 'tax-and-spend' debate that Labour always lost.

The duo's fundamental pre-election insight was that it was in Labour's interest to under-promise in the build-up to an election, thereby reassuring Middle England, who seemed to be suspicious of any pledge from Labour that cost a substantial sum of money. The insight was counter-intuitive and constraining once power had been won. After eighteen years of tight public spending and declining public services, voters might have hoped for glowing promises of incomparably better-funded public services, a vision of a fractured country working coherently under a new Labour government. Yet Blair and Brown instead chose to offer hope and reassurance through incremental changes with a hint that more might follow. Like Thatcherism, a product of the late 1970s and early 1980s, the approach was rooted in the era it took shape. In 1997 the economy was growing rapidly and the challenges for the UK, though considerable, were far less daunting than they were when Keir Starmer began to make his moves as leader of the opposition. This did not stop Blair and Brown offering much advice to Starmer based on their experiences of winning in 1997.

In January 1997, Brown appeared on the BBC's *Today* programme and announced that the next Labour government would stick to the Conservatives' spending plans for the first two years following victory and would retain the income tax rates for the entire parliament. This was an extraordinary moment with much significance. It followed an internal debate between Blair and Brown and their respective advisers on whether there should be a new top rate of tax for high earners. Blair was against and, at first, Brown was in favour. His spokesman at the time, Charlie Whelan, observed mischievously, 'We've got to do something that's bloody Labour, haven't we?'[1] But in the end, Brown also opted for absolute clarity of message: Labour would not touch income tax rates. Later Brown admitted that it was the right call as part of the reassuring, unthreatening message leading up to the election. By the time the campaign got under way there was no room for the Conservatives to revive the tax-and-spend debate which had, in effect, helped them win the four elections from 1979 onwards and most spectacularly in 1992. Brown finally raised the top rate of tax when he was prime minister after the financial crash of 2008. There was a part of him that had always wanted to do it. Blair never did.

There were other significant defensive moves from the New Labour leadership. The party had lost ideological debates during the never-ending election defeats and the leadership was not going to repeat their strategy in 1997. The most fundamental victory for the Conservatives and Margaret Thatcher in particular was over ownership. Thatcher's privatization programme had defined the 1980s and 1990s more than any other policy area. Blair and Brown did not challenge her ideological victory. They did the opposite. To show their conversion to privatization, they pledged to sell off the air traffic control system, a relatively small move but a symbolic one. They had accepted the arguments against a return to forms of state ownership.

With strict limits on tax and public spending and with little to say about how to improve the privatized services, Blair, Brown and a few other trusted figures had to find other ways of conveying change. Blair had the public personality to excite while being cautious, hailing in one early party conference speech with evangelical zeal a 'new Britain . . . a Britain reborn'.[2] The prospect of a different party ruling, however cautiously, more or less made the metaphor work at the time.

The most important policy area to convey 'change' was constitutional reform, one that conveniently avoided the nightmare of the tax-and-spend traps. Changing the way the UK is governed does not cost any quantifiable sum of money and therefore was safer terrain in opposition. New Labour went into the 1997 election proposing possible reforms that, if they had all been implemented, would have been a real turning point in terms of substance, not just in terms of the art of winning elections. The proposals included a referendum on electoral reform. Blair was working closely with the leader of the Liberal Democrats, Paddy Ashdown. He met Ashdown more than he did some members of his shadow cabinet. The basis of the bond was the pledge to hold a referendum on the voting system. There was much more to the partnership but there would have been no engagement if electoral reform had not been on the table. The condition highlighted the ambiguity of early New Labour. Shadow cabinet members observed nervously the close rapport of Blair and Ashdown. Yet Blair was never keen on electoral reform and had inherited the referendum policy from John Smith. He would only hint at his wariness before the election, pointing out that changing the voting system could not be an alternative to reforming a party that lost elections under the existing 'first-past-the-post' mechanism.

Referendums were also pledged in advance of establishing a Scottish Parliament and Welsh Assembly. There was the prospect of an array of referendums under New Labour. Like the Conservatives, Blair pledged to hold a referendum before joining the euro. That was never held, nor was the one on electoral reform, but the idea of them added to the sense of heady excitement that the UK had reached another turning point after eighteen years of Tory rule. And also, by deferring to the population, they hinted at change, while still being non-threatening to voters and the media. The referendum on electoral reform wasn't held because Blair was not especially keen and a significant section of his party was passionately opposed, not least when Labour had won with ease under the existing system. There was never space for a referendum on the euro. Gordon Brown was opposed and Blair would anyway have risked losing it. No prime minister holds a referendum he fears he will lose.

Beyond constitutional change the reforms being proposed were some of the most incremental and cautious that any party had put forward in a manifesto since 1945. Famously, Labour published a card of five pledges that would be introduced under a new government. They were revealing partly because of the limited scope of ambition, but also by the way they were framed. Alone the 'five early pledges' explain fully the approach Blair and Brown took to winning an election in a country that usually votes Conservative.

The first pledge was 'we will cut class sizes to 30 or under for five, six and seven year olds by using money saved from the Assisted Places Scheme.'[3] Blair had proclaimed that his number-one priority was 'education, education, education'. This was the policy he chose to highlight his commitment. The Assisted Places Scheme was a small arrangement that enabled a few pupils to go to private schools who would otherwise not have had the money to do so. Because Labour was committed to sticking to the Conservatives' spending plans Blair's passion could not be expressed in policy terms with anything that cost very much money.

Both Blair and Brown were convinced that, because of all the previous allegations that Labour's sums did not add up, every proposition had to be paid for down to the final halfpenny. Evidently there had to be a pledge about education, and yet the pledge would only benefit five-, six- and seven-year-olds in terms of slightly smaller classroom sizes. They opted for limited ambition to prevent the media from screaming: 'How are you going to pay for this?' They had an answer. They would scrap the Assisted Places Scheme.

The next pledge related to law and order, one of the big New Labour themes. Blair became famous as shadow home secretary for his soundbite about being tough on crime and tough on the causes of crime. At the time, this was seen as a big departure from Labour's usual positioning. The soundbite was one that Gordon Brown had devised. Blair benefited from it considerably in terms of his personal profile. The words were a statement of the obvious, but sometimes the obvious can cast a spell over the media. They were an implicit and unfair attack on Old Labour. The party had always been tough in terms of its approach to crime. James Callaghan, a former Labour leader, home secretary and prime minister, represented the police in the House of Commons for a time. So it was not as if the likes of Harold Wilson and Callaghan were negligent in terms of crime, but there had been a perception formed that Labour was somehow 'soft' on the issue. The soundbite indicated a new approach.

The pledge card stated: 'We will introduce a fast track punishment scheme for persistent young offenders by halving the time from arrest to sentencing.'[4] This was being 'tough on crime' in a way that did not cost huge sums. The pledge was about efficiency, speeding up a process; there was no pledge to recruit more police officers, although that became an objective in government, because again in the crazy tax-and-spend pre-election debate there would be impossible questions about how this would be paid for.

The NHS was inevitably going to be the subject of a pledge. Once again, the promise was relatively small: 'We will cut NHS waiting lists by treating an extra 100,000 patients as a first step, by releasing £100 million saved from NHS red tape.'[5] By 1997, waiting lists were dauntingly long. They had become a big story that haunted the Major government. On a regular basis front pages were dominated by images of elderly people on trolleys waiting to be seen for hours and sometimes days. Waiting times for operations often extended beyond a year. Senior Labour figures had protested noisily about the state of the NHS and with good cause. Given the scale of the crisis, the proposed remedy was modest.

There was an acknowledgement that this tiny pledge was not enough. Note the phrase, 'as a first step'. Here was almost a celebration of the incrementalism: a first step was all they were pledging to take in the election manifesto, having become so aware of the way anything more ambitious was treated as a terrible own goal in British elections. Even so, this was the only pledge where the source of the additional money was vague, being 'saved from NHS red tape'. But given that cutting bureaucratic inefficiencies is often a refrain of the right they got away with it.

The next pledge was, 'We will get 250,000 under-25-year-olds off benefit and into work by using money from a windfall levy on the privatised utilities.'[6] The one-off tax on the privatized utilities was a rare example of a proposed tax rise from Blair and Brown, but they made sure it would be popular. The privatized utilities had made substantial profits because of the generous way in which the transfer from the state to the private companies had been mediated, and then as a result of being near-monopoly services. Here was a safe tax rise, a popular tax. If there were any doubts about that there was further reassurance. It was a one-off tax, not to be repeated. In addition, Blair and Brown also had the protective shield of the Conservative chancellor, Geoffrey Howe, in the early 1980s proposing a one-off windfall tax as well. So if they were attacked from the right on this proposition they had an example to cite from the altar of Thatcherism.

The final pledge contained a fundamental reassurance to those that did not 'trust' Labour to run the economy: 'We will set tough rules for government spending and borrowing and ensure low inflation and strengthen the economy so that interest rates are as low as possible to make all families better off.'

Here was the essence of the economic policy that Brown and his senior adviser, Ed Balls, had been working on intensely: tough new rules for government spending and borrowing when public expenditure had already been constrained for years. Ken Clarke, the outgoing chancellor, later described his future spending plans as 'eye-wateringly tight'. If he had remained chancellor he had no intention of adhering to them. But Labour was committed to doing so. Hidden within those words of fiscal prudence was their plan to make the Bank of England independent. Brown had a sense of history that went back further than the 1970s and 1980s. He was aware that markets set the bar higher for Labour governments. Labour chancellors were traumatized by devaluation crises in 1949 and 1967, while enduring sterling emergencies in the mid to late 1970s. For Brown, the independence of the Bank of England was a protective shield. There would be no significant currency crises while he was chancellor. Before the successful implementation of the plan, Brown had also looked to the single currency as a possible shield. Soon after the 1997 election he became an opponent of Britain joining the euro, while Blair regarded signing up as his historic mission.

Given the limited nature of the five early pledges, there was only a narrow dividing line between the tottering John Major government and New Labour as they presented themselves. In effect, Blair and Brown had decided that the ideological debates of the previous four elections could not be won. For Blair, it became a matter of conviction that New Labour's cautious programme was not only electorally necessary but what he called, with an apolitical flourish, 'the right thing to do'. Brown's view was slightly more nuanced. His clever soundbite in the early years was that he was pursuing 'prudence for a purpose'. The overriding purpose, as far as he was concerned, was narrowing inequality. He assumed that in England at least, any talk of 'redistribution' or tax rises would risk another election defeat. Ironically Brown became famous for taxing stealthily, a contradiction in terms. Still, Brown managed to pull off the trick for several years before being rumbled.

In advance of the 1997 election, Blair and Brown insisted the divide on public spending was between wasteful expenditure with the Conservatives and a productive alternative under Labour. They did not argue that another division was between high versus low spending, fearing the 'tax-and-spend' trap that had undermined Labour in previous elections, especially the 1992 campaign. The 1992 defeat did much to define New Labour. Similarly Blair and Brown spoke of fair taxes under Labour versus unfair taxes under the Conservatives, but not high versus low tax. That divide was pushed back into the Old Labour era, the convenient but dismissive device whereby policies perceived to be unpopular were cemented in a partly mythologized past.

The caution of New Labour in the build-up to the 1997 campaign was disguised by Blair's political personality. He seemed new, exciting and young. As a result, he made the incremental appear exciting. He managed to persuade many columnists who might be otherwise sceptical that New Labour's break with the past was an act of breathtaking radicalism in itself, that limited reforms represented profound change. Blair himself used the word 'radical' often. In his public speeches he had, like Bill Clinton, a capacity to hold a room. He could simultaneously inspire and reassure.

On his reassuring road Blair announced that Labour needed an updated constitution. He did so in his first party conference speech as Labour leader in 1994. In effect, he was proposing the abolition of Clause Four, the clause in Labour's constitution that committed the party to various forms of state ownership. Clause Four had already been disowned by those that came from so-called Old Labour. Harold Wilson used to joke about Clause Four and he left office in 1976. But as a symbol that New Labour genuinely was new, Blair campaigned for it to go. The party voted for the new constitution, including the abolition of Clause Four, by a big majority the following year.

Under Blair there was a constant focus on 'change' and 'reform', his favourite words, but the nature of the change was never threatening to those Conservative voters and newspapers that he sought to woo. Meanwhile, Blair's press secretary, Alastair Campbell, worked around the clock with a tireless passion in order to try, at the very least, to neutralize those newspapers that had been so viciously hostile to recent Labour leaders, specifically Michael Foot and Neil Kinnock. Blair and Campbell were not sure at the beginning of their venture whether they would ever get the endorsement of *The Sun* newspaper, which in the mid to late 1990s was at its most influential and powerful, but they did. They courted the newspaper's owner, Rupert Murdoch, assiduously. When Murdoch effectively summoned Blair to his annual conference in Australia in 1995, Blair went. He dropped all plans and flew out with Alastair Campbell and Anji Hunter, his long-time adviser. They left Heathrow airport on a Thursday evening in July and they were back by the Tuesday. Blair gave a speech to the Murdoch conference, and the event proved to be one factor of many in the conversion of Murdoch from being an ardent supporter of Conservative governments, to telling *The Sun* newspaper that they should back New Labour, which they did at the general election in 1997.

To appease Murdoch, the Labour onslaught on the Conservatives was not ideological. There was a focus on so-called 'sleaze' – that the long-serving and exhausted Conservative government had become corrupt. It was one of several themes connected to 'trust' that created the impression that the Conservatives could not be trusted to govern. These apolitical themes joined another about competence and which party would govern more efficiently. Blair and Brown were fully united in making the fundamental dividing line with the Conservatives one of competence versus incompetence. This was safe terrain. Who was in favour of incompetence? They made the most of what had become the chaos of the John Major government, the Tory revolts, the sense that Major was not fully in control of his party and therefore of the country, and put forward a New Labour leadership that was strong and capable. Meanwhile Blair suggested, as he highlighted sleaze in particular, that his ministers would be purer than pure and would need to be perceived as such when Labour came into power.

A Turning Point that Wasn't?

Could this turning point have been much greater? Could much-needed change have been implemented more speedily? Was it necessary to pledge such tight spending constraints? Would they still have won with a substantial majority by being more daring at a point when voters were aching for something more than near fatally wounded public services? We will never know. But like all successfully coherent projects the New Labour rise to power was rooted in its time and was the product of a few distinct personalities. The relentless self-discipline had a military quality. At one point Blair, conscious that Labour campaigns had often fallen apart in the middle of an election, went away for a day or so on his own to analyse the offering that they were going to put forward in the election. The aim, as he put it, was to 'bomb-proof' the manifesto to make sure the programme did not suddenly explode unexpectedly with propositions that failed to stand up to scrutiny.

As one example, he noted that Labour was proposing a referendum on the single currency because of the constitutional implications. At the same time he was planning for a Scottish Parliament after the election without a referendum. With all the neurotic instincts of someone who had never been on the winning side since becoming an MP in 1983, he envisaged how this could fall apart in an election campaign, with the media asking, 'Well, hold on a second, why isn't there a referendum on the Scottish Parliament, which is arguably a bigger constitutional change than the single currency?' So he returned from one of these bomb-proofing sessions to his office and said, 'Right, we're going to announce a referendum on the Scottish Parliament . . . the Scottish Labour Party won't like it but we've got to make sure this manifesto stands up to any allegations of inconsistency or contradictions.'[7]

There had been no election like it. The Conservative path to victory was blocked by Labour ceding political ground on the past eighteen years since it was last in government. It decided it could not win an election by promising to spend a lot more, even though public services were on their knees. Any such promises could be greeted by claims of hidden tax bombshells in the newspapers and by

the broadcasters asking, in a way that made them sound like account-
ants, how Labour would pay for them. So they did not make the
promises and therefore deprived the broadcasters of their favoured
line of interrogation when they faced senior Labour figures. Labour
did not even argue that it would improve public services by spending the 'proceeds of growth' as David Cameron did in his first party
conference speech as opposition leader in 2006 and for several years
after that. For Labour in opposition the bar is much higher. Every
penny had to be accounted for.

Such defensiveness limited what Labour could do in government
but did lead to a landslide of epic proportions, the biggest majority
since the war. The size of the majority had an immediate impact.
There was no formal arrangement with the Liberal Democrats in
terms of them joining the government. There had been much speculation, and Blair was inclined to encourage it, that whatever the
result, Paddy Ashdown and two or three other Liberal Democrats
would become cabinet ministers. This realignment on the centre left
did not happen. With Labour winning by such a margin, there was
no need to work with other parties. New Labour was a broad coalition in itself. Fairly quickly Blair also decided that there would be
no referendum on electoral reform. Potential further turning points
were falling by the wayside.

Blair did, however, compensate Ashdown with a more proportional
voting system for the Scottish Parliament. He did this fairly willingly,
assuming that the very act of introducing the Scottish Parliament
would diminish the impact of the case for independence advanced by
the Scottish National Party. He calculated that if there was a more proportional system Labour would still do pretty well and the SNP would
lack the potency of a cause when Scotland had its own parliament.
That proved to be a grave misjudgement. The voting system was one

of the principal reasons why, before very long, Labour struggled to be the dominant force and the SNP rose to be the biggest party in a hung parliament and then ruled with an overall majority. The partially proportional voting system for the Edinburgh parliament greatly helped those that were at the time seen as the smaller parties. One of them speedily became the mighty party in Scotland.

Here was a turning point with several consequences. The rise of the SNP and the collapse of Labour in Scotland changed the political map in two ways. Scotland was ruled by a political force that wanted to leave the UK in spite of acquiring significant new powers through the Edinburgh parliament. Labour struggled to win UK general elections after 2010 because its vote collapsed in Scotland. More fundamentally the new divisions of power aided the peace process in Northern Ireland. The assembly in Belfast, established after the Good Friday Agreement, did not need to be seen as an awkwardly contorted aberration but as part of a wider new settlement in which Scotland had a parliament and Wales an assembly.

On the domestic front, there were some substantial reforms in Labour's first term, not on the scale of the 1945 government but still significant and in some respects enduring. The government introduced a minimum wage, and did so with the minimum of fuss. It set up the Low Pay Commission to agree on the level of the wage. Leading Conservatives had predicted unemployment would rise as a result of the minimum wage. This did not happen. Meanwhile Gordon Brown began his elaborate and complex introduction of tax credits that meant those earning relatively low incomes started to get a bit more money each month in their pay packet.

The most substantial early social policy, one that for a time had an impact to compare with the welfare reforms of the 1945 government, was the introduction of SureStart. The aim of SureStart

1. Clement Attlee celebrates after Labour's victory in the general election, July 1945.

2. Aneurin Bevan, the minister of health, on the first day
of the National Health Service, July 1948.

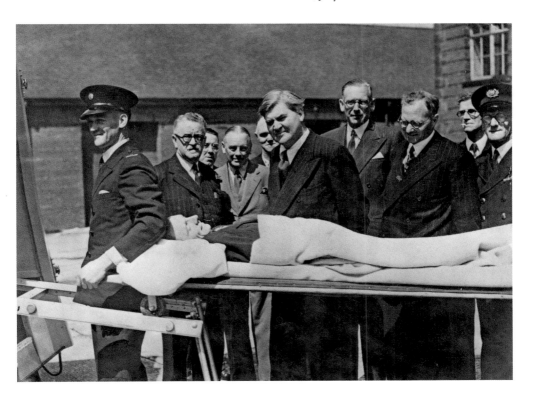

3. The Suez Canal is blocked by ships sunk by the orders of Egyptian President Gamel Abdel Nasser, November 1956.

4. Nasser is carried through the streets of Port Said after the British evacuation, November 1956.

13. Boris Johnson during a press conference as Gisela Stuart and Michael Gove look on following the results of the EU referendum at Westminster Tower, June 2016.

14. Key workers are applauded during the Covid pandemic at Salford Royal Hospital, May 2020.

15. Liz Truss and Rishi Sunak, at the announcement of the winner of the Conservative Party leadership contest, September 2022.

16. The royal family follow the coffin of Queen Elizabeth II as it is carried out of Westminster Abbey during her funeral, September 2022.

was to coordinate schemes for relatively poorer families in ways that brought together local services and allowed families who might have become wholly disconnected from state services to benefit from them. They particularly targeted families with young pre-school children. Initial funding was substantial: £540 million was allocated for spending between 1999 and 2002. Two hundred and fifty Sure-Start local programmes were set up, reaching up to around 500,000 children in areas of deprivation. In 2003 Brown announced the government's long-term plan was to transfer SureStart into the control of local government and to create a SureStart children's centre in every community.

What is so illuminating about the SureStart programme was the sequence that brought it about. Blair and Brown had to wait until securing power before the potential of SureStart and its funding could be explored. The manifesto in 1997 made fairly imprecise commitments to reduce poverty and improve children's health, education and wider life chances. Once the election was won, the original miserly spending plans aimed at achieving these vague goals began to grow significantly. Expenditure on early years education, childcare and SureStart increased almost fourfold in England for under-five-year-olds from £671 per child in 1997 to £2,514 by 2010 when Labour lost the election. Spending across the UK on cash benefits, including maternity benefits, more than doubled in real terms to £3,431 per child under the age of five. Other related policies included longer maternity leave, free early education for all three- and four-year-olds, more affordable and higher quality childcare and more generous financial support for families with parents both in and out of work.

According to the independent Education Training Inspectorate, SureStart helped parents to gain 'confidence, skills and knowledge to support the development of their children's speech, language and communication' as well as improving children's health.[8] Overall, child poverty fell, with particularly strong improvements in households with a child under five. If New Labour had expressed such ambition in the 1997 manifesto, Blair, Brown and others would have been interrogated relentlessly about where the money was going to come from. Every shadow cabinet member, when they appeared on the BBC *Today* programme, would have been asked which taxes were going to have to go up to pay for these objectives. In reality, rather than the absurd fantasy of the media-led tax-and-spend debate, an economy can grow and governments can sometimes receive unexpected windfalls.

Labour got several big financial bonuses, some of their own making. Brown auctioned off the electromagnetic spectrum to mobile phone operators in 2000. They needed the new bandwidth to launch third-generation or 3G services for mobile internet access. In doing so he raised £22.5 billion. Characteristically he used the cash to pay off national debt, prudence for a purpose, constantly reassuring markets that this was a government that could be relied on to preside over stable economic policy, thereby giving him and others the space to increase spending on services, tax credits and the rest.

The other key turning point in the first term was the successful conclusion of the Northern Ireland peace process. John Major had instigated talks in a way that was politically courageous, not least with the strong Unionist inclination in his own fractious party, but he had reached a point where a breakthrough had proven impossible. For Blair, Northern Ireland was relatively safe political terrain. Although highly complex, and though he was dealing with opposing forces that demanded patience and subtle negotiation, the process was safe in the sense that this was not an area where *The Sun* newspaper would erupt or Middle England would turn on him and say, 'You've let us down.' He could take risks because the rewards were potentially huge and the political fallout in UK politics would be minimal if the talks failed to progress.

Blair had an astute sense of where there was political space. In the darkness of Northern Ireland he sensed he had room to move. The Good Friday Agreement, signed in April 1998, was an astonishing achievement in which all parties agreed to work together. The Northern Ireland Assembly was formed with an executive of both Sinn Fein and the Unionists. Given the context of the Troubles in the 1970s and since, here was an unambiguously positive turning point. The outcome reflected Blair's ability to work with, and then use, a wide range of big and complex personalities. His friendship with Clinton was an asset and the president made calls to some of the participants at key moments. Separately Blair formed a constructive relationship with Bertie Ahern, the Irish leader. He gave his first Northern Ireland secretary, Mo Mowlam, some freedom to form bonds of trust with Sinn Fein leaders while he worked constructively with David Trimble, the leader of the Ulster Unionists. Blair's chief of staff, Jonathan Powell, who identified an opening for the process before the 1997 election, was a tireless negotiator.

Another significant change was the programme of devolution. The introduction of an elected mayor of London was in some respects an accidental achievement for the New Labour leadership, but one that proved to be transformative for the capital, and a new model for delivering public services where the elected figure at the top can be held directly accountable for what happened – rare in the UK, where blurred lines of responsibility are a more familiar structure.

The first mayor of London was Ken Livingstone, against the wishes of Blair and Brown, who tried to stop him from standing.

He had been leader of the old Greater London Council abolished by Thatcher and had then become a Labour MP on the left of the party. As mayor, Livingstone provided a model for public-service delivery in his first term. First of all, he found a way to raise revenue that was broadly popular. While New Labour was still constrained over how much it could spend because of its pre-election commitments, Livingstone raised money through the 'Congestion Charge', a tax to drive a car in central London. This was a courageous move in terms of both the politics and the practicalities. Blair often spoke about being 'bold' when he was being cautious. Livingstone was bold without making a great performance about it. He pledged to spend the cash raised by the Congestion Charge directly on public transport. There was a direct, tangible connection between the tax raised and outcome in the form of improved public transport. When voters can recognize the connection between taxes and outcomes they are much less likely to see tax as a 'burden'.

As the first elected mayor, Livingstone fought hard to overturn the convoluted public–private partnership for the London Underground that had proven to be both costly and ineffective. The PPP had been introduced by Gordon Brown and was an example of how New Labour was keen to devise any scheme to involve the private sector, almost as a test of credibility. While seeking to create order out of Brown's chaos, Livingstone brought in the very best from New York and other cities from around the world who had been involved in successfully transforming their own public transport systems. He looked abroad knowing that in Britain there had been such indifference to capital projects that there were few specialists available.

The transformation of public transport in London happened quite quickly. Suddenly London had a decent, more affordable Underground service with the Oyster card as an alternative to long queues for tickets at Tube stations. There were many more bus routes and buses and in the early stages there was less congestion on the roads. The transport improvements were one of the many factors in the revival of London as a dynamic economic and cultural centre. The Thatcherite reforms in the 1980s led to a boom in the City of London, but the capital suffered from dismal and expensive public transport. Livingstone's improvements in public transport were a key element in the transformation of a city that was in the doldrums during the 1970s to one that had become self-confidently fashionable. As an essential part of the new structure, the elected London mayor had to be held to account for what happened. He won a second term. New Labour had stumbled on a way to devolve power and deliver better local services. Soon some other areas elected mayors too, a turning point in the distribution of power.

Blair publicly apologized for refusing to back Livingstone at the beginning and added: 'People ask me why I changed my mind, and the reason is because I was able to judge the record that he had.'9 The attempt to block Livingstone from standing was Blair's only stand against an individual MP from the left. Somehow or other Sir Keir Starmer thought he was following the Blair model in his more ruthless approach after he became Labour leader in 2020, including his refusal to allow his predecessor, Jeremy Corbyn, to stand as a Labour candidate. On the whole Blair got on, or was determined to get on, with the likes of Dennis Skinner and Chris Mullin, who had both, in their different ways, been followers of Tony Benn.

While there were significant changes implemented in Labour's first term, voters required immense patience in terms of the biggest challenge the Labour government faced when it came to power: the state of the NHS. The government had as one of its five pledges a modest commitment to reduce waiting lists, a commitment that was met by the end of the first term. However, the NHS was still in crisis. Because of Blair and Brown's pre-election desire to have no bombshells in a tax-and-spend debate, there were limited options in terms of substantially increasing investment in the NHS. By the end of Labour's first term, overall spending was not much higher than in the John Major era. New Labour had weakly paid the ultimate tribute to the long period of Conservative rule by emulating it.

A Second Landslide Majority

The major domestic project during Labour's second term became a huge increase in spending in the NHS, almost by accident. This was not part of the 2001 manifesto, because once more Blair and Brown sought to avoid the tax-and-spend debate, although by the time of the 2001 election campaign, they at least had the confidence to frame an argument around the fear of Conservative spending cuts. They were not making big claims for their own spending intentions but they made them seem fairly grand in comparison with what they suggested the Conservatives would do, which would be to cut spending in order to pay for what the Conservative leader William Hague had described as a 'tax guarantee' – a range of tax cuts. They were confident enough at least to warn of spending cuts to pay for reductions in taxation. But they had acquired that confidence by being extremely cautious about investing in public services that were in desperate need of additional cash.

What happened early in the second term was the inevitable crisis in the NHS, in which spending had been pretty static in the years leading up to the 2001 election. The cries of despair about NHS treatments were impossible for a leader like Tony Blair to ignore.

Some came from charismatic figures within Labour's ranks. The Labour peer, doctor and TV presenter Robert Winston argued that health provision in parts of Eastern Europe had now become more reliable and better resourced than the NHS. Significantly, even the *Daily Mail* had started campaigning for higher pay for nurses and was also highlighting the chaos within the NHS. The combination of the two was enough to convince Blair that action was required as a matter of urgency. Such was his ragged relationship with Brown, Blair decided that he would make an announcement, without any consultation, on the TV sofa of David Frost's Sunday morning programme. In January 2002 he was a guest, the opening interview of the year. Blair declared with a flourish that 'Spending is too low at the moment, so we'll bring it up to the average of the European Union'.

Such an aspiration should have been seen in a country more capable of a mature debate about public spending as a reasoned and pretty mild objective. Why should not the UK, one of the wealthier countries in the European Union at the time, not expect to have the same level of investment in health as other countries in Europe? Why is it always the case, almost as an accepted assumption, that Britain will spend less on services like health and transport? But those were the orthodoxies and Blair finally challenged them nearly eight years after becoming Labour leader. Here was an extraordinary moment. Because the UK had fallen so far behind the EU average in terms of investment, he was making a bigger spending pledge than Labour leaders had made in the 1980s, the party's vote-losing decade that he normally defined himself against. He had no idea at this point how the money was going to be raised.

Brown hit the roof. He did so for complex reasons. Partly he felt his forthcoming budget had been taken away from him, the one that he was planning for March, in a couple of months' time. He was furious about not being consulted in relation to such a major spending commitment. But Blair knew if he had consulted him he would have been stopped from making the announcement. The third reason was that he felt Blair was making the popular announcement that spending would increase, whereas he, the chancellor who yearned to be prime minister, was left with the arduous and unpopular task of finding the means to pay for it.

The awkward dance between the two of them had got them to a strange place, where suddenly out of the blue Britain was committed to joining countries which had a more sensible approach to public spending. But it was quite a leap for Britain to make. In effect, Blair had promised to inject at least £12 billion of extra money into the NHS over the coming years and the immediate background was a winter flu crisis that had triggered dark news stories, not least in the powerful *Daily Mail*.

Ironically, as Brown worked out how to pay for the spending, he moved towards a budget that gave him the greatest satisfaction of his long tenure at the Treasury. Haphazardly, Blair had released Brown to be more like himself. As we shall see in a later chapter, the wily chancellor got there subtly by appointing a senior banker to commission a review that reached an outcome Brown had wanted in the first place. In his 2002 budget he announced that national insurance would be increased, a rare moment when a substantial tax rise would pay for improvements to a specific service. On entering the Treasury he had worked on the assumption that he would not be able to increase taxes that had an impact on voters' income because of the electoral risk. He did so in this budget, a major turning point for New Labour and the country.

On the eve of the tax rise announcement, Number 10 and Brown's entourage were extremely nervous. New Labour had been defined by its commitment to stick with Tory plans when it came to any tax relating to income and yet here they were putting up tax in quite a substantial way. One of Blair's closest advisers feared the move would lose Labour the next election.[10]

In a revealing twist the budget was the most popular that Brown had delivered. One of his senior advisers, future Labour leader Ed Miliband, noted that 'at last, Gordon has found his authentic voice'.[11] *The Sunday Telegraph*, assuming it would be unpopular, commissioned a poll on the budget and had to report that a vast majority of voters approved of it partly because they could see the consequence of the tax rise would be a better-funded NHS.

Voters are not entirely indifferent to what goes on in politics. They could see, sometimes from direct experience, that the NHS needed an input of cash and that they would have to pay for it. They were willing to do so when they were told that the money was going to go to the NHS and not into a vacuum. The entire sequence was the most powerful example in post-war British politics that showed that with an earmarked tax, voters could readily accept increases. Arguably it remains the only route for Labour governments to put up taxes on income, by making the connection with outcomes in specific services. Although nerve-racking for those directly involved, the rise proved to be relatively straightforward compared with what followed. In order to ensure that it was not perceived as some reckless act of profligacy, both Blair and Brown stressed that what was required for the NHS was investment plus reform.

'Reform' is a magical term applied to public services in the UK, as if the word itself solves all the problems. The term is normally applied when governments do not want to invest to the degree to which other equivalent countries do. But for nervy New Labour, 'reform' was actually justifying spending increases. The problem in this case was that there was intense disagreement between Blair and Brown about precisely what form any changes in the NHS should take. Blair took his lead from some of the Thatcherite reforms first introduced by Ken Clarke, when he was health secretary. He encouraged his choice of health secretary, Alan Milburn, to be 'bold' in his thinking about the best ways of 'modernizing' the NHS. Like the term 'reform', 'boldness' and 'modernization' are vague. In their imprecision they nearly always indicate there is trouble ahead.

Milburn came up with the idea of self-governing foundation hospitals – self-governing to the point where they would have control over budgets. They were part of a wider set of reforms that sought to develop an internal market, giving patients more 'choice' while keeping the NHS free at the point of use. Brown responded partly by delivering a considered speech in 2003 exploring when markets work and when they do not. Most immediately he was passionately opposed to the notion that the proposed newly liberated hospitals could go bankrupt. Brown pointed out that having made great play of the investment they were making in the NHS it would be hard to explain why some hospitals might close on the grounds of bankruptcy following the increased spending. His broader argument was that in a service where people were receiving treatments and medicines free at the point of use it was not feasible to create a genuine market within the NHS. But Blair believed that if you somehow or other contrived a marketplace the patients would get better outcomes.

The debate went on for some time and in the end Brown prevailed, at least in terms of the degree to which hospitals would acquire responsibility for their own budgets and spending to the point of bankruptcy. Milburn resigned as health secretary, ostensibly to 'spend more time with his family'. The row was damaging, not least because the focus within government and beyond became less about how to invest the additional money and was accompanied by a forensic and transparent analysis of whether every penny was being well spent. That got lost in a protracted row over structure and reform, the most intense between Blair and Brown, with the partial exception of Blair's renewed interest in joining the single currency.

Ed Balls, in his otherwise convivial memoir, described the rows over NHS reform as more damaging for the government than the war in Iraq. Nonetheless NHS patients enjoyed a turning point in the institution's fortunes, a brief era when it was well funded, albeit still chaotically organized.

One additional health-related policy did not cost a penny. It was the introduction of the smoking ban in England in 2007, a policy that was a major turning point for several reasons. The use of the term 'ban' was rare in British politics. The word implied state intervention on a big scale. In this case, a ban was imposed on smoking in public places. In theory a 'ban' can be seen as a constraint on personal freedom, and that was how this measure was regarded by opponents. Yet the constraint was liberating. A ban freed up non-smokers to enjoy public places without being disturbed by those who would normally have smoked. A limit on individuals being able to do whatever they wanted to do created a much more healthy atmosphere in pubs and restaurants and on public transport. The endurance of the ban – no party has sought to overturn it – shone much-needed light on the notion of freedom and where freedom lies. In terms of the NHS, it also showed that one way of coping with the growing demands on the health service was to apply a preventative measure. The British Heart Foundation reported that 'there were 1,200 fewer hospital admissions for heart attacks in the year following the ban – improved air quality and fewer smokers will have contributed to this. In 2006, 22 per cent of adults smoked, whereas in the latest statistics 18 per cent did.'[12]

The build-up to the ban was predictably noisy even though in Scotland a similar policy had been introduced a year earlier. At one point, characteristically, Blair noted that 'people have given us permission to introduce a ban'.[13] In other words, the usual polls were taken, focus groups commissioned, and it had high levels of support. Many Conservative MPs opposed it and there was much shallow talk of the 'nanny state'. Some Labour figures able to exercise influence over Blair, including the cabinet minister John Reid, warned that working-class areas represented by Labour would be up in arms. They loved their cigarettes at the working men's clubs and the pubs, argued Reid, and this would not be forgiven.

Although Labour had already started to do relatively poorly in some of its working-class seats by the 2005 election, certainly compared with 1997, the ban was not cited as a reason by voters who turned against Labour. It was, in many ways, one of the most significant reforms of the New Labour era.

The Limits of New Labour's Turning Point

The caution that framed the first 1997 manifesto and the wider ideological tentativeness that it represented meant that quite a lot of the landscape and orthodoxies that New Labour inherited in 1997 remained in place throughout their tenure. Those ineffective privatizations, monopolies rather than vibrant markets, were largely untouched.

Railways remained privatized. Buses were still deregulated. The NHS reforms incorporated the private sector at sometimes costly expense. New Labour could also not cope with the issue of housing shortages, an issue that became increasingly acute. Compared with the 1945 government, which built houses in their hundreds of thousands each year, and indeed compared to the governments of the 1970s, where amid economic turmoil, hundreds of thousands of affordable rented houses were built, the New Labour leadership could not find the necessary levers. The need to alienate certain areas who would proclaim that they would not have these new houses in their backyard – NIMBYs – meant that Britain was left with the problems of the Thatcherite housing settlement, celebrating the sale of council houses and the new generation of private property owners, but not dealing with the subsequent extreme shortage of affordable housing.

On Europe, Blair began 1997 with a great but ill-defined ambition to put Britain at the heart of the EU. He wanted, in particular, at certain points during his leadership for Britain to join the single currency. That did not happen. Nor did he ever decisively put the case for Europe on a regular basis in the UK. The intense doubts of significant parts of the country about the advantages of being a member of the EU were never adequately addressed. The mighty Eurosceptic newspapers were appeased rather than challenged. At times, Brown especially played the old games in which he would brief the Eurosceptic newspapers that he was going to be tough on Europe in some way or another, fuelling the sense that Europe was a problem for Britain that had to be managed rather than a relationship that Britain benefited from.

Most fundamentally of all, in their different ways Blair and Brown failed to make a case for change in a way that had real lasting depth beyond framing arguments around 'modernization' and 'boldness' – near meaningless terms. Towards the end of his leadership Blair stepped overtly away from any ideological advocacy by insisting that the 'left–right' debate was over and that we were living in an era of 'cross-dressing' in which his followers in Labour were close to those he regarded as Conservative moderates. As Blair put it boldly, 'what matters is what works'. Yet no one goes into politics to implement what does not work. These apolitical terms made it difficult for the Conservatives to win elections but they did not worry Thatcher, who claimed Blair to be her greatest achievement in the sense that she did not feel as if her ideological victories were under threat.

The Labour government did increase spending and improve public services. Through tax credits they also redistributed to those on low incomes. But again, terms such as 'redistribution' were rarely used. As a result, voters sometimes made no connection between an improvement in their lives and the government that had brought it about. The cabinet minister and Scottish MP Robin Cook noted in a fringe meeting at a Labour conference in 2002 that his constituents thought the reason their salaries had gone up was a technical adjustment made by the Inland Revenue and had no idea that the tax credits were part of a deliberate policy that Brown had worked around the clock to introduce in order to attempt to narrow inequalities, or at least to stem the tide towards much wider inequality. Labour did not make the case and gradually some voters turned away.

Although the turning point in terms of policy-making was not as great as 1979 or 1945, and the sense of new orthodoxies, assumptions, ideological fashions was nowhere near as intense as in 1945 or 1979, the UK became better off, had far better public services, and more modern and revived cities. 'Cool Britannia' was only a slogan in the summer of 1997 but there was something genuinely 'cool' about many of Britain's cities during the New Labour era in a manner that could not have been imagined in the 1980s and early 1990s. Free entrance to museums and galleries opened up culture to all, irrespective of income. The right to roam gave access to more of the countryside. Quality of life improved considerably.

But the real proof of the limited way in which this era challenged previous political fashions came with the change of government in 2010, when David Cameron and George Osborne moved into Number 10 and the Treasury respectively after the election of that year. Without winning an overall majority, they led a coalition broadly based on the radical right and moved much faster to implement their plans than New Labour did with its huge majorities in 1997 and 2001, and a decent majority in 2005. In comparison Cameron and Osborne moved at the speed of sound, introducing real-term spending cuts in their first budget within weeks of getting into power, and then tripled tuition fees, which had the effect of almost privatizing the universities because they were now all largely dependent on student fees, and giving vice-chancellors an unjustified sense that they deserved to be paid a fortune because they were in a marketplace. It was another artificial marketplace with all students paying the same fees. The tripling of tuition fees was a radical reform and introduced very early by the coalition and without any sort of the nervy qualifications that tended to accompany New Labour's changes.

At the same speed, the coalition went about reforming public services by expanding mediating agencies, including creating NHS England, which theoretically took direct control over the health service from the health secretary and the government, and beneath them a whole range of agencies to negotiate the role of the private sector. They applied the same reforming zeal to education and to law and order. Police commissioners were elected with supposed responsibility, further blurring the lines of accountability in that public service. They moved fast on constitutional reform, introducing fixed-term parliaments. And it was all conducted with a Euroscepticism from Cameron that was partly a product of conviction and also expediency. He felt he needed to appease his Eurosceptic wing.

By the end of one term of a Conservative-led government with no overall majority, much of the New Labour vision had been overturned. Britain was heading towards leaving the European Union rather than being at the heart of Europe, which is what Blair saw his historic destiny as resolving. The rise of Scottish nationalism challenged the basis of the New Labour devolution settlement. And later, the way Brexit was negotiated ultimately threatened the Good Friday agreement that had brought about the completion of the peace process in Northern Ireland.

Above all there was a sense once more that public spending was a sinful act of recklessness with the revival of Thatcherite economic policies, in a way that she herself would never have dared to do. Thatcher did not introduce real-term spending cuts but the coalition did. It took quite some time for the changes of the 1945 Labour government and the assumptions on which they were based to be fundamentally overturned. The counter-revolution did not take place until 1979. After the removal of Labour in 2010 politics leapt without a moment's pause back to Thatcher's heyday.

Inevitably there is a connection between how a party seeks to win an election and then how it governs if it manages to secure a victory. There were echoes throughout the long period of New Labour rule of the cautious incrementalism of 1997. Yet within that tight framework Blair, Brown and their colleagues managed to win three elections. Without winning, a party is powerless to implement any policy. Winning repeatedly was an achievement not to be underestimated, especially given that the Labour Party went on to lose several elections, beginning with 2010.

The other achievement was to govern for a long period in a relatively economically stable climate, an ambition that went well beyond electoral expediency from the beginning. Brown was obsessed with obtaining the backing of the markets. With his sense of history, he knew that previous Labour governments had become destabilized by the markets hovering over them. The Labour government of 1945 was forced to devalue. Similarly, the Labour government elected with a big majority in 1966 was also forced to devalue. In both cases they never really recovered from the trauma. Not only were the relevant prime ministers and chancellors scarred for the rest of the period in their respective offices, they were also much more constrained as to what they could do in government. They had lost vital political authority and markets were even less forgiving and testing. The battles with the markets and the need to prop up the currency had an impact on growth and there was less money to spend on public services. None of that deadly sequence applied in the New Labour era up to the global financial crash in 2008, and even then, although that was a period of great political and economic torment, the currency was relatively secure following the independence of the Bank of England.

The New Labour plan was to have macroeconomic stability, with measures such as the independence of the Bank of England and paying off debt, therefore having more scope to bring about the eventual changes and improvements they wanted to make rather than promising big and then finding the path blocked by apoplectic markets and the consequences of any imposed devaluation of the currency. None of that happened.

There wasn't a revival of the sort of industrial turmoil that tormented the Labour government in the late 1960s and then again from 1974. Inflation was not an issue. The independence of the Bank of England was cleverly constructed so that although power was being given away, the chancellor Gordon Brown and his advisers retained quite a lot of influence. They determined the remit of the independent Bank of England, which included an inflation target that it should not exceed or go much below. They selected the members of the Monetary Policy Committee and appointed quite a range of economists. They selected the governor of the Bank of England when such an appointment was required. Here was an elegantly constructed transfer of power that created space for the government to invest in public services. Having been given that space, they were finally trusted to spend public money.

Ironically the determination of Blair and Brown to be seen as moving with the prevailing tides of the 1980s and early 1990s led them towards their falls. In the case of Blair the issue that darkened his leadership most was the war in Iraq. The reasons why he backed the war had much to do with his need at all times to establish distance from Labour in the 1980s. For Brown, the torment arose from the 2008 financial crash. Here was a chancellor who recognized that stability from an economic perspective was fundamental to achieving the many progressive goals that he pursued. But in the same way that Blair felt the need to be seen as being close to Bush partly because of the domestic politics of the 1980s, Brown had felt similarly about bankers and the financial sector. He regarded association with these big money-making forces as a form of reassurance for voters and the media that he was a different type of chancellor to other Labour predecessors, one that encouraged and rewarded wealth creation as embodied by the banks and the financial sector.

Then in 2008, and indeed to some extent in 2007, those

institutions that he had wanted to be associated with brought the global economy and the British economy to the cliff's edge. All the assumptions he had made about who was respectable to be associated with and what was reassuring to the voters were turned on their head.

Blair and Brown led the country towards two of the biggest turning points since 1945, but they were not ones they had planned or foreseen. One was a change in Britain's approach to foreign policy after Iraq. The other was Britain after the financial crash.

7

IRAQ

From the Falklands conflict in 1982 until the war in Iraq in 2003 there was a widespread assumption that military action involving the UK would be broadly popular and enhance the standing of a prime minister. After Margaret Thatcher's victory in the Falklands, some newspapers, the Conservative Party, sections of other parties and a lot of voters celebrated – without much reason – what they saw as the return of the UK as a major force to be reckoned with. The country was closer in spirit to the victory in 1945 than the humiliation of Suez in 1956 and the economic doldrums of the 1970s.

After the war in Iraq, a different set of questions were posed. What was the UK doing there? Did Tony Blair lie to the country in order to justify war? Was he too weak to challenge President Bush? The questions reflected the scale of the turning point. Blair moved towards Iraq burdened by the assumptions and orthodoxies post-Falklands only to discover that they had quickly become obsolete. Like Eden in relation to Suez, Blair had become trapped by the past. Blair's journey towards Iraq began soon after he became leader of the Labour Party. It led to a significant turning point, in which direct military intervention by a British government became close to impossible and in which unresolved questions about the UK's place in the world erupted once again.

There also appeared to be another profound and related turning point in the character of Tony Blair. Here was a prime minister who had made winning elections and being popular part of his essence as a leader. Suddenly he seemed to have metamorphosed to an evangelist pursuing a cause irrespective of his popularity. Iraq and Blair's role towards war traumatized a country and a governing party, triggered new forms of confusion about the UK's role in the world and arguably led to the rise of Jeremy Corbyn, an opponent of Iraq. The related apparent turning points, the war and Blair's approach to leadership, had deep roots. In order to make sense of what in some respects seems like an episode of wild irrationality, we need to go back decades and to follow closely what happened on many levels, from Labour in the 1980s to the role of the BBC. Turning points do not happen by chance.

During his first party conference speech as the new Labour leader in the autumn of 1994, Tony Blair declared with a flourish that the party needed a new constitution for the modern era. While he was preparing Labour's new constitution he received a note from his close friend Peter Mandelson. The two had been exchanging ideas on the final wording of the important new document. Mandelson noted that there was no significant phrase about defence policy. He shuddered at the absence, his memories of the 1980s still painfully vivid. He had given up his job as a TV producer to become Labour's communications director shortly after Blair had been elected as an MP following Labour's slaughter in 1983. In the years that followed both had wondered whether Labour would ever win again. Even after the 1992 election, when John Smith became leader and the Conservative government fell apart, they feared eternal opposition. This was an early sign of a paralysing pessimism. Smith would almost certainly have won in 1997 but the duo's fear of Labour's narrow appeal was deeply embedded.

There were not many phrases about a range of policy areas when Blair and his close allies wrote a new constitution for their party in 1995; it was a statement of Labour's broadest values rather than an election manifesto. But Mandelson was aware that defence had been a significant vote-loser for so-called 'old' Labour and therefore merited a special mention in the new constitution. 'Will a Blair government not go to war?' wrote Mandelson across the page of the draft and sent it back to Blair.[1]

Mandelson did not mean by this that a Labour government would seek to go to war. Like the rest of the leadership at the top of New Labour, he had little interest in foreign affairs beyond a passion for Britain's membership of the European Union. His thoughts were related solely to domestic politics. Like Blair he was conditioned to be alert to Labour's weaknesses, actual and perceived. The re-writing of the constitution was an exercise to demonstrate the party had changed, and Mandelson was worried that if there was no reference to defence policy, critics might conclude that Labour was still 'soft' in this highly charged area. Blair followed his advice. In the party's revised constitution there are few mentions of specific policy areas, but defence is included, with the words: 'Labour is committed to the defence and security of the British people.'[2]

There were many reasons for Labour's electoral defeats, but one of them was its attitudes towards defence policy, and what they conveyed about its fitness to govern. Labour leaders before Blair had got caught in more nightmarish knots over this issue than any other. The knots are highly significant in understanding the Iraq conflict.

In resolving not to get trapped, Blair moved towards an even tighter form of political entrapment.

Three and a half years before Blair became an MP, Michael Foot was elected the party's leader. He was a committed unilateral nuclear disarmer and while leader joined CND marches, as he had done for the previous three decades, speaking passionately against retaining nuclear weapons under any circumstances. Foot deployed some arguments that had merit, but once they had been mediated through the influential British newspapers he looked like a dangerous romantic, wholly unsuited to be trusted with the country's defence. His deputy Denis Healey opposed unilateral disarmament and was backed by a significant section of the shadow cabinet. Foot's support for unilateralism was one of the reasons why the SDP was formed, a schism that was fatal for Labour – at least in the short term.

In order to plaster over the internal divisions during the 1983 election the leadership came up with the absurd hybrid that Labour was both a unilateralist and a multilateralist party. Foot proposed that Labour would unilaterally remove the UK's nuclear weapons while negotiating multilateral disarmament with other countries. It was an attempt to allow his deputy, Denis Healey, to focus on multilateralism while he would stay true to his unilateralist convictions. Blair proclaimed his support for unilateralism as a Labour candidate in Sedgefield but never believed in the policy. The policy and the equivocations around it caused Labour harm and were cited widely in the pro-Tory newspapers as a reason why the party was unelectable. Robin Cook, who became Blair's first foreign secretary and who resigned from the cabinet over the war in Iraq, suggested Blair's real attitude towards conflict could be discerned a little earlier than the 1983 election. Blair had been a Labour candidate in the unwinnable seat of Beaconsfield, in the first by-election to be held after the Falklands War in 1982. Cook recalled Blair telling him that everywhere he went during that campaign voters were applauding Thatcher's military victory. Cook believed that during the campaign an assumption formed in Blair's mind that voters expected British prime ministers to be ready for war and that victory would greatly enhance their reputation.[3]

In the 1980s, Labour struggled to get beyond a muddled policy on disarmament inevitably that diminished its reputation. An equally committed unilateralist, Neil Kinnock replaced Foot after Labour lost by a landslide in the 1983 election. While Kinnock bravely began to challenge and reform his party against impossible odds he retained at first more or less the same approach to defence policy as Foot up to the 1987 election. As he continued to resist change in relation to unilateralism a pivotal event occurred during his first term as leader of the opposition, one that was vividly in Blair's mind when he became leader. In March 1987, weeks before that year's general election campaign got under way, Kinnock paid a visit to Washington. The timing had been carefully chosen from his point of view in the hope that a meeting with President Reagan would help him to appear prime-ministerial.

The precise opposite happened. In a calculated snub, Reagan saw Kinnock for the minimum time protocol demanded. The US administration allowed only one photo of the meeting to be released. The documents from Reagan's archive explain why. In one briefing for Reagan, prepared by his senior officials in advance of Kinnock's visit, the president was urged to stress: 'Labour's position on defence would make it difficult for any American administration to carry on as before. Your policies would have a profound, unpredictable effect on NATO, East–West relations and bilateral relations.' The rest of the briefing was equally scathing about Kinnock and his leadership.[4]

The contrast with Margaret Thatcher was striking. At the same time as Kinnock was being cold-shouldered in the US, Thatcher, the Iron Lady who was perceived to have helped to bring freedom to parts of Eastern Europe, was being lauded in Russia. She was treated like a rock idol in Moscow and beyond. But the more vivid and precise contrast was with Thatcher's visits to Reagan in which she got a VIP treatment that no other leader secured.

In their cramped office at Westminster, Blair and Gordon Brown watched the media coverage of politics like hawks, in particular the reporting of Kinnock's weaknesses and strengths. They drew a single conclusion from Kinnock's visit to Washington and the inevitably exaggerated derisive coverage from the British media. A Labour leader is credible only when he or she has a close relationship with US presidents. Thatcher had become an international star and more prime-ministerial at home partly because of her very special relationship with Reagan. The opposite was true of Kinnock.

Labour lost again in 1987. Thatcher won by a landslide. In Kinnock's second term as Labour leader, defence policy became a form of hell for him once more. He asked his shadow foreign secretary, the wily Gerald Kaufman, to effect a very big switch from unilateralism to multilateralism, but the process was draining and traumatic. Kinnock suffered from exhausted depression and contemplated resigning. Nonetheless, he succeeded in changing the policy on nuclear weapons, a titanic achievement given the still powerful internal bodies that had to give assent. In one interview Kinnock was asked, 'As leader of the Labour Party, what is your personal view now on unilateralism?' Kinnock laughed and replied, 'Having personal views as leader is a contradiction in terms. As leader of the Labour Party I don't have personal views.'[5]

Even so, Kinnock was persistently asked whether he would be

willing as prime minister to press the nuclear button. He equivocated. In a speech to his party conference in 1986, admittedly before the change from unilateralism, he came closest to a formula that he was comfortable with: 'While I would die for my country I could never let my country die for me'. It was not a sign of personal weakness or cowardice that he was reluctant to trigger nuclear meltdown. Nonetheless, torn apart by the media, struggling to keep his party united over the issue and tormented by his personal journey from committed unilateralism, most voters only detected weakness.

In the 1992 election, the Conservatives and their newspapers made endless references to Labour candidates' support of CND, even if the leader and others had, by then, moved on. Labour suffered a fourth successive defeat. There were many factors that contributed to Labour's inability to win general elections. Perceptions of weakness in relation to defence was one of them. At the very least, their perceived stance reinforced the views of most voters that Labour was not 'fit' for government.

A 'Strong' Labour Leader Ready to 'Press the Button'

When Tony Blair became leader of his party after the sudden death of John Smith, he was a young shadow home secretary who had never served in government and had no experience of foreign affairs or defence policy. He was elected leader in the most benevolent political context possible. The exhausted Conservative government was falling apart over Europe and by then the Labour Party was desperate to win and would accept nearly any policy its new leader espoused.

Blair's charisma obscured his youthful inexperience. His assertions were taken by much of the media at their surface value. Blair was welcomed as a 'modernizer', the title of Blair's first biography. He was a 'radical'. Above all he was 'bold'. All were conveniently imprecise and yet highly flattering terms. But from the beginning of his leadership, his instinct was to regard whatever so-called Old Labour stood for as electorally dangerous. In reaction to Old Labour's abysmal relationship with much of the media, he fought to forge a new relationship with Middle England and the newspapers it read. As part of this quest, he was uneasy whenever his party was pleased with him. Blair preferred a dynamic where his party felt challenged by his leadership, while previously Tory-supporting newspapers praised the new leader for courageously seeking a new direction for his party. In contemplating how to deal with President Bush's desire to invade Iraq, Blair sought to move as close as possible to his familiar comfort zone, and not away from it.

In the run-up to the 1997 election Blair was absolutely clear where he stood in relation to defence policy. There was no evasion, ambiguity or equivocation. At a press conference on foreign policy in the spring of 1997 he was asked whether as prime minister he would be willing to press the nuclear button. He replied without hesitation: 'Yes.' Like Mandelson's intervention in the discussions over the party's new constitution, Blair was not thinking of taking part in a terrible nuclear conflagration. His unqualified response was an act of symbolism. He needed to purge his party of its immediate past, Foot's unilateralism, Kinnock's contorted evasiveness. In a clear, accessible manner, he had to show he would be strong on defence.

In one of the many Shakespearean twists en route to Iraq, Blair's determination to stride away from Labour's vote-losing history led him towards a war that would be more damaging to his and his party's reputation than any of Old Labour's perceived misdemeanours.

Several biographers of Blair have accused him of being messianic about the removal of Saddam soon after arriving in Number 10. This makes no sense. He knew little about Iraq and the region. He was commendably gripped by the need to improve public services and was obsessed about winning a second election having won the first. Iraq was always on his mind for a different reason. Throughout his leadership successive US administrations were contemplating or threatening military action. How would he respond? From the day he arrived in Number 10 in May 1997, a new leader with no great knowledge or interest in Iraq and the wider region, he was alert to the question and the need to find an answer, along with his determination to be seen to be different from previous Labour leaders.

After his first landslide election victory, in May 1997, Blair stood outside Number 10 to declare that he had won as New Labour and he would govern as New Labour. The declaration was more revealing than it seemed at the time. 'Old' Labour was the party that amongst other vote-losing sins had been 'soft on defence' and 'anti-American'. This was the distinction he sought to highlight in his opening words as a new prime minister. Other incoming prime ministers tended to promote a vision for the nation as they stood outside Number 10 for the first time, however vacuous or misleading that vision might prove to be. Blair chose to stress that there would be no turning back. His vision was defined by his constant urge to prove his party had changed.

Blair's early excursions in foreign policy were part of a pattern that led him towards the nightmare of Iraq. He sought to navigate between two awkward or extreme vote-losing positions and in doing so to keep most voters and the media on board. He was fairly open about this, proclaiming his attachment to 'third-way politics' and acknowledging his 'big tent' of support, arguing politely that he saw little point in suffering noble election defeats. Finding a third way between two unpalatable positions was his political philosophy. Remaining popular was an overwhelming objective. In his early days as prime minister, he said publicly and privately on many occasions that the campaign to win a second election had already begun.

Iraq came onto Blair's radar early on because he knew that President Clinton was contemplating an attack. What would he do in such circumstances? In his mind he had no doubt about where he would be if Clinton chose to strike. He would support his close ally, the most powerful leader in the world. The sequence of thoughts that led to his unequivocal conclusion was not triggered by a detailed study of Iraq, but a sense of what was expected of a New Labour prime minister. In February 1998, Blair paid his first visit as prime minister to President Clinton and was treated like a superstar, as the president's closest international ally.

His visit became famous because it coincided with the peak of the Monica Lewinsky saga. The alleged affair between Clinton and Lewinsky was a sensational theme at the joint press conference between Clinton and Blair in Washington. Did Clinton have an affair with Lewinsky? The question was posed in different forms several times by US journalists as the two leaders stood side by side. Wholly obscured since, and ignored at the time, the other topic of the press conference was military action in Iraq. This was the chosen topic of the two leaders, not what Clinton had got up to with Lewinsky. No one noticed. The BBC headline after the press conference was 'Blair backs Clinton over Lewinsky allegations'. The UK newspapers were similarly gripped. But Iraq was what Blair had prepared for in advance of his visit. Lewinsky was not a challenge for him. In contrast he regarded what he said on Iraq as a huge early test of his leadership.

Clinton had started to become obsessed about Saddam. His critics assumed the obsession was a convenient diversion from the Lewinsky saga. Perhaps they were right. Whatever his motives Clinton could not have been clearer in his introduction to the Washington press conference with Blair:

The best way to stop Saddam from developing an arsenal of nuclear, chemical, and biological weapons and the missiles to deliver them is to get the inspectors back to work with full and free access to all relevant sites. But let me be clear: if Saddam does not comply with the unanimous will of the international community, we must be prepared to act, and we are.[6]

Blair followed with a precise echo to Clinton's opening comments and with some detail of Britain's readiness for action. In tone, and to some extent in substance, he had begun his march towards the war in 2003.

We have of course to prepare in case diplomacy cannot work. In view of the situation, we in Britain have been looking at our own military readiness in case a diplomatic solution does not, in the end, prove possible. We have decided to base eight Tornado GR-1 aircraft in Kuwait, with the full agreement of the government of Kuwait. These are ground attack and reconnaissance aircraft. Their deployment is a precautionary measure, and it will take place over the next few days.

So all the way through, in respect to Iraq, we've agreed that we must educate; we must engage in diplomacy; but we also must prepare.[7]

Why was Blair so gripped by what was happening in Iraq rather than, say, Bosnia? He was gripped because President Clinton was gripped. He knew he might face a decision on military action and he knew he would support Clinton. Subsequently much was made of Blair's observation to the Liberal Democrat leader Paddy Ashdown in November 1997, as reported in Ashdown's illuminating diaries, 'I've read some of the stuff on this. It's pretty scary. He's pretty close to some appalling weapons of mass destruction . . . it's deadly serious.'[8] The quote has been used as evidence that Blair was always sincerely alarmed by Saddam and that his alarm was based on intelligence. The analysis is flawed. Blair was getting intelligence from trouble spots around the world, including Bosnia. He seized on the specific intelligence from Iraq as evidence to build his case for military action, or to be more precise, to support Clinton, who was planning military strikes. He cited the intelligence to Ashdown because he wanted to keep the Liberal Democrats on board if the moment came when he would stand shoulder to shoulder with a US president. He knew the Conservatives would support him and that was an important part of his calculation, but he did not want the Liberal Democrats to oppose action in a potentially troublesome alliance with the left of his party. He wanted his big tent to survive a possible military partnership with the US. Ashdown had been a key figure in the big tent and he wanted him to stay in it. The reference to the intelligence was more than an observation. It was an early act of persuasion.

In the autumn of 1997 for a leader of Blair's mindset every calculation pointed unambiguously towards supporting Clinton. They were similar calculations to the ones he was to make nearly six years later. He was a different type of Labour prime minister, who would not shirk tough decisions, including military ones. He was Clinton's closest ally. The Conservatives would support any military action and

Blair did not want to give them the space to look more 'responsible' as an opposition than the new Labour government. The newspapers, especially those he cared about, would support military action. Labour MPs would be supportive, partly because they admired President Clinton. Blair wanted at some point to win a referendum on the euro so it was important as far as he was concerned to show that he was pro-American in order to build up credit with Rupert Murdoch and his newspapers that he knew would be ready to attack him in a referendum on the single currency. Politically there were no downsides.

Blair had no idea for certain whether Clinton would strike but he prepared the ground. On 17 December 1997, US and British forces began a four-day bombing campaign against Iraqi command centres, airfields, weapons storage facilities and radar and missile sites. This was Blair's first experience as a war leader, one that he had prepared for and had psyched himself up for. In a statement after the bombing had begun he told the Commons: 'There is no realistic alternative to military force. We are taking military action with real regret but also with real determination. We have exhausted all other avenues. We act because we must.'[9]

The statement was disingenuous. In the view of many other world leaders the timing was arbitrary and connected more to providing a distraction from the Lewinsky scandal still traumatizing Clinton. Blair was the only other world leader to offer active military support for the strikes. In doing so he was widely hailed as courageous in the British media; he kept his big tent intact, and purged Labour of its perceived weak-kneed past. Here was a Labour leader who could authorize military action with a Thatcher-like resolve.

The action went nowhere. There was no follow-up from Clinton and therefore there was no follow-up from Blair. Saddam remained in place. The erratic dance with UN resolutions and UN inspectors continued. Clinton's attentions moved on and therefore Blair's attentions moved on. He had passed his first major test as a prime minister, supporting military action, proving a strong ally of the US and securing strong support in the UK across the political spectrum.

No cabinet member dissented from the attacks. The foreign secretary, Robin Cook, was wholly supportive. The international development secretary, Clare Short, did not demur. The military action was very limited. And of course this was early in the life of the first Labour government for eighteen years. Political appetites of new ministers were still far from sated. No minister was going to resign over an attack on Iraq instigated by President Clinton, ambitious Labour MPs were not going to rebel when they ached to be ministers. Blair was not the only politician making multi-layered calculations. They all were.

In April 1999 Blair made a speech in Chicago setting out his 'Doctrine of the International Community'. The speech was widely seen as his distinct, personal approach to intervention. Subsequently Blair, his admirers and his critics cited the speech to justify whatever argument they were advancing, as if the address was the product of intense and intensive thinking. This was another misreading.

In fact most of the speech had been written quickly, based on notes from Professor Sir Lawrence Freedman, who was astonished to hear his hastily assembled thoughts become the basis for an entire prime-ministerial approach to matters of peace and war. A few days before the speech Jonathan Powell had asked Freedman to write some reflections. He did so, linking Saddam and Serbia's Slobodan Milošević as challenges facing the international community. He listed five factors to consider in relation to possible military action.

Blair made the same connection and listed the five factors as if they were the outcome of his own long, considered, deep thinking. Here is part of what Freedman wrote and Blair spoke. The speech is quoted at length because it was presented as Blair's doctrine and should therefore provide important clues as to why he went to war in 2003.

Many of our problems have been caused by two dangerous and ruthless men – Saddam Hussein and Slobodan Milošević. Both have been prepared to wage vicious campaigns against sections of their own community. As a result of these destructive policies both have brought calamity on their own peoples. Instead of enjoying its oil wealth, Iraq has been reduced to poverty, with political life stultified through fear. Milošević took over a substantial, ethnically diverse state, well placed to take advantage of new economic opportunities. His drive for ethnic concentration has left him with something much smaller, a ruined economy and soon a totally ruined military machine.

One of the reasons why it is now so important to win the conflict is to ensure that others do not make the same mistake in the future. That in itself will be a major step to ensuring that the next decade and the next century will not be as difficult as the past. If NATO fails in Kosovo, the next dictator to be threatened with military force may well not believe our resolve to carry the threat through.

First, are we sure of our case? War is an imperfect instrument for righting humanitarian distress; but armed force is sometimes the only means of dealing with dictators. Second, have we exhausted all diplomatic options? We should always give peace every chance, as we have in the case of Kosovo. Third, on the basis of a practical assessment of the situation, are there military operations we can sensibly and prudently undertake? Fourth, are we prepared for the long term? In the past we talked too much of exit strategies. But having made a commitment we cannot simply walk away once the fight is over; better to stay with moderate numbers of troops than return for repeat performances with large numbers. And finally, do we have national interests involved? The mass expulsion of ethnic Albanians from Kosovo demanded the notice of the rest of the world. But it does make a difference that this is taking place in such a combustible part of Europe.

I am not suggesting that these are absolute tests. But they are the kind of issues we need to think about in deciding in the future when and whether we will intervene.[10]

The doctrine was not only rushed and based on a single hasty contribution from a distinguished academic, the words were also evasive. The doctrine could have been deployed to justify not intervening in Iraq in 2003 on the grounds that diplomatic options had not been exhausted. The words left Blair with a protective shield. He could cite the doctrine to justify military action if the US decided to go to war, or not to do so if the US took a different course. No doubt he also believed in the words. Few could not do so in the abstract.

The liberation of Kosovo later in 1999 also made a deep impression on him. In domestic policy Blair had Gordon Brown breathing down his neck every day. Separately he bore the 'scars on his back' in his early attempts to reform resistant public services. But in Kosovo he had grateful parents naming their babies after him and chanting their appreciation when he visited. For Blair the war in the Balkans seemed to tick all the boxes. He showed once more he could be a war leader. The Conservative leadership could do little more than express its admiration. For once, Blair had pulled levers and there had been clear responses.

An Attack on New York

Virtually every day of his premiership Blair had kept an eye on what was happening in Washington, making sure he was more or less singing from the same hymn sheet, often using the words of Clinton or Bush as if they were his own. When the terrorists attacked the US on 11 September 2001 he knew instinctively what to do, hardly needing to pause as he switched from being a British prime minister working on a solid but unspectacular agenda to becoming a global leader.

Here was another test of his leadership as a New Labour prime minister. At such moments of immediate history a leader responds on many different levels – horror, outrage, surprise, a sense of personal challenge – and always making political calculations. Blair was in Brighton ready to deliver a speech to the TUC, largely about the virtues of the euro, the historic mission he had in mind for his second term. The speech was never delivered. Instead he spoke briefly and with sparkling eloquence about the threat posed by new forms of terrorism and then quickly left the hall. He and his team rushed back to Number 10 and engaged with Washington with an intensity and persistence that were never going to be easy to break away from. The adulation that greeted Blair when he visited New York and Washington later that month became a trap. How could he ever step aside from this post-9/11 administration after such a coming-together? A decade earlier he had been an obscure front-bencher belonging to a party seemingly doomed to eternal opposition. Now he was the prime minister receiving standing ovations in Congress, thanked by a US president for his loyalty. The dynamic was both intoxicating and politically convenient.

There were many other important and substantial calculations as the relationship between Blair and Bush intensified. By being close to the US, Blair exercised a degree of influence in the timing of the inevitable attack on Afghanistan and in his argument that a new international coalition could be formed to address the threat. There were some in the unruly, divided Bush administration who wanted an early strike on Kabul. Blair was one of those who urged a short delay. His advice was continuous: calls, personal notes, and that visit to the US in which appreciative adulation exceeded anything that Thatcher had experienced. Superficially Blair was offering advice to Bush, but it was in the context of unquestioning support for military action in Afghanistan. The advice was peripheral in relation to the big military call, which was to follow what President Bush had already decided.

Of course, the human tragedy of 9/11 and its implications weighed heavily on Blair as it did on other international leaders. They were human beings. But all that had happened to Blair in his career and was happening at the time appeared to have prepared him for this moment of international crisis. The EU and the US were at one in their horror, making him the ideal third-way navigator between the two. His experiences of Kosovo and Northern Ireland, where near miracles were achieved, propelled him towards more optimistic diplomacy, including a futile visit to Syria in an attempt to persuade President Assad to join the still vaguely defined international cause.

From a domestic perspective, Blair had a new raison d'être as prime minister. Gordon Brown's demands for him to go ceased for the time being. The chancellor was at the margins of another mission for the prime minister who was fast becoming an international super-star. The new Tory leader Iain Duncan Smith even paid homage to Blair's leadership, privately and publicly expressing his admiration for what he took to be the prime minister's courage. Such was the focus on Blair, the election of the new Tory leader was not the main news story even on the day the result was announced. The second term that had seemed a little lifeless in the immediate aftermath of the election had acquired for Blair a sudden and distinct sense of purpose.

In January 2002 Bush used his State of the Union address to out-line his theory on what he called the axis of evil. This was a pivotal event, the moment when Blair knew for sure that war in Iraq was probable as far as the Bush administration were concerned. The Tali-ban had been removed from Kabul with relative ease and Bush wanted to move on. There was little focus from Bush, and therefore little focus from Blair, on how to prevent the Taliban from re-grouping around Kabul or how to retain the unity of the remarkable inter-national alliance of support that had arisen after September 11th. Instead it was clear that Bush had his eyes on Saddam.

The impatience of the Bush administration to move from Afghanistan to Iraq was without reason or logic. The switch would divert military resources from Afghanistan when the new regime was far from secure. Saddam was an enemy of al Qaeda and there-fore would not be part of the new threat that the US was supposed to be confronting; in fact Al Qaeda would welcome his removal. A consistent message of intelligence reports from the US and UK was that an invasion of Iraq would heighten the threat posed by terrorists. Instead of reflecting on these obvious themes Bush returned to the arguments deployed by Clinton when Blair first gave his support to military action in Iraq, although his language was cruder and more sweeping in its simplicity.

In his State of the Union address in 2002, Bush said:

Iraq continues to flaunt its hostility toward America and to support terror. The Iraqi regime has plotted to develop anthrax and nerve gas and nuclear weapons for over a decade. This is a regime that has already used poison gas to murder thousands of its own citizens, leaving the bodies of mothers huddled over their dead children. This is a regime that agreed to international inspections, then kicked out the inspectors. This is a regime that has something to hide from the civilized world.[11]

Towards the end of his address Bush declared, 'States like these and their terrorist allies constitute an axis of evil, arming to threaten the peace of the world.' It was the framing of the global challenge as an axis of evil that confirmed to Blair what he always knew was probable. Bush was moving on to Saddam. As he always had done with a US president, Blair moved on too, deploying almost exactly the same words in describing the threat posed by Saddam. In relation to the axis-of-evil speech, Blair could have cast his forensic gaze and challenged the assertions made. He was smart enough. If a left-wing leader, perhaps from Chile, or a nationalist leader in Russia, had made the speech, provoking opposition from a US president, he may well have raised pertinent questions. But it was President Bush. Immediately, without wider discussion in his cabinet or beyond, he supported the assertions and started looking for evidence to back them up.

But this time he had to be careful. There would be no automatic political consensus – Blair's comfort zone – as there was in relation to the earlier, more moderate strike on Iraq. As far as his party was concerned, Clinton was an admired leader but Bush was widely loathed. A significant section of his party would be opposed to war in Iraq. Blair knew also the section would be a lot bigger if Bush acted unilaterally without seeking support from the UN.

Blair's Dilemma

After the axis-of-evil speech, the issue of Iraq started to dominate British politics. As far as Blair was concerned, it would never go away again. He knew that one way or another Bush would seek to remove Saddam, and he could either back him or oppose him or seek a third way. As ever, he sought a third way, but one that even the navigator of the Northern Ireland peace process could not follow without getting desperately, pathetically lost. The dilemmas facing Blair were deep, complex and not explored at the time or subsequently.

There was no question from Blair's point of view that he would remain Bush's closest ally. The determination to do so was his deepest instinct. He could only breathe politically in a comfort zone where he was as close to a US president as Thatcher had been and where there was no space for a Conservative leader of the opposition to make hay. What about the substance of the issue? Even for Blair, who acquired a reputation for evangelical interventionism, the case for removing Saddam was not straightforward. Even before considering the complex composition of Iraq it does not take a genius to recognize the risks of invading another country. Yes, Blair saw the case for removing Saddam. He had convinced himself long ago, when he became prime minister, that the tyrant was a threat to international security. He had seen the benefits of 'liberation' in Kosovo. But the proposition that war in Iraq was obviously the way forward for the US and therefore the UK was not one of which he could be 100 per cent sure. He was much surer about the political imperative.

He was still no expert on Iraq, its history or the wider region. After the attacks on September 11th, Blair read the Quran in an attempt to understand why fundamentalists could seek guidance from the text. But although he was a quick learner he was not a specialist in the politics of the region. If he had become an expert he would have discovered too many complexities and ambiguities about Iraq and what might happen if a tyrant was removed. It was better not to know.

But as a political leader Blair could not imagine opposing President Bush. Indeed it takes quite a leap to contemplate the alternative scenario, even now when the calamity of what followed is known: Blair standing up at a press conference in Number 10 and declaring that he disagreed with Bush, the leader he had spoken to so many times since September 11th, the leader who he had rushed over to visit following the atrocity, the leader with whom he had worked as they went to war in Afghanistan. Blair was not going to walk away from a presidential desire to remove a tyrant and join a Continental consensus.

He would be horrified at the idea of Iain Duncan Smith being given the space to become Bush's ally while he moved closer to the position of previous vote-losing Labour leaders.

But how could he persuade his party? Bush was a right-wing Republican and widely dismissed in his party and beyond as being recklessly stupid. One of the reasons Blair had removed his foreign secretary, Robin Cook, from the Foreign Office was his fear that Cook would not want to work closely with an unruly right-wing US administration. Cook was a pro-European socialist who loathed

Bush's politics, so Blair replaced him with the more expedient Jack Straw, a figure who reflected more deeply on policy than him, but who was much less troublesome. In this new context of a possible conflict with Iraq, Blair knew parts of his party and possibly some in his cabinet would be deeply alarmed. He also knew he had to keep as much of his party with him as possible. He was aware that the so-called hard left would be opposed and was not remotely bothered by that, but he needed most of his party to be on board and in particular most of his MPs.

He knew the Conservative leadership would back him, an extremely important element in the equation. If the Conservatives had opposed the conflict he might not have acted as he did. Similarly if Murdoch's papers had been opposed he would have had more doubts. A bigger political figure, more courageous, less burdened by his party's vote-losing past, a deeper thinker, might at this point have foreseen what was going to happen in Iraq and moved away from Bush. But moving away from Bush might have risked a different form of hell, at least for Blair. So he faced a nightmarish decision in early 2002. If he had declared his opposition to Bush, opinion-forming newspapers would have turned away. The Tory leadership would have been given a distinct position. There was no easy course for a Labour prime minister in early 2002, the period when the course was set. And once it was set there could be no going back. Later, angry voters would ask in TV studios why Blair ignored the biggest demonstration since 1945 against UK military action. Some fickle newspaper columnists wondered why he was so determined to press ahead. The answer is that by then he was trapped. He could not stand up and state that he had changed his mind. That would have been more disastrous for him than continuing.

In advance of his key meeting with Bush at his ranch home in

Crawford, Texas, in March 2002, Blair came up with a characteristic plan, not a risky aberration but one wholly consistent with his cautious, expedient approach to politics in which he sought to find a position that commanded the widest possible support. He correctly calculated that most of his party, including the likes of Robin Cook, would support military action if authorized by the UN. At the same time he assumed that Bush would be seen as a less villainous character if the US president could be persuaded to pursue the Middle East peace process while planning an attack on Iraq, and a renewed focus on the peace process was a virtue in itself. Above all, Blair needed time to build up support for dealing with Saddam. If Bush acted quickly he would not have the time he needed.

Of course there was more to Blair's calculations than the need to secure a wider coalition of support. The Bush administration was in danger of becoming a superpower disengaged from allies and international institutions. By supporting him Blair gave him no choice but to engage. But for Blair the political context was key. We know this because if he was bothered only by whether or not Saddam was removed he could have let Bush and his administration get on with it: senior figures in the US were irritated by Blair's involvement and wanted to get on with removing Saddam unilaterally. Blair could have let them and Saddam would have been removed.

His involvement was necessary because that was what a British prime minister did, or Blair assumed that this was what was expected of a British prime minister.

The Crawford summit in March 2002 has been the subject of endless speculation. After their private discussions Bush announced he would take the UN route although before it had appeared that he was ready to act unilaterally and had viewed the UN with impatient disdain. The change was solely because of Blair. Blair persuaded him to go to the UN when he might have caused an even greater international crisis by attacking Iraq and bypassing the UN entirely.

This was a significant shift from Bush, annoying his vice-president, Dick Cheney, and his defense secretary, Donald Rumsfeld, who were impatient to strike and at times found Blair an irritant preventing them from doing so. Bush viewed Blair very differently. He knew that invading Iraq was quite a leap and could hardly believe that he had this supposedly left-of-centre prime minister proving to be so supportive at every juncture. When the two of them were together at press conferences Bush, a transparent public figure, could not altogether disguise his bewildered disbelief that he had come upon a leader who could articulate a case for military action more effectively than anyone in his administration, including himself. Bush was willing to go to the UN knowing that his loyal ally would be with him whatever happened.

Blair secured this change of approach from Bush by making clear he would be constant as an ally, taking part in military action with the US even if the UN route failed to deliver their joint objective, the removal of Saddam. Blair also pressed the importance of the Middle East peace process as fundamental in securing long-term stability for the entire region. We know he did because Bush started to mention it in vague terms. After their private conversations the two leaders held a brief press conference in Crawford. Joint press conferences with US presidents were part of Blair's comfort zone, a Labour prime minister working closely with the world's most powerful leader. In this case Blair stated revealingly: 'This is an opportunity for the UN to rise to its responsibilities and not to evade those responsibilities.'[12] In effect Blair declared publicly that Bush was putting an overwhelmingly powerful case to the UN when he might not have bothered, and the UN should behave responsibly by supporting him. As the war approached, Bush would regularly praise Blair as a 'man who sticks to his word'. The constant reiteration was never explored at the time. The words could have only one meaning. Blair promised to stick with Bush when military action became necessary and he had done so.

Blair's success in persuading Bush to seek a new UN resolution in relation to Iraq had several profound consequences. Above all it meant that for both leaders the route to war would focus on the weapons of mass destruction (WMD) that Saddam was supposed to possess. The UN might support the removal of such weapons. It would never sanction the removal of a leader. From Crawford onwards, Blair and Bush had to frame their case in relation to the threat posed by WMD. Before Crawford it was probable that Bush would strike Baghdad openly, arguing that Saddam must be toppled. Blair had stopped an act of illegal unilateralism from a US president but in doing so became dependent on an argument about the need to remove Saddam's WMD.

The second consequence for Blair was that he had to prepare for the possibility of military action and to follow a military timetable largely determined by the US. Blair had bought more time to make his lawyerly case in the UK and he had stopped the US acting unilaterally. Following their talks he knew that Bush would not move speedily but in consultation with him. Blair had some space, but the space was narrow. He needed support from the international community and if he secured it he sensed there was a decent chance of winning over most of his party, and the wider electorate.

Around-the-clock advocacy soaked up nearly all his efforts in the months that followed. He had no choice but to become an advocate, advancing a one-sided case in the build-up to war. He had voters, the media and parliamentary colleagues to persuade. But in persuading he had little time for practical reflections on what would happen in

Iraq after the war. September 2002 was the most important month in the build-up, when the act of persuasion began in earnest, with his monthly press conference dominated by the issue and when he published the dossier on Saddam's alleged possession of weapons of mass destruction. The events of this month were to be viewed very differently in retrospect, but at the time it was starkly obvious that Blair was putting a case. Like all advocates, he was selecting the evidence to make the case. He was not the chair of a seminar on how best to deal with Saddam. But later he was accused of deception and lying, as if he had claimed to be a neutral communicator of the 'facts'.

His comments at his monthly press conference echoed those he made at Crawford. He made clear that the UN had to act with him and Bush. If not, the coalition would act without the authorization of the UN. There can be no other interpretation of this vital quote from the press conference:

Obviously it is better to have the international community with us again. The important thing, however, because this is a problem for the world, is that the United Nations has to be the route to deal with this problem, not a way of people avoiding dealing with this problem. After all it is the United Nations resolutions that Saddam is in breach of. So it makes perfect sense to say that this is an issue for the international community and should be dealt with in that way. All I am saying is it has to be dealt with because we cannot have a situation where people simply turn a blind eye to a situation in which Iraq continues to develop these weapons.[13]

Shortly after the press conference Blair published the WMD dossier, once again as much an act of advocacy as his press conference.

On the day it was recognized as such. Here was a prime minister putting a case for the need to act. On the whole the media concluded that there was nothing much surprising in the document, as did those politicians who were opposed to military action in Iraq. Nonetheless some of the newspapers went over the top in their reporting, highlighting the claim that Saddam possessed weapons that could be targeted at the UK within forty-five minutes. If Blair were conducting a seminar he would have urged caution in relation to such assertions. But as an advocate putting a case he was delighted at such coverage, hoping it might help to change the public mood.

After the war, the dossier became totemic, the publication an act of deception by Blair and his press secretary, Alastair Campbell. Reading the dossier now is a darkly comic experience. Every single item of intelligence, presented without qualification, proved to be wrong. It contained a number of allegations that Iraq also possessed chemical and biological weapons, and even alleged that the country had reconstituted its nuclear weapons programme. Plucked out of context, the dossier is shocking. But the context in which it was published was that Blair had become dependent on intelligence asserting Saddam possessed WMD. He wanted UN backing and the intelligence was his ammunition. Major General Michael Laurie, one of those involved in producing the dossier, wrote to the Chilcot Inquiry in 2011: 'the purpose of the dossier was precisely to make a case for war, rather than setting out the available intelligence, and that to make the best out of sparse and inconclusive intelligence the wording was developed with care.'[14] On 26 June 2011, *The Observer* reported on a memo from Sir John Scarlett, head of the Joint Intelligence Committee (JIC), to Blair's foreign affairs adviser, released under the Freedom of Information Act, which referred to 'the benefit of obscuring the fact that in terms of WMD, Iraq is not that exceptional'.

If Blair had been a free agent he would probably have backed Bush in the toppling of Saddam, bypassing the UN. The Conservative leader, Iain Duncan Smith, had said he would support the US if they went to war without seeking fresh UN resolutions. But Blair was leader of a party committed to international law as determined partly by UN resolutions. So the intelligence became paramount. The dossier was signed off by Scarlett and the JIC. Later the BBC claimed that the document had been 'sexed up' against the wishes of senior intelligence officers. Yet the most senior intelligence officers had given the go-ahead for publication.

There is one very big pertinent question arising from the dossier. Why was the intelligence so wrong? For all the qualifications surrounding the assertions in the intelligence, there was still enough of it to suggest that Saddam possessed WMD. The question was rarely posed. Instead, soon after the war the questions focused on Blair's integrity. Why did he lie? Iraq was a turning point on many fronts. One of the most important was the breakdown in trust.

Yet the answer is that he did not lie. He placed a preposterously excessive weight on intelligence that was obviously unreliable. He did so because it had become his only route to war in which he might be able to retain his big tent of support. Having taken the decision to publish the intelligence, his sole worry in advance of the dossier was that the public and media reaction would be indifference: 'We knew all this already . . . this does not justify war.' So the dossier was an attempt to dramatize the intelligence in order to make a case. Blair might have had doubts about some of the intelligence but at that moment he could hardly say, 'Obviously some of this intelligence might turn out to be wrong.' He was not in a position to be nuanced.

He had promised Bush he would stand shoulder to shoulder with the US and he was using every resource available to him to ensure that pledge commanded wide support.

Blair can be accused of being out of his depth, making poor judgements about the complexities of Iraq and the wider region, of not being bold enough to challenge Bush (although a challenge would not have changed US policy towards Iraq). But it is wholly wrong to frame the position he was in by the autumn of 2002 in terms of his integrity. The framing has not only made it impossible for a considered view of Blair's leadership but has polluted British politics. More than ever, the vacuous but dangerous slogan is asserted by voters: 'You can't trust those bloody politicians. They even lie to take us to war.'

By the autumn of 2002, Blair appeared to be in a precarious place in his party, with polls suggesting most Labour members were opposed, but from his perspective the march to war was largely going to plan. He looked in desperate trouble, but he remained the loyal ally of the world's superpower, the Conservatives supported what he was doing – a backing that meant anti-war voters had no alternative governing party to support – and he was generating rave reviews in much of the UK media. He was still hanging on in his comfort zone and he even secured backing at the UN but all was not what it seemed.

Towards the end of 2002, an apparent triumph for the UK was in fact a deadly defeat. The resolution text was drafted jointly by the United States and the United Kingdom, the result of eight weeks of tumultuous negotiations, particularly with Russia and France. The resolution stated that Iraq would face 'serious consequences' if it did not fully cooperate with weapons inspectors. The consequences were not specified. If the resolution had said clearly that one consequence was international military action, it would not have been passed. France questioned the phrase 'serious consequences' and stated repeatedly that any 'material breach' found by the inspectors should not automatically lead to war; instead the UN should pass another resolution deciding on the course of action.

Nevertheless, most of the media, as gullible in advance as it was hysterically hostile later, was awestruck at what it took to be Blair's courageous leadership. Leaders who are not especially courageous derive intense satisfaction when they are hailed for their perceived bravery. The former Tory cabinet minister and *Sunday Times* columnist Michael Portillo was typical of many in praising Blair for his 'principled boldness'.[15] Portillo wrote that he had wrongly assumed Blair would do anything in order to be popular. Instead his approach to Iraq showed he was a much bigger leader than that. For a leader with Blair's background in a vote-losing Labour Party, Portillo's observations were a form of political perfection, praise from a former Conservative for the depth and strength of his leadership. Much media commentary was along similar lines. Although under huge and varying pressures Blair was still being praised by credible figures on the right.[16]

On the domestic agenda Blair and Gordon Brown were involved in blazing rows over public-service reform. In contrast, as far as Iraq was concerned, Blair was still free to act without Brown challenging him. Brown had some doubts about Iraq but he was not a fundamental opponent. If he had been, he would have stopped Blair one way or another. He blocked other policies with which he disagreed, or sought to; he never made any attempt to prevent Blair from going to war in Iraq. On this he was in a similar place to Blair. As far as Brown was concerned, the politics were overwhelmingly in favour of backing war. He did not want to alienate Rupert Murdoch and the usually gung-ho middle-England voters when he assumed he would soon be prime minister.

Blair's confidence in his ability to lead unimpeded was soaring at precisely the moment he should have had self-doubt. What seemed like a bleak phase in the build-up to war was, on some levels, a heady time for him. The Conservatives were going nowhere and Iain Duncan Smith was already struggling as a leader. Apart from intellectually self-confident heavyweights such as the former Conservative chancellor Ken Clarke, and Blair's old friend Roy Jenkins, the prominent opponents of war were less convinced than they appeared to be. The leader of the Liberal Democrats, Charles Kennedy, became distinctive for opposing the conflict, but only after much agonizing. His predecessor, Paddy Ashdown, was a supporter of the war at first and put considerable pressure on Kennedy to back Blair. It was only later that Blair's big political tent deserted him. As he made his moves towards war, he had the admiring support of most newspapers; the leader of the Conservative Party and nearly all Conservative MPs; Rupert Murdoch, who Blair spoke to several times in the days preceding the war; all but one or two of his cabinet; and the former Liberal Democrat leader Paddy Ashdown. Against him was a nervy Kennedy and some Labour MPs.

The voters were proving more of a problem. Blair's persuasive arts had not convinced the majority of them. But at this point he was not too alarmed. They could hardly turn to the Conservatives, who were even more hawkish about Iraq than he was. He was always at his most politically content when the Conservatives offered no credibly distinct alternative. Equally important, he was still convinced that he would ultimately have been more unpopular if he had allied himself with France and Germany against the US.

He sought a second UN resolution because as usual he also

wanted wide support, including Robin Cook, the vast majority of Labour MPs and voters. But if he did not get it, he had what he regarded as the key part of his coalition behind him. His attempt was doomed from the beginning and a small part of him was smart enough to realize this. Part of him knew that he needed to be *seen* to be trying to secure the resolution in the hope that critics would recognize he had tried his best. But there was also a part of him that was naively optimistic that such a resolution might be possible.

He overestimated his power to persuade. The Northern Ireland peace process and Kosovo had given him a confidence that was partly justified, but in relation to Iraq he was entering another league of challenges. Towards the end of 2002 the scale of the obstacle was strikingly obvious, but by then he was trapped. He had no choice but to try to secure UN backing for war. There was no going back. For him it would have been politically impossible and undesirable to state that he was having any doubts about his third way, an attempt to get UN support for war.

Blair had to try to convince himself that a second resolution was possible. Hans Blix, chairman of the Weapons of Mass Destruction Commission (WMDC), produced a relatively positive inspection report on 14 February 2003, and Britain began the quest for a second resolution authorizing military action. On that day, only two other members of the Security Council – Bulgaria and Spain – were willing to vote for military action. A month later, on 17 March, when Britain finally gave up its quest, nothing had changed. Blair's solution was to blame France, to claim that France was being utterly unreasonable: not only was it opposed to military action in principle, it had sabotaged support on the Council for a second resolution authorizing military action by threatening to use its veto. In that regard, a remark by President Chirac in a TV interview broadcast on 10 March was a godsend to Downing Street. The remark in question was: 'My position is that, regardless of the circumstances, France will vote "no" because she considers this evening that there are no grounds for waging war in order to achieve the goal we have set ourselves, i.e., to disarm Iraq.'[17]

The use of the phrase 'regardless of the circumstances' allowed Downing Street to pretend that Chirac had ruled out force for all time – and by so doing had torpedoed a second resolution. This was not true. On the contrary, in the interview that Monday evening, Chirac made it very clear that there were circumstances in which France would *not* veto a resolution for war: if the UN inspectors reported progress in finding the weapons or if the inspectors said that their task was impossible. In either case, in his words, 'regrettably, the war would become inevitable'.

But as time went on Blair was closer to being a lawyer putting forward a case than a balanced, deep-thinking prime minister contemplating the multi-layered complexities of invading Iraq. He needed to blame Chirac largely in order to convince Labour MPs that he had sought tirelessly to pursue the UN route but France was never going to challenge Saddam.

This proposition, wrapped in a remarkable outburst of anti-French hysteria, was repeated ad nauseam in the week leading up to the Commons vote on 18 March. It covered Blair's retreat from his promise not to take military action without, at the very least, majority support on the Security Council. It was referred to over and over again in the Commons debate on 18 March and played a major role in limiting the Labour backbench revolt that day.

Blair could not wait any longer. The reason had nothing to do with his own impatience: he was operating on a US military timetable and it was him who had kept the US waiting. He could not turn to Bush and say one more time, 'Look, we might get France on board at a future date.' Bush, who had grown to like Blair, would lose patience. He did give Blair the option of pulling out of the planned military action, but although that would have thrilled the growing numbers opposed to the war in the UK, it would have ended his alliance with Rupert Murdoch and with those voters who saw him as a different type of Labour prime minister, one who was strong on defence. He would have been seen as 'weaker' than Michael Foot or Neil Kinnock, calling back UK troops on the eve of war. For Blair, it was not an option he could contemplate because to pull out in such a humiliating way would destroy the coalition of support that he cared about most, those that were singing his praises as he headed towards war. Once again domestic calculations were playing a big part in determining his moves even if it appeared he was acting with disregard to the way he was perceived in the UK. The opposite was closer to the truth. He had not suddenly and weirdly lost interest in his relationship with the electorate and the media.

Blair Sticks to his Course

Without a second UN resolution Blair knew he would have to face significant opposition within the Labour Party, but he calculated that he could manage the dissent as long as most Labour MPs continued to back him. But he was surprised by the size of the demonstration against the war. On Saturday 15 February up to a million people marched against in London, descending from all parts of the UK, a demonstration of unprecedented size on a freezing day.

The march marked the most important moment in Blair's transition from a leader who ached to be popular to one who sought a new rationale for his leadership. In response to the astonishing images of the march, Blair declared he did not 'seek unpopularity as a badge of honour but sometimes it is the price of leadership and the cost of conviction'.[18] These are the most important words he uttered in the entire Iraq saga. He had apparently metamorphosed into a leader who was guided by evangelical belief irrespective of popularity.

But leaders do not change from one human being into another. They are who they are. These words were uttered by a leader who when faced by a smaller demonstration of the Countryside Alliance a few years earlier was so alarmed that he sent his environment minister on the march, even though the marchers were protesting against the government. Poor Michael Meacher, the minister in question, had to join the protest directed at his own department. Blair wanted to signal that he understood the concerns of these middle-England types. One of their concerns was the abolition of fox-hunting. So keen was he to respond to their worries that he contrived measures to abolish fox-hunting that allowed fox-hunting to continue. Now, faced with a march of a million people on a much bigger issue, he was seemingly defiant, the crusader who did what he believed to be right.

What had happened to bring about such a change? The answer is that Blair had no choice but to be defiant. He had tried to secure a broad alliance of support, his normal third-way approach, by persuading Bush to seek UN backing. But because he had pledged long ago to support Bush if the president at least tried to seek UN resolutions to authorize military action, there was no way he could at this late stage back down without looking pathetically weak, the leader who gave up when the going got tough. He was trapped. The only escape route was the one he chose, to play the leader who would defy popular protest out of conviction. This became his persona for the rest of his leadership. He was facing a turning point in the UK he had not dared to contemplate. Voters well beyond the regular anti-war protesters were passionately opposed to the conflict. In response he posed as the strong war leader, when in reality he was in a very weak position and having to follow a US military timetable while needing to appear as if he was in control.

After the conflict Blair was widely condemned for not paying enough attention to what would happen afterwards in Iraq and the wider region. The condemnation is justified in that the post-war planning was shallow and chaotic. But there is a simple explanation for his lack of focus on the aftermath. Quite simply he did not have enough hours in the day to make the case for war *and* pay assiduous attention to what would happen afterwards. The former *Times* editor Peter Stothard was invited into Number 10 to record a diary of the build-up to war. The intense focus, written sympathetically, was on the final political obstacle, winning a vote in the Commons on the eve of war. What would Gordon Brown do? He declared his support for war, but Blair was not sure of his intentions until he made a public statement. Could they persuade Clare Short to stay in the cabinet? Blair managed to keep her in the tent (for a while). What would be the impact of Robin Cook's resignation, the only cabinet minister to resign in advance of war? Could he persuade the majority of Labour MPs to support the war? The aftermath could wait.

As far as Blair was concerned, the invasion went more or less to plan, as it was bound to do. Step back from the intense politics of the year that had preceded the war and it was always going to be a one-sided conflict. Far from being courageous, Blair had chosen to fight with the world's only military superpower against an ageing tyrant. In the short term there was only going to be one winner and Blair had assumed that the controversial arguments about what happened before the war would be forgotten in the light of another military triumph.

So Blair had expected that once Saddam fell he would at worst be not be too badly damaged and, at best, he would get a 'Baghdad bounce' to compare with Margaret Thatcher's 'Falklands factor', a factor that made her electorally invincible. Voters forgot quickly that it was Thatcher's errors that opened the way for Argentina to invade the Falklands. Instead they remembered her victory and that they had supported her the moment she sent the task force to win the islands back. The same applied to Iraq, as Blair had assumed it would. In *The Sunday Times* there was this analysis a few days later:

> The British participation in the American-led invasion of Iraq was, at the moment it began, possibly the least popular war with the British public of any in which British troops have joined since opinion polls first began. But no sooner had the first shots been fired than public opinion started to swing in favour of British involvement in the war and kept on going. Within a couple of days the polls were finding solid majorities in favour where previously they had found solid majorities against, a movement which even reports of civilian casualties, 'friendly fire' incidents and later widespread looting and lawlessness apparently did nothing to check. The scale of the change of opinions makes it one of the most dramatic turnarounds that MORI has measured.[19]

The turnaround was confirmed on 29 April, soon after Saddam had fallen. The *Financial Times* reported: 'As the prime minister turns his attention to domestic matters, he will be pleased to receive news that the Baghdad "Bounce" is working well for him . . . According to an FT state of the nation opinion poll, the British are feeling patriotic.'[20]

Once again Blair had navigated the safest political course, however hazardous it appeared to be on the surface. Having served his political apprenticeship in the aftermath of the Falklands War, he was conditioned to assume that wars are electorally popular in the UK if victory is secured. There was never any doubt that the US would remove Saddam. Sure enough, the war was popular, but only briefly. The pre-war demonstration marked a deeper change in the country's mood since the Falklands.

For many years, long before Iraq, the issue of trust had dominated British politics. Very quickly complex issues were reduced to whether a leader was lying or not. The fall of John Major was partly caused by allegations that raged in the media about 'sleaze', a term that came to torment him. Ministers were forced to resign over 'sleaze'. Major ceased to be trusted because of 'sleaze'. So central was the issue that when Blair came to power he insisted that his ministerial team must not only be 'purer than pure' but perceived to be as well, a striking ambition.

Very quickly perceptions of impurity gathered around the new Labour government, most of them without much justification. The BBC in particular became obsessed with the issue of 'spin'. Before Labour came to power *Panorama* broadcast a lengthy programme about Alastair Campbell and his team. The programme revealed nothing of significance because there was nothing of significance to reveal. Campbell sought to present Blair in the best possible light and was the first Labour press secretary to understand the media since Joe Haines had worked for Harold Wilson in the 1970s. The BBC employed far more managers, producers and reporters at its Westminster base in Millbank than Blair employed spin-doctors.

As a result of the BBC obsession virtually every ministerial announcement was reported partly on the basis of how a policy was presented. The substance of the policy was underplayed. The question of whether Blair had lied to justify war, with the help of Campbell, was therefore guaranteed to make waves. On 29 May 2003 the journalist Andrew Gilligan generated massive waves with a series of reports on the BBC that began with two interviews with the presenter John Humphrys – on the morning *Today* programme. The BBC headlines throughout the day implied that senior intelligence officials were disowning the dossier on the alleged weapons of mass destruction.

All hell broke loose after Gilligan's broadcasts. Blair was on a visit to Iraq when the allegations were made. He and Alastair Campbell were both bewildered. Had John Scarlett, the head of the Joint Intelligence Committee, briefed Gilligan in a strange act of betrayal? What precisely were they being accused of? Then on the following Sunday Gilligan hyped up his allegations in *The Mail on Sunday*. The first two columns of the first page of the article carried a photograph of Alastair Campbell with a smaller photograph of Gilligan below, with the words in the headline: 'I asked my intelligence source why Blair misled us all over Saddam's WMD. His response? One word . . . CAMPBELL'.[21]

Here was a senior BBC correspondent asserting as an assumed truth that 'Blair misled us all over Saddam's WMD' and offering an explanation from his 'source'. Again there was confusion in the article over whether Gilligan was saying there had been unhappiness over the inclusion of intelligence about WMD being ready for deployment in forty-five minutes, or whether he was making the much more sweeping claim that Blair 'misled us all' over the entire dossier. Because the seniority of the source was unclear, no one could make a fair judgement. But the BBC had given its weight, the weight of supposed impartiality, in deciding that Blair had 'misled us all' in making the case for war.

It was a sensational allegation and Campbell was livid. In the scattergun of vague accusations he was in effect being accused by the BBC of writing a dossier of fiction against the wishes of the intelligence agencies even though the JIC had signed off the document. The BBC's director of news, Richard Sambrook, gave an interview in which he defended 'every word' of Gilligan's reports, even though a close reading of those reports would reveal it was not at all clear what precisely Gilligan was alleging. Normally sheltered in a management structure of many levels, senior BBC managers misread what was happening when exposed in a political battle involving the outside world. They assumed Campbell's anger was an act and that the spin-doctor was trying to divert attention from the fact that no WMD had been found in Iraq.

But Campbell and Blair had every right to be genuinely angry – and the anger *was* genuine – given the sweeping nature of the allegations being made, apparently on the basis of one source. The director-general, Greg Dyke, also gave his full support to Gilligan even though he had not read the transcripts of the reports and had been on holiday when the broadcasts were made. Dyke had been accused by some newspapers of being a Labour stooge. This was his chance to prove his independence and for once he was being praised by newspapers who loathed Blair and Campbell more than they did the BBC.

The row was close to boiling point when a tragedy occurred that raised the temperature even further, in a way that none of the protagonists could have anticipated. On 17 July, two days after Dr David Kelly was interrogated by the Foreign Affairs Committee about his role as the source of Gilligan's story, his body was found in woodland near his Oxfordshire home. Kelly was a distinguished and well-informed senior weapons expert but had not been directly involved in compiling the controversial government dossier on Saddam's alleged weapons of mass destruction. The inquest recorded a verdict of suicide; conspiracy theorists have claimed Kelly was murdered. There is no evidence for such a wild claim, and what followed proved that his tragic death was in no one's interest. A row between Number 10 and the BBC now became one about what had led to the death of the source, a terrible twist that made the row much bigger. When Campbell heard the news, he was distressed enough to know immediately that he would leave his role at the earliest opportunity. Blair heard the news on arrival for a brief tour of Japan. At a press conference one journalist asked him whether he had blood on his hands. On the other side Gilligan and his senior managers, some of whom had previously declared how much they were enjoying the row, also suffered various forms of hell and guilt in the aftermath of Kelly's death. Gilligan lost his job. Ultimately Dyke and the BBC chairman, Gavyn Davies, lost theirs.

The assumption that Blair lied in advance takes some explaining. Did Blair say to his closest fellow crusaders that he would lie about the WMD even though the lie would be exposed when no weapons were found? Of course he did not. The sequence was more complex. Blair was desperate to put forward a case. He deployed the evidence he had to win it. He was not conducting a debate on whether or not to invade Iraq. He needed the backing of voters, the media and most of his party in order to stand shoulder to shoulder with President Bush. He could not lead in a different way.

So, like a lawyer in a tight corner, Blair had put his case on the basis that the intelligence *suggested* Saddam possessed WMD. As he was engaged in an act of persuasion he did not spend time pointing at the many qualifications in the intelligence. He could not afford to put the case for the opponents of war. The opponents were doing that already. Contrary to the Gilligan reports, he placed a disproportionate focus on the intelligence with the cooperation of the senior intelligence officials on the Joint Intelligence Committee. There are many important questions that arise, not least why did the head of the JIC, Sir John Scarlett, so willingly cooperate, and why was the intelligence so wrong? These questions were not asked. Instead a row erupted between Number 10 and the BBC over whether Blair lied in order to justify war.

A Breakdown in Trust

From the Gilligan/Kelly saga onwards there was no calm for Blair in relation to Iraq. Bloody chaos erupted in the country and no weapons of mass destruction were found. Evidence surfaced that suggested US troops had brutally tortured Iraqi prisoners. A bloody civil war broke out as various terrorist groups fought for control. Opponents of the war had claimed that an invasion without the sanction of the UN would lead to a form of anarchic hell in Iraq, disrupt the wider region and divide the international community. They proved right on all fronts, to the point where it was difficult to find anyone defending the war retrospectively. Blair had to do so. British troops had died. He could never admit they had died needlessly or for a cause that made matters much worse in Iraq and beyond.

Iraq was in some respects a more profound turning point than the Suez crisis in 1956. It raised fresh questions about the UK's role in the world as well as those whirling around leaders in relation to trust. Was it the duty of a UK prime minister to support a US president when he decided to go to war? In the late 1960s, Harold Wilson did not provide military support as the US went to war in Vietnam. Perhaps Wilson was closer to the national mood, an expedient approach to war, than the post-Falklands jingoism that Blair had identified in the by-election he contested in Beaconsfield. After the calamitous consequences of the war, would later UK governments be more wary of intervention?

The fact that the questions were posed illustrates the scale of the change. Blair's answers were clear from the moment he became prime minister. It *was* the duty of a UK prime minister to back the US, as he had first of all in December 1997 when Clinton dropped bombs on Iraq without any clear purpose. He was not wary of intervening militarily and did so several times. Many argued subsequently that wariness should be an essential approach after Iraq. Blair showed no sign of regarding a less hawkish attitude as being a virtue. He had decided to back Bush from the beginning with few questions asked of the deeply divided, dysfunctional Bush administration.

The scale of the turning point was illustrated when a later prime minister, David Cameron, planned to join President Barack Obama in a military assault on Syria, as a response to Assad's illegal deployment of chemical weapons. As Blair did in relation to Iraq, Cameron granted a vote in the Commons before going ahead with the intervention. The debate was held on 29 August 2013, as parliament was recalled from the summer break, adding to the sense of heightened drama. Whereas Blair won his vote by a big margin, Cameron was defeated by 272 votes to 285, an opposition majority of thirteen. Thirty Tory MPs joined forces with Labour. The Liberal Democrats were part of Cameron's coalition but some of the party's MPs also voted against. Immediately after the vote Cameron said it was clear parliament did not want action and 'the government will act accordingly'.[22]

Iraq hovered over the debate. Early in his speech Cameron went out of his way to explain why what he was proposing was unlike Iraq: 'I am deeply mindful of the lessons of previous conflicts and, in particular, of the deep concerns in the country that were caused by what went wrong with the Iraq conflict in 2003. However, this situation is not like Iraq. What we are seeing in Syria is fundamentally different. We are not invading a country. We are not searching for chemical or biological weapons. The case for ultimately supporting action is not based on a specific piece or pieces of intelligence.'[23] All the arguments that Blair had deployed a decade earlier were overtly not made and Cameron still lost. Cameron was slow to realize that he was leading a different country to the one in which Blair had won a landslide in 1997 with assumptions and orthodoxies formed in the 1980s. After the vote the Labour leader, Ed Miliband, said, 'People are deeply concerned about the chemical weapons attacks in Syria, but they want us to learn the lessons of Iraq.'[24] The following day, the chancellor George Osborne told Radio 4's *Today* programme there would now be 'national soul-searching about our role in the world'.[25] But the soul-searching had begun long ago, before and after the war in Iraq. A lesson had been learnt about the UK's rush to support the US without much consideration of the reasons and consequences. The Commons debate was about timing and evidence, not whether action might be required at some point to address Assad's use of chemical weapons. As Miliband put it, 'The people don't want a rush to war. They want things done in the right way, working with the international community.'[26]

Miliband received much scathing criticism then and since for opposing the intervention. Evidently he had his own doubts. It was the defeated Osborne who appeared on the *Today* programme the following morning. Miliband was nowhere to be seen or heard in the immediate aftermath. But he was part of a changed era. The Tory MP and future cabinet minister David Davis was even more forensically opposed during the Commons debate on Syria. Contrary to mythology, Iraq had not generated automatic opposition to any military intervention but it had transformed assumptions and orthodoxies. No longer was it assumed that the UK would side with the US as a matter of course. There needed to be compelling evidence of the case for war. There had to be a convincing case that the aims of war were clear and achievable. As Blair argued in his conveniently imprecise Chicago speech, there had to be evidence that all other options had been fully explored before the final card of military intervention.

The twist in this case was that President Obama was almost relieved when Cameron phoned him to say that the UK could not take part in the planned missile strike on Syria. Ben Rhodes, his deputy national security adviser at the time, wrote later:

> [W]e got word that the British Parliament had voted 285–272 against joining U.S.-led strikes on Syria after a debate filled with demands that the United Kingdom not follow the United States down the path to war as Tony Blair had followed George W. Bush. A shell-shocked David Cameron called Obama to apologize, explaining that he could no longer offer his support. The hangover from the Iraq War had left us staggering toward military intervention with next to no international support, and a Congress demanding that we go through the same divisive process of seeking authorization that had just failed in London.[27]

Rhodes reports Obama as quoting himself from a few years earlier:

'It is too easy for a president to go to war'.[28] Iraq had made it more difficult, a welcoming constraint as far as Obama was concerned.

British foreign policy was as confused and uncertain after Iraq as it was after Suez. There was one big difference. Following Suez various prime ministers sought to join the Common Market, recognizing that the UK could no longer be a dominant power on its own. After Iraq, a prime minister accidentally triggered a sequence that led to the UK leaving the EU. The UK had chosen to be on its own once more, an even bigger turning point than Iraq.

8

BREXIT

The outcome of the Brexit referendum in the summer of 2016 was both a historic turning point and yet, at the same time, it was another familiar bomb exploding on the British political landscape as a result of the country's complicated relationship with Europe. The explosions had been erupting more or less continuously since the UK joined the Common Market in 1973. In this case, the British prime minister, David Cameron, who called and lost the referendum, resigned. He was by no means the only Conservative prime minister to be forced out over Europe. His successor, Theresa May, secured her elevated position because of Europe and met her demise because of it too.

The eruptions might have begun when Britain joined the Common Market but they did not stop with the 2016 referendum. The noise became even louder. In the UK, prime ministers call referendums in an attempt to make their leadership easier. They offer a false allure, resolving nothing for very long. On one level this turning point is the most striking since 1945. The UK was a member of the European Union. After the referendum, and then following much traumatic navigation towards the exit, it was not. Brexit marked a seismic change for the country's economy and place in the world. But the turning point is more complex because the trauma at Westminster had been constant since the UK joined in 1973. Nothing in politics happens by chance and in order to make some sense of Brexit there is a need to go back several decades, well beyond Cameron's shallow decision to call a referendum in 2016.

A referendum was required early on in the UK's formal relationship with Europe. Another brought about the end. From the beginning, British politics – or at least the two major parties – struggled to cope with the UK being part of what became the European Union. No other issue wrecked careers in quite the same way. Even the related debates on tariffs versus free trade that split the Conservative Party from the mid-nineteenth century onwards were less intense. The rows over Europe threatened at different times to destroy both the Labour and the Conservative parties.

The first referendum, held in 1975, two years after the UK had joined the Common Market, was the counter turning point to leaving. Contrary to mythology the debates were precisely the same then as they were in the build-up to Brexit. Later Eurosceptics argued that Britain joined in 1973 without a proper debate around the issue of sovereignty and democratic accountability. The opposite was the case. The opponents of membership in the early to mid-1970s were as obsessed by the issue of sovereignty as Michael Gove and Boris Johnson. They were at least as articulate and better orators.

Edward Heath was the prime minister who finally managed to agree terms with the other members of the Common Market. Harold Macmillan tried after the Suez crisis had highlighted the fragility of the UK after the Second World War. Harold Wilson also made an attempt in the 1960s when he became prime minister. Both got nowhere. For Heath, after the 1970 election, the negotiations with the other members was the relatively easy part. The struggle would be persuading the Commons to back him.

Here was an early portent of what was to follow. From the 1970s onwards negotiations with Europe were never that tricky. UK prime ministers nearly always got what they had sought, whether it was Margaret Thatcher demanding a rebate or John Major insisting on opt-outs in relation to the single currency and the social chapter of the Maastricht Treaty. The nightmarish element for prime ministers was always what happened at Westminster. Their parties could barely withstand the strain from the beginning. At first it was Labour that was almost torn apart by the issue of the UK's membership, although there were also significant stresses in the Conservative Party from the beginning. Heath refused to even contemplate a referendum on membership but allowed a six-day debate in the Commons on the principle of joining under his negotiated terms.

As Labour leader, Harold Wilson reflected the view of the majority in his party by opposing membership. But he did so with typical wiliness. Here he is speaking on the final day of the marathon debate in October 1971: 'In a free vote the Parliamentary Labour Party took their decision by a substantial majority against entry on the terms negotiated.'[1] Wilson had given himself a way of keeping options open. He was opposed but only on the terms negotiated by Heath. At one point during his speech Wilson was asked a pertinent question by the gloriously named Conservative MP Sir Tufton Beamish, who wanted to know whether Wilson would accept other terms of membership. Wilson's response evokes perfectly his delicate ambiguity: 'We saw great advantage in getting into Europe if the terms were right, but that, if the terms were wrong, we thought that Britain was strong enough to stand outside and prosper.'[2]

Wilson was the first of many opposition leaders and prime ministers who opted for a crafted evasiveness in relation to Europe. In the early 1970s this was enough to keep Wilson's front bench, backbench MPs and party members content, since most of them were opposed to membership, but he also avoided wholly alienating his pro-marketeers. They included his deputy leader, Roy Jenkins. In his memoir, *A Life at the Centre*, Jenkins devotes a chapter that relates his agonizing over reconciling his passion for Europe with his party's hostility. At the end of the six-day debate he led a Labour rebellion in favour of Britain joining in principle, backing Heath and opposing Wilson. In total, sixty-nine Labour MPs rebelled and twenty abstained. One of them was Roy Hattersley. who was also later to become deputy leader of his party. In his memoir, *Who Goes Home?*, Hattersley argues that Jenkins's path towards setting up a new party, the SDP, began that night in the autumn of 1971.

One of those who spoke in the debate was the Labour anti-marketeer Peter Shore, who was soon to be a prominent cabinet minister when Wilson returned to Number 10. His arguments against membership combined economic policy and sovereignty implications. Two decades later it was prominent Conservative MPs who were to make similar arguments against the Maastricht Treaty. As Shore put it on the first day of the debate:

> We are not dealing with small or light matters. We are dealing with economic and social policies which affect the people of this country, their prosperity, employment, the distribution of incomes and the things which matter most to them. I cannot accept that what is involved is, in the terms of the White Paper, a minor cession of sovereignty. On the contrary, major transfers are at stake.[3]

The other issue of concern was legitimacy, equally potent when future EU treaties were passed without referendums. Enoch Powell, still a Conservative MP, cited Edmund Burke as he challenged the right of Heath to go ahead with a major constitutional and economic turning point without the direct assent of voters. Powell acted often in tandem with Michael Foot from the left of the Labour Party, the duo raising provocative 'points of order' in the chamber one after the other before delivering similar speeches about the perceived loss of sovereignty. Uniquely the issue of Europe brought together unlikely allies from the two main parties.

Heath's speech that ended the six-day debate also had a modern feel to it, which again challenges the mythology that issues were avoided when the UK joined the Common Market. They were not. Heath explored the notion of sovereignty in depth, as he was to do again during the 1975 referendum. He was also gripped by the UK's place in the world and the need to refute arguments (made repeatedly decades later by Brexiteers) that it would flourish more outside the European bloc:

As to whether Britain is European, I fail entirely to understand the argument about cutting off our links with the outside world, when the members of the Community itself are the great trading countries of the world; when the Community itself is the greatest trading bloc in the world; when, as the Leader of the Liberal Party [Jeremy Thorpe] pointed out this evening, when the enlarged Community is created, it will have arrangements with 80 countries. Twenty-nine of the Commonwealth countries and 19 dependencies will be associated with the Community. What on earth do critics mean by our cutting off our links with the outside world?[4]

Heath won the vote with the help of the Labour rebels, but it was a troubled beginning, an early example of many debates about

Europe to follow. Jenkins and his fellow pro-Europeans were tormented about what to do in relation to the Labour Party. He was deputy leader. He wanted to be leader. Should he continue to vote with Heath in a series of related votes to come in the following months? Having made his stand should he back Wilson's various contortions?

There is a vivid vignette in Jenkins's memoir where he meets Michael Foot for lunch at the club Brooks's on the elegant St James's Street near Westminster, a favourite haunt for Jenkins. Here were two big figures in British politics who were soon to become even more clearly defined opponents. Foot became Labour leader, facing Jenkins, who led the SDP into the 1983 election. At first, the lunch went well. This was the era when some of the most prominent politicians were great writers and readers: 'We gossiped easily for an hour on books and history.'

What a shame there is no recording of that exchange. But then the conversation took a turn for the worse as they focused on Europe.

> Then I tried to make him see that his hope of defeating Heath rested on the intolerable premise that Enoch Powell and the other Tory rebels were men of honour who would stick to their beliefs in contrast to the Labour Europeans who would show themselves to be men of straw. He could not see the point at all. 'But surely you must regard the opportunity to defeat the most reactionary government for a hundred years as more important than a particular piece of legislation' was the unyielding essence of his position.[5]

Fast forward and recall the many calculations MPs made as Theresa May sought a deal to leave Europe after the 2016 referendum.

Boris Johnson and others acted partly to secure his leadership. Some opposition MPs wanted to bring down the government. Lots acted out of principled belief that either her deal was not a proper Brexit or that it was too hard a Brexit and needed to be defeated on that basis. Now return to Jenkins and Foot at lunch. In part, these two political giants read the situation poorly: the politics of Europe is persistently misread at Westminster. Jenkins was wrong to suggest that Powell and his allies would not stick to their beliefs. Powell did so to the point of leaving the Conservative Party. Foot was wrong to assume that there was a chance to bring the government down over Europe. There was a majority in the Commons in favour of entry that would inevitably prevail. Equally Jenkins was wrong to emphasize Foot's calculations solely in terms of bringing down Heath, though evidently that was a factor in his thinking. Foot was sincerely opposed to membership, as he was to demonstrate in the lead-up to the 1983 election when he led Labour with a pledge to leave the Common Market. Deeply held principles, crude calculations and misplaced assumptions shaped the political debate about Europe from the eve of Britain's entry to the departure.

The UK's formal entry to the Common Market in 1973 changed its place in the world as Heath had suggested. It was part of a bigger project. But in terms of the politics surrounding the issue, it changed nothing. Wilson went into the February 1974 election with a pledge to hold a referendum on the issue once a Labour government had 'renegotiated' the terms of membership. Unlike Jeremy Corbyn in December 2019, Wilson made the most of his dramatic pledge. The idea of a referendum had come from Tony Benn. Wilson was initially wary, but came to recognize it was a device that might keep his party together. Neither Wilson, nor David Cameron later, called a referendum on Europe because they had suddenly discovered an enthusiasm for this form of direct democracy; they did so in order to keep their parties more or less united. Wilson made the most of it first of all by wooing Enoch Powell. On the day Heath announced the February election, Powell announced he would not be standing as a Conservative candidate. During the campaign he told his followers that he was backing Labour on the basis of the referendum pledge. Internally Wilson made the divisions on his front bench seem like a triumph. He would give them 'a right to differ' during the campaign. The phrase sounded positive; he was granting a right.

Although leading a minority government after the February election, and then an administration with a tiny majority following the October election, Wilson managed to negotiate new terms of membership. Most argue the changes were cosmetic. A few, including Nick Thomas-Symonds in his illuminating biography of Wilson, argue that they were substantial, not least in relation to the import of butter and lamb from New Zealand. Cleverly Wilson had made much of this in advance. He knew voters worried about the price of butter in an era of soaring inflation and he made one of his pitches 'butter will be cheaper under a Labour government'.[6]

In the summer of 1975, the UK voted to remain in the Common Market with 67 per cent in favour, a substantial majority. But the outcome resolved very little. The Labour anti-marketeers were still as determined and resilient as their Tory counterparts became from the late 1980s onwards. After Labour was defeated in the 1979 election, Tony Benn and others made a pledge to leave the Common Market, a defining issue as he travelled the country putting the case for Labour to move to the left. Eight years after a referendum that was supposedly aimed at resolving the issue of Britain and Europe, Labour went into the 1983 election pledging to leave without another plebiscite. Foot's position on Europe was one of the main reasons why Jenkins, David Owen, Shirley Williams and Bill Rodgers formed the SDP, the biggest schism in British politics for decades. All four were Labour cabinet ministers in the 1970s. Europe had torn apart the Labour Party to the point of a formalized division in 1981. The schism within Labour, much more than her victory in the Falklands War, propelled Margaret Thatcher to her landslide victory over Michael Foot.

Then it was the turn of Thatcher and the Conservatives to fall out over Europe. One of Neil Kinnock's first moves as the new Labour leader was to announce that his party would no longer be committed to withdrawal. Gradually the party became more pro-European. However, Thatcher's wariness intensified with the selection of Jacques Delors as president of the European Commission in 1985. Delors emphasized some of the great social benefits of being part of the EU as well as the benefits of deeper integration. Thatcher delivered her totemic Bruges speech in 1988 partly in response to Delors. Her address framed the thinking and attitudes of a growing number of Eurosceptics in her parliamentary party and among Tory activists. Her words became mythologized to the point where the Eurosceptics formed the Bruges group in honour of the speech. In actual fact, Thatcher's arguments were more measured than those of her ardent followers in future years: 'Britain does not dream of some cosy, isolated existence on the fringes of the European Community. Our destiny is in Europe, as part of the Community.'[7]

She also highlighted her active support for the single market and why it was important for the UK to be part of a wider entity when faced with competition from other emerging countries: 'The aim of a Europe open to enterprise is the moving force behind the creation of the Single European Market in 1992. By getting rid of barriers, by making it possible for companies to operate on a European scale, we can best compete with the United States, Japan and other new economic powers emerging in Asia and elsewhere.'

These sections of the speech were overlooked by her supporters, who focused on the arguments against closer integration: 'We have not successfully rolled back the frontiers of the state in Britain, only to see them re-imposed at a European level with a European super-state exercising a new dominance from Brussels.'

But even in this assertively provocative section Thatcher navigated a Tony Blair-like 'third way': 'Certainly we want to see Europe more united and with a greater sense of common purpose. But it must be in a way which preserves the different traditions, parliamentary powers and sense of national pride in one's own country.' At this point at least Thatcher was seeking more common purpose with the EU while retaining powers within the UK.

What followed is one of the many twists in the saga of the UK and Europe. While her devotees in parliament focused solely on her critical words, Thatcher and her successors prevailed in securing the third way that she highlighted in her mythologized speech. The substance of Britain's membership was relatively smooth in the sense that UK prime ministers tended to get what they wanted. But as increasingly defiant Eurosceptic MPs also got what they called for, they then went on to get worked up about something else. During the 1990s, Tory rebels were calling for a wider EU membership and for the UK to remain outside the euro. They got their way on both. The EU expanded to the east and the UK has never been close to joining the single currency. They won and got angrier still.

The political turmoil at Westminster intensified. A key moment in the history of the Conservative Party was the dramatic exit of the UK from the exchange rate mechanism (ERM) in September 1992. The UK had only joined the ERM in October 1990, thereby formally aligning sterling to the other EU currencies. Thatcher had ferociously opposed the move until finally persuaded to act a few weeks before she was removed from power. The objective had been to strengthen the currency by a formal mechanism, as a previous chancellor, Nigel Lawson, had sought to do when unofficially shadowing the German Deutschmark, again to Thatcher's fury.

In relation to the ERM, Thatcher's instincts proved to be correct. The markets hovered over a weak pound and struck. After raising interest rates to absurd levels within hours, in an attempt to keep the pound in the ERM, Major was forced to announce a humiliating devaluation. Far from traumatized, his chancellor, Norman Lamont, was delighted, one sign of many volcanic tensions at the top of the government and below.

The Conservative Party and Europe

Brexit had many causes but the most fundamental of them all was the changing nature of the Conservative Party. A majority of voters in England back the Conservatives at general elections unless given monumental reasons not to do so. Therefore, a modern history of the UK is partly a history of the Conservative Party. The party changed at its annual conference in Brighton in 1992, weeks after the pound fell out of the ERM. The mood was closer to Labour's yearly gatherings from the late 1970s to the early 1980s in its intense acrimony. Before then Conservative conferences had been docile affairs with members gathering to pay homage to their leader and the front bench. In 1992 all hell broke loose. Inevitably, the cause was Europe, in particular the question of who was to blame for the

ERM humiliation and its implications in the immediate future as to whether the UK should sign up to the Maastricht Treaty.

For John Major the contortions over Europe had begun before the historic conference in Brighton. At his most resolutely self-confident soon after winning the leadership contest, he delivered a speech in Bonn that became almost as emblematic as Thatcher's Bruges speech, for opposite reasons. A great deal of effort was made in preparing the speech with the objective partly of wooing Chancellor Helmut Kohl in Germany, but also of reassuring his Eurosceptics that he would not go too far in seeking a closer relationship. While expressing the desire to be 'at the very heart of Europe' he also stressed that the UK would be bringing its own proposals on the single currency and political union. He would 'relish the debate' with other EU leaders.[8] The balance was not greatly different from Thatcher's Bruges speech and yet marked a genuine attempt to establish a warmer partnership. Major's new party chairman, the pro-European Chris Patten, played a part in preparing the ground for the speech. One of Major's advisers, Sarah Hogg, helped to write it. Hogg was a supporter of the single currency as a way of bringing down inflation. As ever with UK prime ministers and Europe, the calculations were multi-layered.

By the time of the 1992 Conservative Party conference, Eurosceptics were scathing about Major's contortions even though he had won a general election victory only months earlier. Fringe meetings were punctuated with passionate speeches opposed to Maastricht and equally fervent ones in favour. The names of pro-Europeans from the cabinet, Michael Heseltine and Ken Clarke, were jeered or applauded depending on the fringe meeting. In the main conference hall there were unprecedented scenes for a Tory conference. Dissenters included the former party chairman Norman Tebbit, who was cheered to the rafters.

Tebbit's speech in the conference hall had provocative echoes with Mark Antony's at Julius Caesar's funeral. Mark Antony's address appeared to praise Brutus while damning him. Mischievously, Tebbit claimed to be supportive of Major while inserting a very large blade in the back of the suddenly fragile prime minister. Tebbit began by expressing the hope the prime minister would resist calls for the dumping of Norman Lamont, the chancellor. Lamont had not taken sterling into the European exchange rate mechanism in 1990. It was Major who had been chancellor at the time. In seeking to protect Lamont, Tebbit was attacking Major's record as chancellor as well as in relation to what had happened since he became prime minister. He added: 'The cost in lost jobs in bankrupt firms, repossessed homes, in the terrible wounds inflicted on industry, has been savage . . . But we have established our credentials as good Europeans.'[9]

Tebbit went on to prompt pantomime-style responses from his audience, asking them whether they wanted a single currency, and whether they wanted Brussels meddling in immigration controls, foreign affairs, industrial policy, education and defence. Each question was greeted with a chorus of 'No'. 'Do you want to be citizens of a European Union?' he asked, to a final roar of opposition. He continued:

Now is the time to negotiate anew. Kohl and Mitterrand no longer speak for Europe. John Major should raise the flag of patriots of all the states of Europe . . . Let's launch the drive for Maastricht Two; a treaty with no mention of more power to Brussels, no mention of economic and monetary and political union. It's a task in which I stand ready to join John Major whenever he is ready to begin.[10]

He might as well have declared, as Mark Antony had of Brutus, 'And John Major is an honourable man.'

Major was sitting on the podium as Tebbit played to the crowd, looking pale while trying to convey a mild-mannered calm. He knew he was in the midst of a tempestuous drama with many more acts to come. Although Tebbit did not raise the possibility of leaving the EU, the Conservative Party was beginning its march towards Brexit. Where the Conservative Party marches England tends to follow. They did not meekly follow the will of voters in England; the voters followed them.

For the rest of his leadership Major endured various forms of hell over Europe. He could not focus on any other issue before Europe erupted once more in the form of parliamentary insurrection. If the 1992 conference marked a change, then the period going forward to the 1997 election marked a near revolution in the parliamentary party. Tory MPs became insurrectionary over Europe and, significantly, seemed to enjoy their new role. Rebels queued up at the newish BBC studios at Westminster, Four Millbank, to articulate their contempt for Major with joyful venom. The author bumped into two of them, Teresa Gorman and Tony Marlow, one early morning at the *Today* programme studio in Broadcasting House. A few hours later they were at Four Millbank putting the same case on another outlet. The author noted he had seen them at Broadcasting House. Gorman replied: 'We're available around the clock. We do parties, bar mitzvahs.' They were enjoying themselves. Both called on Major to resign, a proclamation that became increasingly common as Tory prime ministers wrestled with Europe.

Major danced painfully, a preview of what was to follow with David Cameron, Theresa May and, in a different way, Boris Johnson. In July 1993 Major lost a key Commons vote in relation to

Maastricht. He had made clear to his MPs the authority of his leadership and the entire government would be near fatally undermined if he lost the vote. He was still defeated and was forced to hold a vote of confidence in the government the following day, which he won. Conservative MPs had become rebels but were not ready to trigger an election slaughter. In the immediate aftermath Major gave a range of interviews. In one with the ITN political editor, Michael Brunson, he assumed the mic was off and referred to the 'bastards' in his cabinet. The mic was still on and the comment became part of the frenzy: a prime minister attacking his ministerial colleagues with a term rarely deployed against political opponents.

The chaos intensified. In July 1995 Major resigned as leader of the Conservative Party to fight a leadership contest, willing his critics to challenge him. One cabinet minister, John Redwood, did so. The issue that united Redwood's band of MPs was Europe, although at this stage none was calling for the UK to leave. Major won the contest but not by an overwhelming margin. He staggered on to the 1997 election, the last contest in which the top of the Conservative Party were all pro-European. Ken Clarke was chancellor and Michael Heseltine was deputy prime minister. The foreign secretary was Malcolm Rifkind, who had replaced Douglas Hurd. But below them the rebellion was intensifying even during the campaign. Elections normally discipline a party. The issue of Europe creates its own rules. At a press conference during the October 1974 election one of Harold Wilson's favourite cabinet ministers, Shirley Williams, announced she would resign if the referendum led to the UK leaving the Common Market. In this the issue of Europe was freakish, making parties fragile even in the middle of an election campaign.

Labour and Europe

Open warfare over Europe was a key factor in the Conservatives' slaughter in 1997. The intense ambiguity at the top of British politics took a subtler form in the New Labour era, but the tensions concerning Europe were far from resolved. Both Tony Blair and Gordon Brown, the duopoly that took all key decisions in the New Labour era, wanted the UK to be a constructive player in the EU after the chaos of recent years, but also yearned for the support of Eurosceptic newspapers. During the 1997 election Blair told readers of *The Sun* newspaper that he 'loved the pound' while hoping vaguely that he would lead the UK into the single currency. Before heading off for meetings of the EU's finance ministers, Brown's advisers briefed Eurosceptic newspapers about the tough line he was going to take, hoping to secure positive coverage compared with Blair's apparently more pro-European position.[11]

Both got into a mess over what to do about the single currency, an issue of intense passion in the main political parties and the media during the mid to late 1990s. After the 1997 election Brown made the Bank of England independent and the internal dynamics changed in relation to the euro. Brown no longer worried as much about a currency crisis now markets had been reassured by the independence of the bank. Blair became much keener. At times with a crusading equivocation he decided his historic destiny was to resolve Britain's ambiguous relations with Europe. He saw joining the euro as a means to do it. Soon after 1997 Brown realized that the issue of the UK's membership of the currency needed a speedy solution. He gave an interview to *The Times* that hinted the UK would not join before the next election. His press secretary, Charlie Whelan, briefed chaotically from the Red Lion pub in Westminster that the interview meant the UK was out for the entire parliament. Blair was as surprised as anyone to hear such unequivocal clarification.

He became more determined to revive the issue after the war in Iraq, largely for superficial reasons. He wanted to show he was as much a pro-European as he was pro-American by holding a referendum on the euro. By this time Brown and his senior adviser, Ed Balls, were resolutely opposed. At one meeting to discuss the issue Balls was unflinching in what he said to Blair about the dangers of pursuing such a course, a special adviser telling a prime minister about policy consequences. The two did not speak again during the rest of Blair's period in Number 10.

There were many tensions between Blair and Brown. Europe came to be the most prickly of them all, although public-service reform and several other policy areas were not far behind. Oddly, while Blair and Brown agonized over the single currency, freedom of movement was given the go-ahead almost casually. Both issues raised similar questions in relation to sovereignty and control. Should a government relinquish control over its currency? Should a government have no control over the size of its population and the implications for the labour market?

Seeking answers to the first question was fraught. Blair answered the second question without much hesitation and with no resistance from Brown. When ten new countries joined the EU in 2004, he decided to allow their citizens to exercise the right of free movement to come to live and work in the UK from day one. The decision contrasted with the approach of Germany and France, which were to impose temporary restrictions on free movement for the first few years. But it was a decision made by default, according to Balls, who noted later: 'We didn't see the extent to which low-wage people would move. Fundamentally, we didn't think they would.'[12]

By 2016, there were two million more EU-born people in the UK compared with 2004. Most came to work, meeting a demand. There would have been little point in coming if there were no demand. They wanted to earn money. But their sudden arrival in such large numbers transformed the debate about EU membership.[13] The seething row moved on from control of currency to control of borders. Why did freedom of movement get the go-ahead when the single-currency debate led to fearful paralysis? The answer was that the Conservative Party and its newspapers had become obsessed with the single currency and had barely noticed that permission had been given for millions more to move to the UK.

This phase of the debate over Europe was without ideological coherence. Increasingly, right-wing, free-market Conservative MPs opposed freedom of movement. Instead they advocated a big-state intervention in a market, the labour market. They called for tightening of borders to the point where people from the EU would not be able to work in the UK any longer, a form of import control supported by the left-wing Tony Benn in the early 1980s. Much of the Labour Party, usually more at ease with intervening in markets, opposed any intervention in the free movement of labour.

Under William Hague, the first leader of the opposition following the 1997 election, the Conservatives became increasingly strident and even more obsessed about Europe. By the 2001 election, the naturally calm Hague was heading for Dover declaring that the UK had days 'to save the pound'. Hague was defeated as heavily as John Major, but that did not stop the 2001 leadership contest revolving around Europe and which candidate took the toughest approach. The only issue that mattered to members meant the candidate least suited for leadership won the contest. With no experience of government, Iain Duncan Smith, a Maastricht rebel, defeated Ken Clarke, popular with voters but pro-European.

The biggest twist came during the 2005 Conservative leadership contest. Once again Clarke stood and was defeated over his support for Europe. David Cameron posed as the 'modernizer' and beat David Davis, supposedly the more orthodox Tory on the right. Yet it was Cameron who pledged to withdraw Conservative MEPs from the centre-right parliamentary group in the European Parliament, a move that Davis opposed. From the beginning Cameron was appeasing his Eurosceptic wing in ways the more Eurosceptic candidate in the contest thought went too far. Cameron's only stricture to his now strident anti-European wing was to stop 'banging on about Europe'. Of course, he was to be disappointed.

Cameron personified the unresolved ambiguities over Britain and Europe. He appeared to be in one place on the political spectrum but was in reality in another, posing as the modernizing centrist when on Europe he was neither a modernizer nor a centrist. His internal party challenges became more important to him than any other factor in addressing issues relating to Europe, although he actually shared quite a lot of the views expressed by his Eurosceptic wing. In seeking to appease his more militant MPs, Cameron assumed he could play Europe to his advantage, but it was Europe that was to bring him down.

Cameron's decision to offer a referendum was based on a misreading of the strength of UKIP, the party led by Nigel Farage during Cameron's phase in Number 10. Farage boasted constantly that several Tory MPs were planning to defect to UKIP. Later, Cameron's director of communications, Sir Craig Oliver, said that the prime minister feared up to forty MPs might switch sides unless the Europe question was resolved.[14] This was why Cameron pledged a referendum against the advice of his chancellor, George Osborne, and his fellow cabinet minister (and Brexit opponent) Michael Gove. He assumed that if he could win a referendum that would end the threat from UKIP and the eternal debate within his party. He both overestimated the threat posed by UKIP and that the offer of a referendum would end Farage's potency. In 2014, UKIP went on to win the European elections, in terms of votes cast, even after Cameron had made his offer to hold the referendum. Meanwhile the number of defections to UKIP was never going to be that high. The two that did defect, Douglas Carswell and Mark Reckless, were loners. Both defected after the offer of a referendum had already been made.

The assumption of victory in a referendum was an even more fundamental mistake. No prime minister offers a referendum assuming he or she is going to lose, but Cameron misjudged the mood of his cabinet and the wider country when he made the pledge and placed it at the heart of the 2015 manifesto. It is a myth that Cameron hoped there would be a hung parliament, with another coalition with the Liberal Democrats, formed on the basis that he would not call the referendum. Cameron knew he would have to stick to this pledge and was confident with justification that if another coalition was necessary he could persuade the gullible Liberal Democrat leader, Nick Clegg, to go along with it.

After Cameron won by a small majority, the referendum pledge moved centre stage. Immediately he made his next mistake, announcing that the referendum would be held the following year. He learnt no lessons from Wilson's approach to a referendum in 1975, who only named a date when the polls suggested he was on course for a big victory. Wilson also assumed from the beginning that some of his cabinet would argue for leaving the Common Market. Therefore he did not have to focus his negotiations with Europe in ways that would please his ministerial doubters. He recognized that there was nothing he could do to persuade them.

In contrast Cameron wanted a united government and the support of the London mayor, Boris Johnson. He approached the negotiations with the hope of reassuring committed Eurosceptics and those whose personal ambition chimed with support for leaving the EU. He thought friendship would trump personal beliefs in the case of Michael Gove and one or two others. He hoped to appease Johnson with legislation protecting the Westminster parliament's 'sovereignty'. Meanwhile the EU had only limited patience for Cameron after his game-playing over the years. His new deal was insubstantial and followed years in which he had given vent to his own Euroscepticism. Cameron's memoirs, written after he left Number 10, are infused with his doubts about the European project, unsurprising to those that followed him closely during his wayward leadership.

The Brexit Turning Point

The 2016 Brexit referendum campaign was far more dishonest and frenzied than the parliamentary debates that were the prelude to the UK joining the Common Market in the early 1970s. Indeed, the contrast between the Commons debates in the early 1970s and those held during the referendum is the best example as to why they should not be held. If a referendum is called, do not expect a public education exercise: it is a battle between two sides, and what matters for both is the result. Unsurprisingly the UK voted to leave. It would have done so if there had been no Nigel Farage or Boris Johnson or

Dominic Cummings, the three men widely credited with bringing about a historic turning point. Since the early 1980s voters had heard little that was positive about Britain's membership. As far as they followed politics, some would have known about Margaret Thatcher's handbag, a symbol of her early haranguing of other EU leaders; her 'no, no, no' against further integration; the foreigners arriving to do their jobs and using depleted public services; John Major's 'beef war', a contrivance to appear to protect 'British beef'; various prime ministers vetoing possible EU Commission presidents; Tony Blair siding with President Bush over Iraq while attacking the weak-kneed French; Gordon Brown acting 'in Britain's interests' in taking on EU finance ministers. They read in their newspapers about 'EU rules' that bordered on the insane, except that the reports were often not true.

Lurking under these shenanigans there was a serious debate to be had about sovereignty, where power lies in an interconnected world. This did not get much of a look in. Referendums are not about serious debates. As President Macron was to observe later, if France were to hold a referendum, it would probably vote to leave too.[15]

Some of the lies that punctuated the referendum became famous, the huge sums that would be available for the NHS after the UK left the EU being the most notorious. But the biggest distortion was the lack of any clarity about what form Brexit would take. There were preposterous jingoistic claims about Britain holding all the cards in a negotiation, but no precision about which model the UK would follow after its withdrawal and therefore no detailed analysis as to the implications. The referendum was a vote on the drab status quo versus an exciting future in which powerless voters would 'take back control'. It was a near miracle that as many as 48 per cent voted to remain, not least when Cameron and his chancellor, George

Osborne, were ready to regard victory as an authority-enhancing boost as they prepared to embark on another round of misjudged spending cuts. One of Brexit's many origins was the austerity programme launched by Cameron and Osborne in 2010. They became its political victims.

The lack of clarity about what Brexit meant shaped the next, equally stormy phase of the UK's relations with Europe. Obviously the referendum marked a significant turning point on many levels but at Westminster the outcome meant merely that the tempest took different forms. Parties still fell apart over Europe, but in different ways from the splits that arose from the early 1970s when the UK was seeking to join.

The new prime minister, Theresa May, had been a low-profile Remainer who felt the need to reassure her Brexiteer MPs that she was deadly serious about delivering. In March 2017, less than a year since becoming prime minister, and without knowing what form of Brexit she wanted or could secure, she triggered Article 50 of the Lisbon Treaty. Once the clock started ticking, the UK had two years to depart. If reason had ever played a part in the UK's approach to Europe, May would have at least decided on the details of the type of Brexit she wanted, negotiated them with the rest of the EU, and then triggered Article 50 to give UK businesses time to prepare. None of this happened.

Compared with Cameron, Johnson and Truss, by some margin, May was far more serious-minded and diligent. She did not come close to resolving the Brexit challenges, agreeing a deal and selling it effectively to a parliamentary party that was becoming even more restive. Unsurprisingly May soon came to the conclusion that to get any deal through parliament, she needed a bigger majority than the tiny one she had inherited from Cameron. Way ahead in the polls, enjoying a heady prime-ministerial honeymoon, she announced the day after the Easter holiday in 2017 that there would be an election in May. The 2017 election has been more or less airbrushed out of history. Most commentators in the UK media had expected an altogether different result and could not cope with what happened. Jeremy Corbyn's Labour Party made substantial gains standing on a manifesto that would not have been out of place in northern Europe but was seen as dangerously left wing by the UK's media. It was the first election for decades that attempted to show that the state could be a benevolent force. May was a hopeless campaigner but she attempted a leap away from Cameron's reignited Thatcherism by highlighting 'the good the state can do' in the party's manifesto. She secured the highest number of votes since Thatcher's landslide in 1987 but Labour's success meant the Conservatives lost seats. May's gamble had failed sensationally. The 2017 election led to a hung parliament.

The hung parliament from 2017 to the December election in 2019 merits an entire book. Brexit was the overwhelming issue and became as hellish for both principal party leaders as Europe had been for their predecessors. Now Labour was in as big a mess as well. Corbyn's electoral triumph led to his doom. Lacking the guile, depth and experience of Wilson, he could not turn the party's layers of division to his advantage. The hung parliament gave Remainers in the parliamentary Labour Party and the wider membership the hope that Brexit could be stopped. Yet a considerable proportion of Labour voters in the Midlands and the north of England had backed Brexit in the referendum. This was a conundrum without an obvious solution.

May faced the bigger challenge as she had to actually deliver Brexit. Soon she came across the Irish question, the main dilemma that made the UK the least suited of any EU member to seek withdrawal. The UK and Ireland had joined on the same date in 1973. The borderless single market between Northern Ireland and Ireland was a key part of the Good Friday Agreement, the climax of the peace process agreed, after tortuous negotiations, in April 1998. If the UK, including Northern Ireland, left the single market and the customs union, there would have to be a border with Ireland, an entry point to the single market. But a border threatened to jeopardize the always precarious Good Friday Agreement.

At first there was much talk that 'technology' could address the problem. 'Technology' could monitor movement around the vast porous border between Northern Ireland and Ireland. Now the foreign secretary, Boris Johnson suggested that if an Oyster card worked on the London Underground a similar device would solve the border issue. Like many of Johnson's interventions in relation to Brexit this proposition went no further after the original utterance.[16] With good cause, May placed most faith in the unelected senior civil servant whom she asked to conduct the details of the negotiation with Europe. Olly Robbins understood the layers of complexity. May's Brexit secretary, David Davis, took a more swashbuckling approach in his dealings with the EU, fantasizing that he would be able to agree bilateral deals with the likes of Germany and France, bypassing the formal EU structures. They never happened. If Davis had bothered to probe more deeply he would have discovered those countries were committed to the negotiations being conducted on behalf of the whole EU. Never lacking in self-confidence Davis thought he knew better. Even less reliable, Johnson was kept well away from the negotiations.

With the clock ticking, May set out her original proposals in July 2018. The Chequers Plan, as it became known, looks in retrospect almost dream-like in its ambition. Her plan aimed to establish a close relationship between the UK and the EU with continued access to the single market for goods and a common rulebook on state aid preventing either side from subsidizing their own industries, thereby jeopardizing the so-called 'level playing field' that made the single market fair for all EU members. The Irish question would be addressed by a 'facilitated customs agreement' that would remove the need for customs checks by treating the EU and the UK as 'a combined customs territory'. In a convoluted proposal May wanted the UK to apply the EU's tariffs and trade policy on goods heading for the single market but would control its own tariffs for the UK market.

Although May was working arduously, the issue of Europe had brought about a metamorphosis. She had become a fantasist. The EU was never going to agree to the 'customs agreement' as she envisaged, one in which the UK had its cake and ate it. Yet her Chequers Plan was at least an attempt to square the Brexit circles, retaining a close enough relationship with the EU while establishing a key Brexit 'freedom': the end of free movement.

This was nowhere near good enough for the Brexiteers in her cabinet and the wider parliamentary party, who had been fantasists for so long that they could no longer deal with the hard grind of reality. Her Brexit secretary, David Davis, resigned two days after the cabinet met at Chequers to consider the plan. Davis set a precedent. A series of Brexit secretaries resigned rather than face the consequences of their convictions in the form of detailed negotiation with the EU. They could proclaim from the backbenches or in newspaper columns. This was much more fun than making their vision of Brexit work. Her foreign secretary, Johnson, had no choice but to follow. He resigned the following day.

May had failed to manage her party or reach agreement with the EU for her plan. Yet she kept going. She had resilience, one of her few qualities as a leader. She possessed this quality to the point of weirdness. After every tumultuous setback she returned to an admiring Number 10 and carried on almost as if nothing had happened. This stoicism was her response to the resignations of Davis and Johnson. She made new appointments and carried on.

Her deal finally negotiated with the EU was far removed from her Chequers fantasy and yet much better for the UK than the final deal agreed subsequently by Johnson and his soon departed Brexit secretary, Lord Frost. The biggest difference was that May agreed the UK should remain a temporary member of the customs union until there was a technological breakthrough that prevented the need for a border between Northern Ireland and Ireland. Independent forecasters, including the Treasury's own estimates, agreed that May's deal would lead to a significant fall in GDP but not as big a drop as other Brexit permutations.

In itself, this marked a turning point in British politics, a government pursuing a policy that it acknowledged would damage economic performance, a freakish admission but a measured one based on all available evidence. Brexiteers argued these forecasts were 'Remainer propaganda' without fully refuting the details of the carefully prepared analysis. Some of them did not bother to refute. They argued that Brexit was not about economic performance but about 'freedom', that ubiquitous and simplistic term that has long distorted political debate and has featured in several turning points already discussed.

May's Brexit deal was subject to a Commons vote on three occasions. Each time she was defeated heavily. The first time, in January 2019, she was defeated by the biggest majority for a prime minister in the democratic era, losing by a majority of 230. After that first defeat May returned to Number 10 with an icy calm and continued her negotiations with Tory rebels and Northern Ireland's Democratic Unionist Party (DUP). May was the latest Tory prime minister to assume that in the end some of her dissenting MPs could be appeased with small concessions and their sense of tribal loyalty. May was driven by her commitment to the Conservative Party and struggled to realize that when it came to Europe many of her colleagues had a deeper loyalty to their cause.

Although their arguments were sometimes incoherent and contradictory the Conservative Eurosceptics in the House of Commons were part of the most focused political project since 1945. They organized. They rebelled. They never relented. Leaders sought to appease them. They took the concessions and then moved on to make sterner demands. In policy terms they usually prevailed. They opposed the single currency and the UK did not join. They wanted a wider EU extending to the east. The EU became wider. There were no celebrations from the Eurosceptic parliamentarians. They moved on to their next cause with an angry, determined anxiety.

When Cameron granted them a referendum, most Conservative MPs in the Eurosceptic camp gave up on the cause of staying in a 'reformed' EU and moved towards full support for Brexit. When they won the referendum, they did not pause for a second to wallow in victory. They wanted the hardest possible Brexit, one that ended all ties with the EU. They achieved that aspiration too as far as that was possible. In doing so they transformed the Conservative Party into a more revolutionary force.

They were the most successful parliamentary force in modern times. The leader of UKIP and then the Brexit Party, Nigel Farage, gets much credit or opprobrium for the Brexit sea change, but he operated outside the demands of an elected House of Commons. He had the easier task, framing arguments, changing them at times, without much scrutiny. Cameron's fear of UKIP was a major factor in his decision to call the referendum, but his parliamentary rebels were ferocious enough to make his party impossible to manage. The likes of Steve Baker, the MP who headed the so-called European Reform Group at a key phase in the Brexit saga, were more significant and influential than Farage. Baker personified the modern Conservative parliamentary party in his loyalty to his vision of Brexit over any tribal commitment, a huge leap from the old Tory party where loyalty to leader was almost a religious faith.

In the post-2017 hung parliament, the contrast between Baker's wilful parliamentarians and pro-European MPs could not have been more marked. While Baker and his colleagues were brutally determined, their disparate opponents were all over the place, even though they were by some margin in a majority. MPs opposed to a hard Brexit could not agree on a way forward. Some of those who had campaigned passionately for Remain now argued that May's deal was the best available and should be supported. They came from quite a range. From within her government Rory Stewart became a passionate advocate for May's deal. From outside parliament, the former cabinet minister Alan Johnson, who had run Labour's 'Remain' campaign, argued in favour of it. Almost certainly Labour's leader, Jeremy Corbyn, would have been content to back it too. If Labour had done so it would have ensured a relatively soft Brexit and split the Conservative parliamentary party, perhaps fatally. A Brexit brought about by a combination of the Remainer prime minister, May, with support from the largely Remainer Labour Party would have horrified that focused group of dissenting Tory Brexiteers. What a turning point it would have been on many levels.

But Corbyn was not in a strong enough position within his parliamentary party to impose his will. Some Labour MPs backed amendments in the Commons that would have led to the UK being in a similar situation as Norway, inside the single market and customs union while outside the EU. Others wanted a referendum that would include the option to back Remain, the position of the shadow Brexit secretary and future leader, Sir Keir Starmer. On the other hand, Tory MPs who feared a hard Brexit would not work with Corbyn, and neither would the leader of the Liberal Democrats, Jo Swinson, who had concluded she might be the next prime minister if she stuck to her pro-European position that included a commitment to dump Brexit without a referendum.

In the summer of 2019, a desperate May finally engaged with Labour. Her Number 10 team held talks for several days with Corbyn's senior colleagues. There was much common ground but two impossible problems. The Number 10 entourage recognized that a commitment to hold a referendum was Labour's bottom line and that would tear apart the Conservative parliamentary party. Labour's team sensed that nothing they agreed could be delivered by May. Both were right. In her final attempt to save her leadership May did not rule out a referendum and her MPs erupted. They were livid that May was talking to Corbyn although they had barred any alternative. The insurrectionaries were equally furious that a referendum might become part of the mix. May was gone within days, another prime minister to fall over Europe.

The final phase of the hung parliament was the most bizarre. May's successor, Boris Johnson, began his premiership as if he was leading with a landslide majority. Outside Number 10 for the first time as prime minister in July 2019, Johnson declared that the UK would leave the EU with or without a deal by 31 October. There was no majority in the Commons that would back a 'no-deal' exit and yet he behaved as if there was. Johnson's appointed chief of staff, Dominic Cummings, was his guiding light. Johnson had many flaws but was not daft. He could see there was no majority for a no-deal departure within months. One of Cummings's ideas to deal with the impasse was to prorogue parliament, a move that was declared illegal. This gave more shape to the dangerous juxtaposition made by Johnson that it was a case of 'the people versus parliament' and he was on the side of the people. Brexit had become a battle between the will of voters as expressed in a referendum and the Commons that happened to be elected by the people, an awkward factor overlooked in the deadly juxtaposition.

Johnson insisted that the referendum outcome must be implemented. The 'people' must prevail. The majority of MPs argued that voters had not backed a 'no-deal' Brexit and therefore they had the right to block such a move. They passed legislation making it unlawful for the UK to leave without a vote in the Commons, thereby making a rushed exit by the end of October impossible.

Johnson responded by negotiating a deal, more or less the one the EU had proposed in the first place. May had rejected that deal and secured a better set of arrangements in which the UK would be allowed to remain in the customs union while ending freedom of movement. Johnson revived the idea of a border between Northern Ireland and Great Britain, a barrier that would protect the single market without necessitating a new border between Northern Ireland and Ireland. Johnson claimed the deal as a triumph and argued that it was only through his assertive leadership that the EU had been willing to move on from May's agreement. This was nonsense. The EU was relaxed about reverting to arrangements that it had put forward in the first place. The Eurosceptic newspapers hailed the new deal as did the Tory rebels who had been most concerned about the UK remaining in the customs union.

Johnson wanted parliament to consider his proposals for the shortest time possible. Most MPs, including senior figures on his own side, wanted more time. By then Johnson had changed further the nature of the Conservative parliamentary party. He had withdrawn the whip from prominent MPs who had failed to toe the line over his plans for Brexit. Those suspended from the parliamentary party included the former chancellors Ken Clarke and Philip Hammond, along with several recent cabinet ministers and experienced backbenchers. One former minister who had been suspended was Oliver Letwin, an unlikely rebel. At this point, there were at least two sets of potential rebels on the Conservative benches, the so-called European Research Group of hardline Brexiteers and those who were aware of the Brexit dangers and sought scrutiny over any deal. They had become 'independent' MPs.

On a rare Saturday sitting, Letwin led the charge for more time to study Johnson's deal, proposing a new amendment. He was supported by other unlikely rebels such as Hammond, another solid Tory not known for his insurrectionary zeal. His amendment won by sixteen votes, a much lower margin than most Commons votes against the government, but one that meant Johnson's agreement would not pass until there had been time for a proper examination. Johnson started calling for a general election. It was not in his gift to call one because of the Fixed-term Parliaments Act introduced by the coalition. In theory at least, the timing of an election was in the hands of the House of Commons. At this point, around two and a half years since the last election that was instigated by a Conservative government, MPs were not remotely obliged to concede Johnson's demands. They were in a still early stage of a parliamentary term. There had been two elections already in a short space of time, one in 2015 and the next in 2017. More expediently from his opponents' point of view, Johnson was still on a prime-ministerial honeymoon, still a novelty. Yet the opposition parties gave him precisely what he wanted. They backed his call for an early election rather than persist with their wholly reasonable demands to secure some time to scrutinize his deal. If they had done so, the flaws in Johnson's agreement, specifically in relation to the implications of a border between Great Britain and Northern Ireland, might have surfaced in some detail.

Unsurprisingly the SNP leader, Nicola Sturgeon, was up for an early election. The SNP was way ahead in the polls in Scotland and the trial of the former first minister and her once close ally, Alex Salmond, was scheduled for early the following year. Bizarrely the leader of the Liberal Democrats, Jo Swinson, also called for an election. Her party had performed well in that summer's European elections and subsequently some of the MPs who had formed the hastily conceived Change UK party had switched to the Liberal Democrats. This was no rational basis to give a newish prime minister an election precisely when he wanted to hold one. With two opposition parties calling for an election and dissenting Conservative MPs, Jeremy Corbyn, the Labour leader, had little choice but to call for an election too. There was also a part of Corbyn that ached for a campaign after his success in 2017. His life as leader at Westminster was a form of hell with a lot of Labour MPs expressing public venom about his leadership. For leaders struggling to lead, an election campaign can be a form of liberation. Corbyn succumbed too.

Johnson had been defeated many times in the Commons since becoming prime minister. He got his way on his biggest wish. A hung parliament with years to run granted him an election. Three and a half years after the referendum, the December 2019 election was fought around Brexit. A new informal alliance of disparate voters was formed while Europe destroyed another two leaderships.

Johnson won a near landslide on the slogan 'Let's get Brexit done'. Once again the chosen theme was process rather than substance. There was little debate about what form Brexit might take. Instead Johnson asked for the space to carry it out. In doing so he got the backing of many Labour voters in the so-called 'red wall' in the north of England along with more traditional Tory backers in the south. For 'red wall' voters, the cause was partly to do with 'trust'. They had voted for Brexit. They were still waiting. Only Johnson would deliver. The least trustworthy prime minister of modern times formed a deep bond of trust with former Labour voters.

As with New Labour's 'big tent' of support in 1997, there were seeds of tensions from the beginning. Polls suggested Johnson's new voters in the north sought more economic interventions and higher public spending. More familiar Tory Brexiteers had the opposite vision of a small state with low taxes flourishing against what they saw as the sclerotic EU. If Johnson had spelt out a precise post-Brexit vision, his new coalition of support would have been impossible. But he excelled at being defiantly imprecise while avoiding any TV interviewer who might seek clearer definition.

Corbyn lacked the skill to escape the Brexit trap. Like Wilson in the 1974 elections, he offered a referendum without stating which way he would declare, and suggested he would remain neutral in the referendum. But he was proposing a follow-up to the 2016 referendum, the third to be held over Europe. Voters turned away. In addition, he and his equally naive senior team made a fundamental error. They decided that their campaign would not be about Brexit. This was absurd. Johnson had called an election to 'get Brexit done'.

It was the Brexit election but they sought to focus on other policy areas.

Even more naive was the stance of the Liberal Democrats leader, Jo Swinson. She pledged to keep the UK in the EU without another referendum. Once more, the issue was process. There was a case for the substance of her argument, but no substance was argued over. Instead other questions erupted around her. Was it democratic? What did she say to the majority who voted to leave in the referendum? Swinson lost her seat. Labour and the Liberal Democrats were slaughtered. Corbyn announced his resignation in the immediate aftermath of the defeat.

The UK left the EU at the end of January 2020 on the basis of Johnson's deal. But that left the future trade arrangements to be negotiated. The trade deal with the EU was at least as significant as the withdrawal arrangements. Johnson appointed David Frost, soon to be made Lord Frost, to be his chief negotiator with the EU. Johnson had got to know Frost when he was foreign secretary. They got on, as Frost was one of the few in the Foreign Office who enthused about Brexit. Yet their exuberance when it came to leaving the EU was at odds with their pasts. Johnson had always been ambiguous about the EU and had contemplated campaigning for Remain. Frost had been politely sceptical in a restrained way when he was a diplomat, rising to be the UK's ambassador in Copenhagen. Later he was to represent the Whisky Association in Scotland when he became an ardent advocate for the economic benefits of the single market. Emerging from this limited career Frost became a great British 'exceptionalist', wearing Union Jack socks in his negotiations with EU leaders, as if this act of jingoistic assertiveness would deliver the deal he sought.

At first Frost liaised extensively with Dominic Cummings in Number 10 as he embarked on his negotiations. With his genuine interest in detailed policy and outcomes, Cummings was in a different league to Johnson and Frost, both of whom in their own ways regarded Brexit as a means of boosting their own careers. Cummings's instinct was to be aggressive and most emphatically to not rule out a 'no-deal' outcome as a possible end of the talks.

Quite a lot of those who worked with Cummings wanted to please him, a useful quality in an otherwise erratic leader, and Frost carried out the instructions from the dominant force in Number 10 with a willingness that became a form of conviction. His conversations with Johnson were more convoluted but Frost got the impression that the wayward prime minister was keen to play tough too. 'Frosty', as Johnson affectionately called him, was the star of Number 10, doing what was asked of him. But by the end of 2020, Cummings had fallen out with Johnson spectacularly and left Downing Street. Johnson instructed Frost to secure some form of deal and one was rushed through and agreed on Christmas Eve 2020. The cabinet was informed by Zoom. There was no detailed discussions on the proposals and Johnson recalled parliament for a short session on a single day between Christmas and New Year. The deal that few had read passed by a majority of 521 to 73 after a mere four hours of debate. Keir Starmer's Labour Party voted in favour.

Boris Johnson's speech was short and vague, during which he claimed without being challenged that the deal secured the best of all worlds:

In less than 48 hours, we will leave the EU single market and the customs union, as we promised and yet British exporters will not face a sudden thicket of trade barriers, but rather, for the first time in the history of EU agreements, zero tariffs and zero quotas. And just as we have avoided trade barriers, so we have also ensured the UK's full control of our laws and our regulations.[17]

None of this proved to be the case. There was a sudden thicket of trade barriers making access to the single market arduously bureaucratic and expensive. No country, let alone the UK, had 'full control' of laws and regulations. Any trade deal meant agreement between two sides on regulatory arrangements and the laws governing them. Johnson did not mention the Northern Ireland protocol in his speech but that quickly unravelled as the border between Northern Ireland and Great Britain ensured checks on goods that Johnson had promised would never take place. Soon Johnson and Frost were railing against the protocol even though they had negotiated it and the deal arose from Johnson's opposition to place a border between Northern Ireland and Great Britain.

Here was the more perverse twist – in a competitive field. For months, scrutiny, analysis and news reports of Theresa May's Brexit deal dominated parliament, the broadcasting outlets and newspapers. No other issue got a look in. That deal was never implemented. Johnson and the unelected Frost's deal went through without scrutiny from cabinet, parliament or much of the media. This was the agreement that was implemented.

The main agents of Brexit ran away from addressing the consequences. Nigel Farage resigned as UKIP leader the day after the referendum. Following the deal, Frost soon resigned as Brexit secretary, following the speedy departures from the same post of David Davis and Dominic Raab.

The UK and Europe

From 1973 to 2020, the year it formally left the EU, at no point could the British political system cope calmly with membership, as it struggled with the traumas of entering and departing. Yet the storms were at the top of politics. Voters were neither especially angry nor committed for much of the time. Newspaper reports such as those suggesting Brussels was banning certain types of banana got some worked up. But in the 1988 European elections and the 1997 general election when the Conservatives ran intensely Eurosceptic campaigns the party was slaughtered. When Cameron pledged to hold a referendum, the issue of Europe was well down the voters' lists of concerns. But at Westminster, Europe always featured as an issue until January 2020.

Then there was an even more disturbing reaction at Westminster. As the early Brexit consequences played out around the UK with trouble in Northern Ireland, insanely long queues at Dover, companies giving up trying to export to their biggest market because of the costs, artists finding it too complicated and expensive to perform in Europe, there was silence at Westminster. By 2023 the UK economy was performing more weakly than any other in the G7, yet there was only more silence on the issue at Westminster. Labour's leader, Keir Starmer, lacked the agility to expose the Brexit damage while wooing former voters who had backed leaving the EU in 2016. The Conservative parliamentary party had been purged of all heavyweights capable of scrutiny in relation to Europe. The silence was madder than the earlier deafening noise.

The nature of the post-Brexit turning point was unclear because the aims were never clear or coherent. In the early autumn of 2021,

Boris Johnson claimed that a petrol shortage arising from a short-age of lorry drivers was a Brexit triumph. He suggested firms would have to pay drivers higher wages rather than rely on cheaper labour from Europe. Yet when nurses went on strike in early 2023, also demanding higher pay, the new prime minister, Rishi Sunak, insisted the UK could not afford to meet their demands even though there was a shortage of nursing staff partly because of Brexit and the end of free movement. During Liz Truss's short reign, she spoke repeat-edly of 'Brexit freedoms' but her calamitous tax-cutting plans would have been permissible and equally disastrous if the UK had been in the EU.

Johnson spoke often of 'global Britain' but so did George Osborne when he was chancellor after the 2010 election. Osborne was a com-mitted Remainer. The much-heralded trade deal with the US did not happen. Instead, during the presidency of Joe Biden, the US was more distant than usual because of tensions over the Irish protocol. Inevitably the UK was detached from the EU too, determinedly separate but without discovering a distinct new international role. Johnson took much pride in his contribution to assisting Ukraine after Russia's invasion but there were ironies in his self-proclaimed heroism. Ukraine's great wish was to join the EU.

Logically the most significant turning point might have been that British politics became less volcanic after the stormy years join-ing and being part of Europe. But that the country has left without deciding how and precisely why it did so means there have been many more eruptions in the years that followed. In 2022 the UK was ruled by three prime ministers and four chancellors, hardly a model of post-Brexit stability.

Britain's place in the world continued to be confused, but that was the case during its membership of the EU and before. In the aftermath of the Suez crisis, prime ministers sought greater clarity by seeking to join the Common Market. After entry Heath was passionately pro-European and less bothered about the so-called special relationship with the US. Margaret Thatcher was driven by the significance of the relationship with the US and became less bothered by the EU. Tony Blair sought a third way, close ties with Europe and the US, but failed over Iraq. After Brexit, 'global Britain', more than ever, was still little more than a slogan.

The bigger turning point was a constitutional one. This was highly appropriate given the significance of rows about sovereignty from the early 1970s onwards. Who ruled the UK? This question assumed an unresolved urgency after the referendum. Did 'the people's verdict' as expressed in a referendum in 2016 override the majority in the elected House of Commons, or 'people versus parliament' as Boris Johnson put it? Ironically the leading Brexiteers, who had argued for the sovereignty of the Westminster parliament over the EU, now suggested that the referendum must prevail over the Commons. There was no clear resolution. A general election was called 'to get Brexit done' and that was what gave Johnson the space to implement the UK's withdrawal. But after all the heady dramas there was to be no end. Brexit would be a long-drawn-out process and one that would never be wholly 'done'.

Brexit came between two seismic events, the 2008 global financial crisis and the pandemic that spread around the world in the early spring of 2020. Although Brexit was a self-induced conflagration there was a common theme linking it with these earthquakes. Was Brexit about the UK becoming more statist, intervening to narrow inequality and for the government to take back control of the borders, thereby protecting the wages and jobs of British workers? Or was Brexit aimed at securing a small state with low taxes, less public spending and an increased role for deregulation? A succession of Conservative prime ministers struggled to come up with a definitive answer. Similarly, there was no clarity about the implications of the global financial crash in 2008. When some of the world's biggest banks headed towards the cliff edge (and in some cases toppled over) there was an ambivalence in the UK. The state came to the rescue with huge sums of money and there appeared to be a recognition that a lightly regulated financial market was not as benevolent as predicted. Yet within a couple of years the UK had elected a Conservative prime minister and chancellor who sought a smaller state with decisive spending cuts. What lessons had been learnt? Was the idea for the resurrection of a more active state, or was a smaller state the solution for the UK? Several years later, when Covid-19 wreaked havoc in the UK there was a similar confusion. Boris Johnson's libertarian instincts led him to conclude that lockdowns should be delayed for as long as possible and yet the ultimate escape from Covid was a vaccine coordinated by the state. Adults were texted about their vaccine appointment and in most cases recognized gratefully a link between the state and freedom from a terrible illness. The state was back in fashion again. Or was it?

9

THE STATE TO THE RESCUE

According to Thatcherism, the dominant ideology of recent decades, the state undermines 'freedom' and is a barrier to a booming economy. There have, however, been two monumental pauses in this orthodoxy. One was the global financial crash in 2008 and the other was the pandemic that began to cause mayhem in 2020. In response to both, people, businesses and institutions turned to the state to navigate the crises. In 2008, the state became an agent of freedom and security as banks were rescued, allowing people to still withdraw their money. In 2020, it was government that freed businesses and individuals from going bankrupt, while the NHS saved lives. In such circumstances, Margaret Thatcher's view of the state as a malevolent power made no sense. The Labour Party might have failed to counter the force of her personality and ideas. But global events were harder to ignore.

Consider two vignettes, both of which preceded the global financial crash in 2008. At the time, they seemed part of the natural order, but afterwards they would not have happened. For Gordon Brown, the build-up to his budget in the spring of 2002 had been even more nerve-racking than usual. He was going to make the case overtly for a significant tax rise to pay for additional NHS funding. Brown had taxed stealthily, but with the NHS in crisis he needed to resort to more open methods, turning to a rise in national insurance. Except he did not put the case for the tax increase himself. He sought a proxy, in the form of a figure who was guaranteed to command unqualified respect, not least from 'Middle England'. He turned to a senior banker. Since the mid-1980s, the lightly regulated financial sector had been the UK's great success story, with London in competition with New York as the biggest player in the global economy. Politicians worshipped at their altar.

Brown asked the former chief executive of NatWest Bank, Derek Wanless, to reach the conclusion that he had already decided upon. In his budget in 2002, it was not Brown seeking a tax rise. It was a masterful banker. Here is the chancellor in the Commons delivering his budget on behalf of Wanless:

> The report by Derek Wanless states that the NHS needs, in support of reform and modernisation, a long-term sustainable financial framework, and it sets out the financial needs for the next two decades, starting with a five-year period of high and sustained growth and, once we have tackled decades of under-investment, moving to lower rates of growth—4.4 to 5.6 per cent., then in the next five years 2.8 to 4 per cent., and then in the final five years 2.4 to 3.5 per cent. a year in real terms—for the three five-year periods after 2008.[1]

Wanless argued that these big leaps in growth must be paid for by a national insurance rise. Brown was bound to take the advice of a respected banker. Within a few years he would rather have sought association with the devil than a senior banker. But in 2002,

Wanless was the equivalent of a vicar in the 1950s. He could be trusted.

Two years after the Wanless budget, in April 2004, Lehman Brothers established a new European headquarters in Canary Wharf. Willingly and with ebullience Brown presided over the official opening.

> I would like to pay tribute to the contribution you and your company make to the prosperity of Britain. During its one-hundred-and-fifty-year history, Lehman Brothers has always been an innovator, financing new ideas and inventions before many others even began to realize their potential. And it is part of the greatness not just of Lehman Brothers but of the City of London, that as the world economy has opened up, you have succeeded not by sheltering your share of a small protected national market but always by striving for a greater and greater share of the growing global market.[2]

Brown made a thousand calculations before making any public move. He could only see upsides in being associated with the prestigious bank and its decision to base its European operation in London. Personally, he was more concerned with policies that might address inequality in the UK than he was with spending vast amounts of time with bankers, but he saw the two as connected in many different ways. The financial sector provided the Treasury with revenue for other projects related to his social justice agenda. His identification with high-flying bankers gave him the space, as he saw it, to be more daring on other issues such as tax credits and the NHS. Other Labour chancellors had been vilified for being financially irresponsible. How could he be reckless when he was at one with the great wealth creators of the age? How could the Conservatives in opposition frame New Labour as anti-business or economically irresponsible when the long-serving chancellor was at ease with the most senior bankers in the global market? The Conservatives could not answer. Labour won a third successive election in 2005.

Two years after the general election Brown achieved his ultimate personal ambition and became prime minister, a triumph of will and discipline. But he arrived in Number 10 under huge pressure from the media and a section of his party to show that he was as New Labour as Tony Blair, while also having to demonstrate that he was a change from his predecessor. The conundrum, one that he had been wrestling with for years, had drained him by the time he finally replaced Blair.

There were many consequences arising from his relative exhaustion. One was that he could not quite see what was happening in front of him. A year before the global crash there were some ominous signs that the financial sector was not as robust as it appeared to be. But Brown was slow to adapt. In September 2007, he got an early glimpse of the explosion that was to follow when the British bank Northern Rock got into deep trouble. Northern Rock had struggled to raise funds in turbulent money markets and was on the verge of collapse. Queues formed outside branches of the bank as alarmed savers tried to withdraw their cash while they still could. As chancellor for a decade Brown had faced many crises. This one was on a different scale. He had been enjoying a prime-ministerial honeymoon with voters that he had not anticipated. With good cause, he assumed the honeymoon would turn speedily into a political funeral if account holders lost their deposits.

The government had no choice but to lend the bank £3 billion while the new chancellor, Alistair Darling, guaranteed that all deposits would be safe. Darling had a calm temperament and he was going to need it. In the middle of the maelstrom, he flew home to Edinburgh briefly. Seeking a relaxing escape for an hour or two with his family, he switched on the TV to watch some football. Newcastle United were playing. Featuring prominently on each player's shirt was the Northern Rock logo. The bank sponsored the team. Darling concluded there could be no escape.[3]

In spite of the drama, Brown's mindset was still rooted more or less where it had been when he spoke enthusiastically at the opening of Lehman Brothers. Northern Rock had become so fragile that a host of venerable institutions, commentators and politicians were calling for the bank to be taken into state ownership. They included *The Economist* magazine, the *Financial Times* and the widely respected Treasury spokesman for the Liberal Democrats, Vince Cable. None of them worshipped at the altar of 1970s-style interventionism. Nonetheless Brown was terrified how the nationalization of a bank would be perceived.

Under pressure to prove his New Labour credentials, Brown was being asked to adopt a Bennite policy of the 1980s, or at least that was how he saw it. Tony Benn had called for all banks to be nationalized during a messianic party conference speech in 1980. New Labour was framed partly as a repudiation of 1980s Labour. That was old Labour. Brown was fearful how Rupert Murdoch's newspapers would react and how the Blairite wing of his parliamentary party would brief against the move. He resisted nationalization for months. Instead he tried to find a buyer for the bank. Wisely no firm was willing to take on that particular challenge.

Finally in February 2008, Brown and Darling announced that they were bringing Northern Rock into 'temporary' state ownership. Brown repeatedly and nervously stressed the temporary dimension. On one level he was right to be worried. The Conservative leader

David Cameron and his shadow chancellor, George Osborne, held a joint press conference condemning this 'return to the 1970s'. Osborne deployed one of his favourite phrases, arguing that Darling was a 'dead man walking' and if Brown was not so weak, he would sack him. After Theresa May failed to win an overall majority in the 2017 election Osborne described her as a 'dead woman walking' too. Both Darling and May continued to walk for quite some time after Osborne pronounced them as deceased. Cameron insisted vaguely that the best way to protect taxpayers' money was a Bank of England-led administration: 'The nationalisation is a disaster for the taxpayer, a disaster for this government and a disaster for this country'.[4]

Like Brown they were not seeing what was happening in front of their eyes. Polls suggested voters approved of the nationalization. This was not the 1970s or 1980s, but a new crisis that dwarfed the various emergencies of those earlier decades and demanded its own response. Within months the big banks were pleading for the state to intervene on a scale that made the takeover of Northern Rock seem like pocket money.

On 15 September 2008, Lehman Brothers, the American global financial services firm that Brown had venerated, went bankrupt. The European branch that had been opened in Canary Wharf four and a half years earlier ceased to trade on the same day. Lehman Brothers was heavily involved in the subprime lending market, one that targeted consumers with low incomes and poor credit histories on the assumption that economies and property prices would boom eternally. They were the riskiest of loans but in lightly regulated markets banks were free to take risks without contemplating the consequences of financial turmoil.

The crisis spread like wildfire. As Brown noted, governments were facing the first emergency in the era of the globalized market.

The subtitle of his subsequent book was *Overcoming the First Crisis of Globalization*.[5] When Northern Rock was in crisis, he had been tentative, trapped by the vote-losing decades of Labour's wilderness. In 2008, he was more far-seeing than most global leaders and his political opponents in the UK, including quite a few in his parliamentary party who were plotting to remove him. The activities of banks across the globe were interconnected and the crisis fed on itself. Government intervention on a massive scale across much of the globe was the only solution.

In the early autumn of 2008, the state was back in fashion. Up until then, the Conservative leader, David Cameron, was calling for an even more lightly regulated financial sector. 'Light regulation' was seen as liberating and 'regulation' perceived as a threat. The Thatcherite conception of 'freedom' had endured to the degree that Cameron was hailed as a 'centrist' for arguing 'there is such a thing as society but it is not the same as the state'.[6] But then the dynamic and heroic agents of growth were pleading for governments to intervene. In the build-up to the closure of Lehman Brothers, the then minister, Ed Miliband, caught a segment on the radio in which he heard the interviewee begging for the government to step in. Miliband assumed it was a trade union leader. When he realized the voice was that of a senior banker from the doomed firm, he recognized excitedly that the orthodoxies in place since 1979 were being challenged like never before.

At Labour's conference in September 2008, Brown constructed an argument about the role of government that he had always believed but had been fearful to articulate:

Insuring people against the new risks and empowering people with new opportunities is the mission of the hour. Those who say governments should walk away when people face these risks, and need the opportunities, will be judged to be on the wrong side of history. This is a defining moment for us – a test not of our judgement but our values.[7]

The UK was at another turning point as those that argued against state intervention were suddenly in a freakish minority. By October, they had become an endangered species. On 7 October the chair of the Royal Bank of Scotland, Tom McKillop, contacted Brown to declare that he was 'worried about the immediate financial position overnight'. The word 'overnight' was alarming. McKillop was calling for government help on a spectacular scale and without delay.

Brown had no choice but to deliver: 'I was simultaneously furious and shocked . . . it was apparent the banks didn't have a clear idea of what was happening . . . No one trusted anyone in the banking system and people were predicting not a recession but a depression.'[8]

Amidst a frightening emergency Brown noted the breakdown in trust. He had trusted the bankers. He sought association with them because the public had trusted the bankers. No one did now. The following morning, Brown and Darling unveiled a 'comprehensive' bank plan involving huge sums of money. They did so in advance of some other governments but Brown knew they would soon follow. The duo announced £50 billion in capital, £250 billion in funding guarantees, and £100 billion for a special liquidity scheme. Later, when the storm had subsided, Darling reflected that before the crash he and Brown agonized over whether to increase spending here and there by a few million pounds. Then early one morning in October 2008 they announced a package worth hundreds of billions.

Brown and Darling seemed almost at ease with their suddenly defined mission. As they injected equity into British banks and

provided guarantees on bank debt, the influential American economist Paul Krugman praised them for taking the lead in the worldwide
rescue effort. Krugman wrote that 'this combination of clarity and
decisiveness hasn't been matched by any other Western government,
least of all our own.'[9] Brown had acquired a prime-ministerial sense
of purpose even if his own fiscal rules, which had partly defined New
Labour, were broken.

Darling's financial statement of 25 November 2008 was part of
the turning point. It was widely seen as abandoning Brown's so-called
'Golden Rule', adopted in 1998 under the government's code for
fiscal stability. This stated that the government should borrow only
for the purposes of investment, and not for current spending, over
the course of the economic cycle. A further fiscal rule stated that
public sector debt would be held below 40 per cent of gross domestic product over the course of the economic cycle. It was cast aside
as well. Darling predicted that net debt would peak at 57 per cent
of GDP in 2013–14. Although he aspired to balance the budget by
2015–16, a significant underlying budget deficit would persist in
the meantime. A government that prided itself on fiscal prudence
embraced massive reflationary borrowing.

The rest of the world was following suit. On 2 April 2009, Brown
announced a fiscal stimulus at the G20 summit of leaders in London.
Here was an implicit acknowledgement of the good that governments could do from the most affluent economies in the world.
Leaders agreed on a $1.1 trillion injection of financial aid into the
global economy. Brown claimed that the grand bargain he had bro-
kered represented 'a coming together of the world' that would speed
recovery from the worst recession since 1945. The deal also contained
measures to tighten financial regulation, including a clampdown on
tax havens, championed by the glittering new US president, Barack

Obama. He declared at the end of the summit that 'the patient had stabilised and was in good care'.[10] Those who saw Brown in the days following the summit detected a hint of melancholy. He feared there would be no electoral benefit from his efforts at a time when he needed a boost. He and his party were far behind in the polls.[11]

If Brown or Darling had been told that their emergency spending would be a mere trifle compared with what a Conservative government would spend a few years later, they would have needed to lie down in a darkened room. At the time, they were pushing the notion of an active state to its limits. But in 2020, a prime minister widely regarded as a staunch libertarian would make more use of the state than any leader since 1945. In 2020 the state became the means by which most people were protected from a global pandemic and was the agent that enabled businesses across the UK to survive.

Covid and the Active State

As a columnist, Boris Johnson had railed against the 'nanny state', one of his regular themes when governments sought to free people from the burden of illness by some form of state intervention. He saw 'freedom' as the right to do what any individual wanted to do. This was how he had lived his colourful life and he wanted others to have the same opportunity, unimpeded by too many rules. During the Conservatives' leadership contest in 2019, Johnson stayed at his girlfriend's flat. A neighbour noted his car outside was plastered with parking fines. Johnson had not bothered to remove the tickets, let alone pay the fines.[12]

Johnson won the leadership contest and had no more immediate need of his car spattered in parking tickets. He became prime minister in July 2019. Months later he won a near-landslide election victory. Within weeks of his eccentric but triumphant election campaign, coronavirus was spreading from China to Europe.

But Johnson was another prime minister who could not see what was in front of his eyes. In early February 2020, he delivered a speech in Greenwich during which he outlined his vision of global Britain while mocking other countries for putting up barriers in order to protect their populations from Covid. The words were breathtakingly complacent. The UK was on the edge of a lasting turning point. Johnson seemed to have no idea.

> We are starting to hear some bizarre autarkic rhetoric, when barriers are going up, and when there is a risk that new diseases such as coronavirus will trigger a panic and a desire for market segregation that go beyond what is medically rational to the point of doing real and unnecessary economic damage, then at that moment humanity needs some government somewhere that is willing at least to make the case powerfully for freedom of exchange, some country ready to take off its Clark Kent spectacles and leap into the phone booth and emerge with its cloak flowing as the supercharged champion, of the right of the populations of the earth to buy and sell freely among each other.[13]

Johnson joked that he shook hands with patients during hospital visits, attended a packed Twickenham to watch England against Wales in the Six Nations tournament and allowed other major sporting events to take place. England was enjoying itself and so was Johnson. But with his scientific advisers warning that the NHS risked being overwhelmed with sufferers of coronavirus, Johnson suddenly had no choice but to act. Apparently post-Brexit Britain was not immune to the virus. By the middle of March, the freedom-loving prime minister declared that 'now is the time for everyone to stop non-essential contact and . . . travel'.[14] On 23 March, he announced a strict lockdown, ordering people to 'stay at home', a phrase that would come to define his leadership as much as Brexit. The state was determining how people could live in ways that in some respects were far more constraining than during the Second World War. Then, people could still meet up in each other's homes. In the spring of 2020 they could not. Johnson was discovering that freedom took many forms. He was imposing rules on what people could and could not do in order that they had the freedom to stay safe.

At the same time, the recently appointed chancellor, Rishi Sunak, announced an economic intervention that made the spending of Brown and Darling during the financial crash seem miserly. On 20 March, Sunak made clear that he was acting in a way that was unique. It had taken Brown some time to frame his actions around the idea of an active state. From the right of the Conservative Party Sunak did so without any hint of equivocation.

The economic intervention that I'm announcing today is unprecedented in the history of the British state. Combined with our previous announcements on public services and business support, our planned economic response will be one of the most comprehensive in the world. Let me speak directly to people's concerns. I know that people are worried about losing their jobs. About not being able to pay the rent or the mortgage. About not having enough set by for food and bills. I know that some people in the last few days have already lost their jobs.

To all those at home right now, anxious about the days ahead, I say this: you will not face this alone. But getting through this will require a collective national effort, with a role for everyone to play – people, businesses and government. It's on all of us. To meet our commitment to that effort, I am today announcing a combination of measures unprecedented for a government of this nation.

Our Plan for People's Jobs and Incomes will protect people's jobs; offer more generous support to those who are without employment; strengthen the safety net for those who work for themselves; and help people who stay in their homes. Today I can announce that, for the first time in our history, the government is going to step in and help to pay people's wages.

We're setting up a new Coronavirus Job Retention Scheme. Any employer in the country – small or large, charitable or non-profit – will be eligible for the scheme. Employers will be able to contact HMRC for a grant to cover most of the wages of people who are not working but are furloughed and kept on payroll, rather than being laid off . . . I am placing no limit on the amount of funding available for the scheme. We will pay grants to support as many jobs as necessary.[15]

In these responses to the pandemic, the government was establishing a direct and obvious relationship between state and voters. Inevitably voters noticed. They did stay at home because they had been advised to do so. There were few protests. They did notice that in most cases they were still being paid by the government even if they were not working. Although much of the government's response was late and chaotic, Boris Johnson remained fairly popular in England. In Scotland Nicola Sturgeon was in charge and there was a similar connection between the elected leader and voters. The same applied to Labour's Mark Drakeford in Wales.

Sunak was proposing to spend approximately £70 billion to free people from worrying about losing their jobs or their businesses going bust. The connection between the government and the people deepened in the summer when the strictest constraints of lockdown had been lifted and Sunak announced an 'eat out to help out' initiative: the Treasury would subsidize those going to restaurants in order to boost the hospitality sector. It was almost as if Sunak had invited 'the people' out to dinner.

The connection was at its most intimate during the rollout of the vaccine. People were texted with the time and place to attend their vaccination and it was almost as if Johnson, Sturgeon or Drakeford were contacting them direct. The head of the Vaccine Taskforce, Kate Bingham, was praised for the success of the vaccines as they were administered smoothly and speedily in the early months of 2021. Bingham recognized that the NHS itself was fundamental to the vaccines' success, from the vaccine trials to the nationwide implementation of inoculation through GP surgeries: 'So we created the NHS Vaccine Registry. This allowed anyone to sign up on the NHS website and give consent to be contacted about clinical trials. Over 500,000 people enrolled, including 35% of over-60-year-olds, a critical demographic: after all, we had to demonstrate that the vaccines we were trialling would be safe and effective for those most at risk from serious disease and death.'[16]

During the early stage of the pandemic people around the country gathered at 8 p.m. every Thursday evening to clap for NHS workers. There was a connection with the NHS and with all those taking part from Johnson in Number 10 to those gathering outside their homes across the country. Clapping is easier than paying higher taxes for a well-funded NHS, but like the war in the 1940s, there was a sense of a collective struggle rather than individuals acting alone and solely in their own interests. When the New Labour government redistributed through tax credits, few noticed. What a contrast from when the cabinet minister at the time, Robin Cook, feared that his constituents thought their higher pay was a result of a technical adjustment by the Inland Revenue or that patients assumed new NHS walk-in centres had arrived from nowhere. In their early years Blair and Brown were wary of talking about redistribution or higher public spending. The beneficiaries did not make the connections. In the pandemic it was impossible not to do so.

In addition, when the health system creaked pathetically under the strain of the pandemic there appeared to be a new willingness to analyse deeply why the UK struggled, going beyond the haphazard incompetence of some elected individuals. Ministers complained of pulling levers and nothing happening. They had little or no control over social care even though there was a direct link between the strain on NHS capacity and the puny levels of adequate social care. A quango, NHS England, was supposedly in direct control of delivery, yet ministers were accountable for what happened in every hospital. At no point during the daily Downing Street press conferences did the head of NHS England, Sir Simon Stevens, appear with the health secretary, Matt Hancock. There were too many blurred lines of responsibility and accountability between them.

At first, availability of tests for the virus was wholly inadequate. Procurement of urgently needed medical equipment was panic-stricken and possibly corrupt as lucrative contracts were speedily agreed and, in some cases, useless and overpriced equipment followed. Beyond the notable flaws of some individuals at the very top, there were raging questions across government and in the media about why the decision-making could be so chaotic. In their different ways they were all posing one fundamental question: who was in charge of what?

In order to answer that question, or to discover why they could not answer it, some of those involved in the saga dared to look back. There was a context to the structural chaos. Of the many causes, the deepest were the result of ill-conceived reforms.

The NHS and 'Reform'

Andrew Lansley, who became health secretary in the coalition government following the election in 2010, was quick to make his mark. Neither David Cameron, who was prime minister at the time, nor Boris Johnson, who ruled during the pandemic, understood the consequences of Lansley's plans, a case study of shallow thinking in which Lansley emerges at least as a coherent and consistent policymaker. Reactions during the pandemic suggested a turning point away from this shallowness where the word 'reform' is seen as a solution in itself. The likes of Hancock and the chair of the Health Select Committee, Jeremy Hunt, appeared keen to learn what had gone wrong.

In 2010, few seemed to know what Lansley was planning to do with his reforms. As the journalist and author Nick Timmins has argued, there should have been little surprise when Lansley published his white paper. Yet prime ministers and future health secretaries were taken aback when they realized that they had initiated changes that took away their powers. In particular, during the pandemic, Johnson and his Number 10 staff despaired when Hancock spoke of the limited levers available to him because of the party's own reforms. Timmins wrote a detailed analysis of the extraordinary build-up to the changes for the independent health think-tank The King's Fund:

> Pretty much all of it – the commissioning board, clinically-led commissioning with GPs purchasing care, a new economic regulator, 'any willing provider', Healthwatch – had been there in dozens of speeches and documents. So much so that by the time of the 2010 election senior officials at the health department had prepared a dossier of documents in order to prepare for Lansley's revolution. When officials met Lansley in the pre-election access talks that shadow secretaries of state are entitled to ahead of polling day, Lansley himself was armed with detailed proposals, referring to them, at times page by page and line by line, as he set out what he wanted to do. For the shadow health secretary and for Kremlinologists, both in and outside the department, it was all – or pretty much all – as clear as day. Yet on 12 July 2010 – the day of the white paper's publication – the sheer scale and scope of what was being planned took the public and the health service itself aback.[17]

There were plenty of events where Lansley and others spoke candidly before the 2010 election. Two of Cameron's most influential advisers, Steve Hilton and Oliver Letwin, organized a series of seminars in which policy specialists, shadow cabinet members and a few columnists were invited to attend events aimed at exploring what they billed as 'the post-bureaucratic age'. The overriding theme was that the government would stand back, set targets and then allow other agencies to deliver public services. At one of the events, Lansley declared that as health secretary he would have achieved his goals if he was absent from the BBC's *Today* programme during a crisis in the NHS. By then he hoped to be part of a wider recognition that responsibility for delivery lay elsewhere, with NHS leaders account-able to patients, who would be considerably empowered. Cameron attended the meetings, taking extensive notes, almost as if he was a passive observer. Lansley's white paper was all about creating new mediating agencies between patient and provider, with the govern-ment stepping back.[18]

Few noticed the radical implications. Political journalism often follows mood music rather than the substance of policy. Cameron had told the party faithful in his conference speech in 2006 that while Tony Blair had declared his priorities to be 'education, educa-tion, education . . . I can do it in three letters: N.H.S.' He provided further reassurance, promising 'no more pointless and disruptive reorganizations' of the health service. At the same time, however, he endorsed Lansley's developing ideas for how the health service should be run, which would involve disruptive change on a colossal scale.[19]

The full details of Lansley's plans emerged in June 2007 in what the Conservatives dubbed an 'NHS Autonomy and Accountability White Paper', the 'white paper' claim being an attempt at govern-ment loftiness, a move with far more detail than is usual from an opposition front bench. But it was not only Cameron's apparent intense commitment to the NHS that diverted the media from paying attention. The term 'reform' has a mesmeric quality in Brit-ish politics, casting a spell over political journalists and broadcasters. When Gordon Brown replaced Tony Blair in 2007, Rupert Mur-doch's newspapers, columnists and parts of the BBC concluded that a major test for Brown was his support for 'reform' in the NHS and beyond. During the surreal leadership contest in which Brown was the only candidate his team would meet to review the media.

'What do they mean by "reform"?' was a common question.[20] It was a good one.

On the whole the media orthodoxy was vaguely in favour of more use of the private sector and wary of higher investment in the NHS. This did not lead very far. Some of Blair's 'reforms' had resulted in better outcomes for patients, but others had produced an inefficient, convoluted hierarchy involving too many mediating agencies. Such was the disillusionment with Blair within the NHS that Cameron started to get standing ovations when he addressed NHS staff. It was after one such meeting that he dared to wonder whether he could win the next general election.[21] Ironically he planned to go much further than Blair in disrupting the NHS.

Brown knew there were problems with some of Blair's policy changes but the outgoing prime minister's juxtaposition of 'reform versus anti-reform' had intoxicated the media. If he raised any doubts about what Cameron was planning, Brown worried he would be deemed to be 'anti-reform'. Brown therefore adopted a relatively stealthy approach, recognizing the importance of 'reform' while appointing a surgeon, Lord Darzi, to make his own proposals aimed at achieving better outcomes for patients. Most political journalists noted only that Brown continued to place an emphasis on 'reform'. As a result there was an assumption that there was no great difference between what the Labour government was doing and what Cameron and Lansley were proposing. In the 2010 election Labour stressed its commitment to the NHS as it always did but chose not to focus too much on Lansley's plans out of fear of being perceived as 'anti-reform' in the media.

There were echoes with Labour's reluctance in the 1987 election to highlight Margaret Thatcher's plan to introduce a poll tax as a means of raising money for councils, because that might lead to a media focus on the party's so-called 'loony-left' local authorities. The poll tax did not feature in the 1987 election although it came to dominate the next parliament. The same applied to the Lansley reforms. They did not feature in the 2010 election campaign because both parties appeared to be in favour of 'reform' and that was the end of the matter.

The coalition formed in 2010 moved with the same breathtaking speed as the 1945 government, this time from the radical right. The pace and substance were a shock to some who had voted for the Liberal Democrats on the assumption they were to the left of New Labour, part of the topsy-turvy nature of British politics in which nothing is quite what it appears to be. 'Reform' was the coalition's mantra, taking its lead from Blair's rhetoric, but seeking to go much further. There was to be not just the NHS 'reform' but a radical restructuring of tuition fees; the expansion of 'free' schools; a new 'universal' credit in the benefit system; a 'rehabilitation revolution' in the criminal justice system; a major restructuring of the Financial Services Authority and the Bank of England; a merger of the Competition Commission and the Office of Fair Trading; elected police commissioners; more elected mayors; a big reform of public-sector pensions; a new 'localism' offering individuals new rights and powers below the level of local government; a referendum on reform of the voting system; reform of the House of Lords; a redrawing of parliamentary constituency boundaries; and much else. Above all, its economic policies were based on accelerated Thatcherism, theoretically eliminating the deficit, while imposing by far the biggest cuts to government spending in living memory. The austerity programme was also part of the context in which the later Conservative government battled with the pandemic. There were far fewer hospital beds available in the UK compared with equivalent countries in Europe.

Staff shortages were also acute as a result of spending restraints and a Brexit that ended free movement of people.

When Lansley published his white paper in July 2010, both sides of the coalition were relaxed. The Liberal Democrats' leader and deputy prime minister, Nick Clegg, liked the focus on localism and new roles for councils.[22] Oliver Letwin, the Tories' overall policy chief, wholly supported the devolution of commissioning to GPs and the use of choice and competition. Cameron had also argued vaguely that he intended:

> to strengthen society rather than the state; to give more power to the people through increased localisation, transparency, choice and accountability; and to encourage enterprise by liberating individuals, communities and businesses from the dead hand of excessive bureaucracy. And the direction in which the programme seeks to take Britain is into a post-bureaucratic age. The ambition is to liberate the energies and reinforce the social bonds of our people so that they can achieve what has not been achieved and will never be achieved by the mechanisms of centralized bureaucratic micro-management.[23]

Well before the pandemic, when Cameron was still prime minister, he struggled with the consequences of the 'reforms' even after they had been watered down following uproar in the Liberal Democrats, a party that Clegg did not fully understand even though he led it. In December 2014, with a general election in view, Cameron asked his health secretary, Jeremy Hunt, to intervene directly with some hospitals to ensure they were ready for a winter flu crisis. Cameron did not want stories about the NHS being unable to cope under a Conservative prime minister. Hunt pointed out that the government had given away the powers for a health secretary to intervene in such a direct manner.[24]

When a series of scandals emerged at the Mid Staffordshire NHS hospital in 2013, Cameron made a formal apology in the Commons, personally 'vowing' to tackle NHS complacency.[25] This was far removed from the original vision as espoused precisely by Lansley and vaguely by Cameron. They did not expect to appear on the *Today* programme if there was a crisis in a hospital let alone deliver a prime-ministerial statement in the Commons that included a pledge to take full control of the situation. Cameron had discovered the obvious. An elected government that raises the money for the NHS is at least partly responsible for delivery.

During the pandemic, Johnson, Hancock and others rediscovered this in the midst of a global emergency. For the first time since the 1980s the most popular version of 'reform' went out of fashion, to be replaced by another attempt at a different 'reform', one that reversed the earlier orthodoxy. Under constant immense pressure to deliver on a daily basis from Number 10 and beyond, the health secretary Matt Hancock told the BBC's Andrew Marr that the NHS had become too 'atomized', a view echoed by his predecessor, Jeremy Hunt, now chair of the Health Select Committee.[26] There were an absurd number of health secretaries after Hancock resigned for breaking his own Covid rules. They included Sajid Javid, Steve Barclay twice and Thérèse Coffey for a few weeks. Yet out of the chaos the government finally managed to pass the Health and Social Care Act in the spring of 2022. The most significant element of the legislation was that the health secretary regained some of the control over the NHS that Lansley gave away when he set up NHS England and bestowed upon it a quasi-independent status. The aim was to give 'enhanced powers of direction for the government over NHS England, which will support greater collaboration, information sharing and aligned responsibilities and accountability'.[27]

Ministers were fed up of being the fall guys – in parliament and the media – even though, in their view, the real blame lay with NHS England, which was operationally independent – at least in theory. The plans also unwound some of the increased privatization of services that the 2012 act had forced on the NHS. In the future, integrated care systems would not have to put out to tender contracts for care, unless they believed doing so would help patients. The legislation represented a drastic U-turn on the earlier ideas of Cameron, Lansley, Hilton and Letwin and the policies that arose from them.

Such was the scale of the apparent turning point, it seemed that the government was finally going to get a grip on social care. One of the great tragedies of the pandemic was the rushed attempt to create more hospital beds by removing elderly patients into care homes. There were many tragic layers. In the early months, the patients were not tested and the virus spread at horrendous speed within the institutions. Predictably there was not much capacity in care homes either, a lightly regulated sector over which the government had chosen to have limited or no control. The need for an adequately funded social-care system formally connected with the NHS, rather than linked by necessity without any established ties, was a lesson that the government had claimed to learn.

For Johnson, a leader with a selective short-term memory, there was a more pressing imperative to resolve the thorny issue. In his opening statement as prime minister outside Number 10 in July 2019, he pretended to have a plan for social care. He had not wanted to make his entire address about Brexit so threw in a casually made pledge to remedy one of the biggest gaps in public-service provision. Fast forward and by the summer of 2021 Johnson was worried that on his second anniversary as prime minister he would be asked about what had happened. So far no plan of any sort had surfaced. He was desperate to have a concrete answer.

There were frenzied, panic-stricken conversations with his chancellor, Rishi Sunak, and his health secretary, Sajid Javid. By then Sunak, a self-declared 'fiscal conservative', wanted to focus on 'balancing the books' after the biggest state intervention since the war during the pandemic. Johnson had expected Sunak to do what he was told and to his growing anger he had chosen a chancellor who was proving to be increasingly stubborn and self-confident. He could not cope with assertiveness in others. Meanwhile Javid, a health secretary recently given the post having been sacked earlier as chancellor, stressed the huge demands facing the NHS after the pandemic.

Out of these clashing priorities emerged a farcical arrangement. Reluctantly, Johnson agreed to raise the cash through a significant tax increase, a rise in national insurance. This would pay for a much-needed 'social-care levy'. Except that most of the cash would be invested in the NHS. It was a social-care levy that was not for social care. None of it was thought through with any depth. Where would the staff for care homes be recruited from, given the already acute labour shortages arising from Brexit and the pandemic? How would standards be raised? What institutions would regulate the new regime? Still the rushed conversations and shallow outcome meant that Javid had short-term cash for the NHS, Sunak could focus on cutting borrowing and Johnson had his fig leaf. He did have a plan for social care after all, or at least he had a levy to pay for it if the NHS crisis was ever addressed.

The whole episode was absurd and yet seemed to be part of the historic turning point. Here was a Conservative prime minister and chancellor raising taxes to pay directly for improvements in public services. This had not happened since Gordon Brown raised national insurance to pay for improvements in the NHS in 2003. It appeared as if the pandemic had forced the Conservative government to move on from its unyielding attachment to Thatcherism. Johnson had always been rootless: a Thatcherite or a Keynesian depending on his mood at any moment. But in the summer of 2021, there was Javid pleading for big spending increases and Sunak putting up taxes to pay for a specific service in a way no chancellor had done since Brown. A year later the same party was seeking to recalibrate NHS structures towards the state after the chaos under Cameron. England's governing party of choice was moving on from the orthodoxies of the 1980s. Or was it?

The State Goes Out of Fashion Again

Both the financial crash and the pandemic promised fundamental changes to the relationship between the state and the people – and the scale of resources required. But before very long the more familiar orthodoxies in the UK reasserted themselves as if they had never been away. Following the financial crash in the autumn of 2008, David Cameron and George Osborne became the only leaders of a mainstream party in the G20 to oppose a fiscal stimulus. Even President Bush in the US, not known for his Marxist tendencies, had supported emergency spending in the early phase of the crisis. Cameron and Osborne proposed real-terms spending cuts. They did so for several reasons. The duo were returning to their ideological comfort zone having pretended to support higher spending on some services than Gordon Brown was planning. Now they were able to return to their own instincts and those of their party. There was too much public spending and they would cut it. The stance also realigned them with the influential Conservative-supporting newspapers, from *The Times* to the *Daily Mail* and *The Sun*, that tended to regard spending as a 'waste'.

Above all, the political positioning was perfect. They were able to claim that Brown's public-spending levels were the cause of the crash and that he could not be trusted with the nation's finances. 'Don't give the key back to those that crashed the car' was one of many accessible soundbites crafted by Osborne to make sense of his position. The claim was not based on what had happened. The crash had led to the gaping deficit. The deficit did not cause the crash. All previous assumptions about economic growth and tax revenues were undermined in weeks as the UK headed for a recession and possible depression. Instead of the Treasury receiving revenues from a booming banking sector, the government had been forced to spend billions to save the banks from collapsing. It did not matter. Cameron and Osborne pledged to wipe out the deficit in the next parliament and Brown was under constant pressure to explain how he would do the same or something similar.

No left-of-centre politician in the UK has found a way of making Keynesian arguments accessible to the wider electorate. After the crash the task became harder. There was a deficit crisis and yet one way of addressing it was to borrow in order to stimulate economic growth. This was how the G20 responded to the initial emergency and the widely anticipated economic depression was avoided. But no one in the Labour leadership could counter Osborne's simplistic assault. There were fuming tensions at the top of Brown's government about the substance of the economic response as well as the language to make sense of it all. His chancellor, Alistair Darling, wanted to make clear that big cuts were required, much deeper than Thatcher's in the 1980s. Brown feared that such assertions fell into Osborne's trap, essentially accepting the premise of the onslaught. With justification he feared that arguing Labour would cut more effectively than the Conservatives would not be a great vote winner.

There were endless meetings involving Ed Balls, Peter Mandelson and others about how to move on from the initial fiscal stimulus by accepting that some cuts would be required but not as many as Osborne was proposing. By the time of the election Labour was proposing to halve the deficit in a single parliament, a more realistic proposition than Osborne's and closer to what actually happened when the Conservatives formed the coalition in 2010. But this policy was formed after many energy-draining internal rows. After the 2010 election Darling was open about how he saw the situation: 'My frustration is that we could have got through this, we could have charted a political way through this. We could have come through this but we didn't.'[28]

Mandelson and Darling concluded that Brown and Balls had a 'psychopathic' loathing of the Treasury.[29] Brown's doubts were more complex. He did fear that Darling had been 'captured' by Treasury orthodoxy and sought an alternative course without finding one.

His worries were well founded. Labour did walk into Osborne's trap. Every BBC interview asked why Brown and his colleagues were not prepared to go much further given the scale of the deficit that they had brought about. Broadly the Blairite wing of Labour accepted, or almost wanted to accept, that Brown had been too profligate when he was chancellor. Quickly the UK's response to a financial crash triggered by lightly regulated and reckless banks was to move towards a smaller state, even though an active state had been required to prevent even more turmoil.

Cameron and Osborne did not win an overall majority in 2010 but they managed to persuade Nick Clegg, the leader of the Liberal Democrats, to fully back their austerity programme for the following five years. In doing so the Liberal Democrats moved towards their electoral doom. In the longer term, the consensus in relation to regulation also broke down. At first there was acceptance that lightly applied regulation was a significant factor in causing the crash. Yet by December 2022 the new chancellor, Jeremy Hunt, in another desperate search for economic growth, wanted to free up the banks to take risks once again. Hunt declared that he planned to repeal some of the post-crash regulations. Amongst several proposals, he sought to roll back ring-fencing rules that Osborne had introduced to protect customers by separating their deposits from riskier investment plans being considered by banks. Hunt's package was enough to prompt Sir John Vickers, the senior economist who led the commission that reviewed the UK banking industry after the crash, to warn about an 'extremely dangerous and wrong path': 'We want safe and sound institutions, we want well-functioning financial markets . . . What I think would be a great mistake would be to put the financial services sector on some kind of pedestal, warranting a kind of special light touch regulatory treatment, when we all need that sector to be safe and sound for the competitiveness of the economy as a whole.'[30]

The package also included plans for a central bank digital currency and changes to the rules on short-selling – where investors bet that the price of an asset will drop. That was on top of introducing new targets for City regulators that would force them to consider how their rules could increase competition and UK growth, including by boosting venture capital funding for growing companies, unlocking funding for infrastructure projects and helping first-time buyers. Hunt was hoping risk-taking would lead to growth, as if the 2008 crash had never happened.

The same pattern applied before very long in relation to managing the NHS and social care. New forms of chaos took hold rather than any serious attempt at working out where power should lie. By early 2023, the NHS was facing what many of its leading players agreed was the biggest emergency since its formation. The waiting lists had risen rather than diminished. Staff shortages remained acute. Nurses went on strike for the first time since the NHS was launched. Once again it was not clear who was in control. NHS England was theoretically responsible for delivery but delivery was dependent on staff levels, a responsibility of government. The latest health secretary, Steve Barclay, met unions to discuss the various pay disputes, but it was the Treasury and Number 10 pulling the strings.

The national insurance rise to pay for a social-care levy was dropped. The scrapping of a much-needed, revenue-raising measure was one of the few policies that survived Liz Truss's moment at the centre of the stage. Sunak's heart was never in it. Johnson had demanded the money for social care. Whatever his motives, he was right to do so. Sunak could not see that the costs were worth it. Although assiduous, Sunak was not an empathic politician, one who recognized instinctively the challenges of life with under-resourced, fractured public services. He was extremely wealthy and perhaps that played a part. He was not dependent on chaotic services where the users felt far from empowered. Some wealthy politicians are capable of such empathy but he could not make the leap. Social care remained as under-resourced and lightly regulated as it was before the pandemic. The turning point had passed.

The nebulous term 'reform' became fashionable once again. After the initial post-pandemic attempts to make the NHS less atom-ized, both Conservative and Labour politicians looked to the earlier 'reforms' for inspiration. Keir Starmer became at ease as a leader when he chose, perhaps out of conviction, to identify with Tony Blair, Labour's great election winner. He began to stress the import-ance of NHS 'reform'. He got cheers from the commentariat when he declared support for a greater use of the private sector, although he did not specify how the sector would be deployed beyond meet-ing short-term capacity demands. He spoke of giving more power to patients, using the language of Blair, Cameron and Lansley. Sunak did the same.

Ultimately the turning points once again did not take the form of more considered reflections on the role of a modern state, its respon-sibilities and how it should meet them. Instead the turning points arising from the pandemic took different forms, partly to do with lifestyle and working patterns. The pandemic made the labour short-ages that followed Brexit even more acute. Some people discovered they enjoyed not working during lockdown and resolved to carry on in the same manner when restrictions were lifted. By the summer of 2022 the Office for National Statistics showed that 'among those who left work since the start of the coronavirus pandemic and had not returned, when surveyed in August 2022 over 3 in 10 left to retire. This was dominated by the older cohort with nearly a half (48%) of aged 60 to 65 years retiring.'[31]

Others opted to continue working from home. In the summer of 2022, the ONS reported that that 23 per cent of workers earning £40,000 or more were still working from home five days a week and a further 38 per cent were in a hybrid pattern, splitting their time between the office and home.[32] Victoria Robinson, a partner at PwC who advised firms on adapting to working from home and hybrid working, argued it was 'unrealistic and unwise' for employers to force workers back to the office full-time: 'This is not a temporary blip; the pandemic has led to a permanent change in working practices and the office as a form of control is gone for ever . . . We're in the midst of a "great resignation", with more than a fifth of workers expecting to change jobs in the next year.'[33]

After the financial crash, people continued to bank warily and had to navigate their way through fragile public services as they had done before both the crash and then the pandemic. As with Iraq, the biggest change was a further intensification in the breakdown of trust between some voters and once-revered institutions. The then governor of the Bank of England, Mervyn King, told a parliamentary select committee after the crash that he was surprised there had not been 'riots on the street'.[34] But across the Western world rebellion took a different and more potent form with the rise of nationalist outsiders from Nigel Farage to Donald Trump.

Indeed, after 2008 British politics became volcanic: a rare peace-time coalition at Westminster after the 2010 election; the rise of the SNP in Scotland; Brexit; and by 2022, three Conservative prime ministers in the same year. The dance between the parties and within them was always tense and complex, but until 2008 had been relatively orderly. From 1979 the Conservatives had led for eighteen years with big or near decent majorities. After 1997 there were three terms of a Labour government more or less in full control of the House of Commons, a party dominant in England, Scotland and Wales. After 2008 and the breakdown of trust, voters looked elsewhere. In the 2010 election the Liberal Democrats were partial beneficiaries but they fuelled the mood of disdainful mistrust when they formed a coalition of the radical right having pitched themselves to the left of New Labour. Disillusioned with the two bigger UK parties, considerable numbers in Scotland turned to the SNP and the hopes of a never fully defined independence. Nigel Farage offered a different form of nationalism with his UKIP and Brexit parties, a vision that made the SNP's proposals for independence a model of progressive clarity in comparison.

A breakdown in trust likewise brought about the fall of Boris Johnson. With considerable ease, he got away with several controversies over policy including Brexit, his early complacent approach to the pandemic and his support for 'levelling up', a notion so vague that not even his levelling-up ministers knew what it meant. However, eventually, the parties in Downing Street during the pandemic fuelled his downfall along with other misdemeanours. Dealing with the issue of leadership and 'trust' is in one sense relatively easy. Leaders can be replaced. Addressing the policy implications of the crash and the pandemic were far more complex. Johnson went. The policy challenges were sidestepped.

Johnson's successor was Liz Truss. Her brief moment in the sun marked another turning point, a prime minister attempting a revolutionary economic experiment without a mandate beyond her party's membership and the Conservative-supporting newspapers that proclaimed the arrival of a true Tory. During the reign of Truss, the Queen died. In the run-up to the funeral many commentators suggested that the end of the Elizabethan age marked a significant turning point. It did not. There was a smooth succession to King Charles and the more ardent royalists got on with their lives as before. But the speedy introduction of an economic revolution and its equally dramatic failure marked another twist in an era of seismic politics. Within weeks, one set of economic beliefs were replaced by another.

10

LIZ TRUSS AND RISHI SUNAK

After a leadership contest lasting much of the summer, Liz Truss was elected prime minister on 6 September 2022. Most prime ministers arrive in Number 10 with a degree of wariness, wondering whether they will be up to the task. Even those that win general elections usually have some self-doubt. Truss did not appear to be burdened by worries about the challenges ahead. She arrived as a new prime minister ready to unleash her economic revolution, one that she had enjoyed espousing during her victorious campaign over the summer.

The final duel in the leadership contest was between Truss and former chancellor Rishi Sunak. Most contests in any political party are marked by a lack of candour about the tasks ahead. This was not the case here. The two candidates outlined their ideas and visions with near total clarity. Initially this was to Truss's advantage, although Sunak became the ultimate victor. Both experienced the wildest of oscillating fortunes. Sunak lost and became prime minister. Truss won by a comfortable though not overwhelming margin, only to return to the backbenches within weeks.

Her radical impatience at the very start of her reign was tested briefly, but not in a way that would throw her off course. Before she could settle into her new role, the Queen died, imposing a strange and rare pause in political activity. For a week or so the ideologically resolute prime minister became little more than a ceremonial figure performing duties that had been carefully prepared long before she had reached the very top of British politics. She yearned to change the political landscape but her first role was to comply with the duties of a prime minister when the monarch dies. Still, she did not have to wait for very long before she could command. She was ready for when the political silence turned to the more familiar cacophony once again.

Her chancellor, ally and friend, Kwasi Kwarteng, unveiled a mini-budget in the House of Commons on Friday 23 September. In the space of a few minutes, Kwarteng and Truss overturned what they regarded as paralysing orthodoxies and sought to recalibrate the entire UK economy. Although Truss and her senior followers had been making their case for years, it seemed to come as a surprise to some that they actually meant what they had been saying. Perhaps the pause arising from the Queen's death had been deceptive. For a short time they had been passive. Yet on her arrival in Number 10, Truss sensed with more good cause than she realized that she had little time to bring about the changes she sought. Every Conservative prime minister since 2010 had moved with reckless speed on various fronts. The coalition government from 2010 introduced ill-thought-through reforms at a breakneck pace. Theresa May had triggered the Brexit timetable at the earliest possible moment without knowing what form of departure from the EU she wanted. Johnson rushed to negotiate his version of Brexit, ready to accept any deal that was not May's. Truss made Cameron, May and Johnson seem like cautious neurotics in comparison.

On that Friday morning in September, Kwarteng rose to deliver the budget of his dreams. They did not want advice from anyone who had flourished under the 'consensus' of recent decades that they were planning to tear apart. In his lofty confidence, Kwarteng also bypassed the Office for Budget Responsibility (OBR), the independent body tasked with making economic forecasts. Truss and Kwarteng saw Tom Scholar, the permanent secretary at the Treasury, and the OBR as being part of the old regime that they were ready to overturn. More immediately they did not want the scrutiny of the OBR; it was an interrogation that might spoil the fun. They sacked Scholar, preferring the unqualified thumbs-up from the right-wing think-tanks and pressure groups that had been urging them on. The think-tanks and pressure groups now had leading representatives working at the heart of the new government.

With a quietly spoken flourish Kwarteng declared on a sunny early autumn morning, 'We need a new approach for a new era, focused on growth.' He pledged to 'turn the vicious cycle of stagnation into a virtuous cycle of growth. So as a Government, we will focus on growth – even where that means taking difficult decisions.'[1]

Yet there were no difficult decisions. Kwarteng made it look easy. He announced £65 billion worth of tax cuts while insisting that the government's expensive but urgently necessary plans for social care would still go ahead. These were tax cuts and spending increases on an astonishing scale. The previous revolutionary steps since 2010 had been partially reinforced by general election victories. This one, the biggest leap of all, was based on a victory in a leadership contest alone. There had been no authority-enhancing general election win to provide a wider mandate for Truss and Kwarteng. Nor had the markets been squared.

Kwarteng announced the ending of the cap on bankers' bonuses. The planned increase in corporation tax to 25 per cent would be scrapped. The tax on business earnings would stay at 19 per cent. Overseas visitors could look forward to VAT-free shopping. The health and social care levy would be cancelled and yet, waving his conjuror's wand, Kwarteng added: 'I can confirm: the additional funding for the NHS and social-care services will be maintained at the same level.' He ended on a climax, as chancellors try to do when announcing new economic policies: 'I'm not going to cut the additional rate of tax today, Mr Speaker. I'm going to abolish it altogether. From April 2023, we will have a single higher rate of income tax of 40 per cent. For too long in this country, we have indulged in a fight over redistribution.'[2]

There was to be no more top rate of tax for higher earners, one example of several in which the more affluent were the main beneficiaries of this radical budget. Truss had made clear during the leadership contest that as far as she was concerned, taxes should not be deployed to redistribute wealth but to generate growth. This took some chutzpah given that she was speaking after a long period of Tory rule in which inequality had widened considerably in the UK and when 'levelling up' was supposed to be the guiding light for the government in which she served. But since becoming an MP she had flourished without much critical scrutiny. From 2012, her assertions had floated in the air and did not come crashing down to the ground until tested by power.

Truss had also unveiled a hugely expensive fuel subsidy scheme, hours before the formal announcement that the Queen had died. Combined with Kwarteng's budget, the government was going on a massive borrowing spree in order to keep homes warm and in what they considered would be a dash for economic growth. In cabinet meetings under Boris Johnson, Truss had argued against some of the tax rises proposed by the then chancellor, Rishi Sunak. She suggested more borrowing should pay for increased spending. Now she had the power. She and Kwarteng were in charge and knew that their vision must be realized before the next general election. They did not have very long.

Volte-face

There has been no speedier turning point in British politics. Within weeks there was a new chancellor, Jeremy Hunt, delivering a financial statement that reversed most of what Kwarteng had announced the month before. As part of the speedy craziness, Jeremy Hunt had moved from being a backbench MP and failed leadership candidate to the new chancellor of the exchequer. He had been the defeated alternative to Johnson in the 2019 Conservative leadership contest and was knocked out in the early rounds of the 2022 campaign. Following his melancholic conclusion that fighting twice was no route to victory, he was readying himself for a long career on the Conservative backbenches. He was a thoughtful chair of the Health Select Committee, a post of some influence, although no direct power. However, on 17 October, Hunt stood up in the Commons to make his speech on the government's new economic direction with Truss sitting next to him, clinging on pathetically as prime minister. By then she was in office but not in power, to revisit the phrase of Norman Lamont in relation to John Major and his government. Lamont made that observation after he had left Major's government in 1993. Major had been in deep trouble by then, but incomparably more secure and powerful than Truss was as her new chancellor delivered his financial statement.

Hunt had supported Sunak in the final rounds of the leadership contest, so Truss did not consider appointing him to her first cabinet, let alone to be her chancellor. Yet within weeks she had offered him the post. Most prime ministers become trapped in the end, facing nightmarish options whichever way they turn: Truss was incarcerated after a few weeks, the period when most new prime ministers enjoy an intoxicating honeymoon. Truss had no choice but to sack Kwarteng amid the storms in the aftermath of his mini-budget. Having removed her close ideological friend, she needed a successor who represented a big step back from her early revolutionary fervour. Hunt's opposition to her original economic ambitions had become a bizarre qualification for the most pivotal post in the cabinet.

He had been abroad when Truss phoned him. At first he thought it might be some form of practical joke. When he realized the offer was genuine, he consulted a few friends, who advised him correctly that he would possess all the power in the new government and that he should take the job. He took it and the mild-mannered politician became instantly mighty. The day before his Commons statement he travelled to Chequers to inform Truss of his plans. The meeting that Sunday had a cinematic quality: a suddenly weak prime minister and a chancellor who had become the most powerful figure in her government. She had become a mere recipient, listening passively to what he planned to say and do. She was again a mere ceremonial figure as she had been in the immediate aftermath of the Queen's death. At Chequers he told her that he was planning to reverse most of the measures Kwarteng had triumphantly announced. The former impatient revolutionary meekly agreed. As a study in the changing nature of power, there was little to beat the meeting between Truss and Hunt. The next day in the Commons, Hunt politely and calmly stuck the knife in.

Firstly, the Prime Minister and I agreed yesterday to reverse almost all the tax measures announced in the Growth Plan three weeks ago that have not been legislated for in Parliament. We will no longer be proceeding with: the cut to dividend tax rates, saving around £1 billion a year; the reversal of the off-payroll working reforms introduced in 2017 and 2021, saving around £2 billion a year; the new VAT-free shopping scheme for non-UK visitors, saving a further £2 billion a year; or the freeze to alcohol duty rates, saving around £600 million a year. I will provide further details on how those rates will be uprated, shortly.

Second, the Government is currently committed to cutting the basic rate of income tax to 19% in April of 2023. This government believes that people should keep more of the money they earn, which is why we have continued with the abolition of the Health and Social Care Levy. But at a time when markets are asking serious questions about our commitment to sound public finances, we cannot afford a permanent, discretionary increase in borrowing worth £6 billion a year. So I have decided that the basic rate of income tax will remain at 20% – and it will do so indefinitely, until economic circumstances allow for it to be cut.

Taken together with the decision not to cut Corporation Tax, and restoring the top rate of income tax, the measures I've announced today will raise around £32 billion every year. The third step I'm taking today, Mr Speaker, is to review the Energy Price Guarantee.[3]

Not only were the original policies scrapped but so was the ideological verve that underpinned them. Truss had become prime minister convinced that lower taxes would spur economic growth and that the higher taxes introduced by Sunak were a key factor in explaining the UK's sluggish economy. Unsurprisingly, after this climbdown, she did not last much longer. Indeed, she did not survive the week. How could she when she had been stripped of political purpose, presiding over a government pursuing economic policies that were the reverse of her own?

On 20 October, Truss resigned as prime minister, the shortest tenure in history. She had lost control, not only of economic policy but her parliamentary party. There were several further chaotic scenes illustrating her powerlessness, at which point even she realized that she could not remain in Number 10. Within days, the candidate who had lost to Truss in the final round of the leadership contest, Rishi Sunak, became prime minister.

Sunak had warned about the dangers of Truss's half-formed ideas throughout the long summer of leadership hustings and media interviews. The more he had put his case, the weaker his position became with his party and the Conservative-supporting newspapers. The rise of Truss can only be explained by the uncritical and exuberant support for her in some newspapers and the party membership. The Truss era is partly a story about the changing nature of the Conservative Party and the power of its newspapers to sway political outcomes. Amid the growing momentum towards her during the leadership contest, some of the party's senior figures who had backed Sunak gave up on him. They switched to Truss when it was obvious she was going to win. These fickle mediocrities comically illustrate the dangerous allure of power. Some were rewarded with places in Truss's cabinet only to return to the backbenches before the autumn was over. Sunak was not going to reward all of those who had moved away from him, though his position was sufficiently fragile that he was obliged to offer some posts to those who had switched to Truss.

With the rise of Sunak to Number 10 the turning point was complete. The loser was the victor. The self-proclaimed fiscal conservative had replaced the tax-cutter dashing for growth.

The Dance Between the Thatcherites and the Revolutionary Truss

As ever in the modern Conservative Party, nothing was quite what it seemed. Sunak was an admirer of David Cameron and George Osborne, the architects of austerity economics after the 2010 election. So was Hunt, the chancellor who remained in place after the fall of Truss. In one of his first moves as chancellor, he appointed Rupert Harrison to join a small team of advisers. Harrison had been Osborne's chief of staff during his reign as chancellor and was now the influential chair of the Council of Economic Advisers at the Treasury.

The reconnection with key players from the Cameron/Osborne era was not such an abrupt change of gear from the leadership of Truss as it appeared to be. During the early phase of the coalition, in 2012, Liz Truss, Kwasi Kwarteng and others published their seminal work, *Britannia Unchained*, a book that became their guiding light as they rose up the government's ranks to the very top. *Britannia Unchained* is closer to a pamphlet than an expansive, deeply considered text. It is a polemic against active government and in favour of a much smaller state. The authors wrote as if they were living in a state so extensive that it stifled all energy and entrepreneurial vivacity. In reality, the book was published as Cameron and Osborne were implementing the deepest real-terms spending cuts since the war. Like Truss and Kwarteng, they were also believers in a smaller state. So were Sunak and Hunt. They had much in common.

In *Britannia Unchained*, the authors declared that, 'In 21st century Britain, more people look to others to solve their problems'. The state is blamed for such hopeless passivity. 'The state has made Britain idle'.[4] What precisely does this mean? Few are ever in a position to solve all their problems as individuals. Even the wealthy are dependent on the state in some aspects of their lives. In one of the more famous passages the authors were candid in their disdain: 'The British are among the worst idlers in the world. We work among the lowest hours, we retire early and our productivity is poor. Whereas Indian children aspire to be doctors or businessmen, the British are more interested in football and pop music.'[5] But sport and music are extremely popular in India too. Quite a few British children want to be a doctor or run a business. Perhaps more would if an active and efficient state gave them a chance.

Non-Conservative reviewers of the book were predictably scathing, but on the whole assumed that the contemporaneous government of Cameron was on an altogether more sensible part of the political spectrum. Here is the Labour MP Jon Cruddas reviewing the book:

> The authors of *Britannia Unchained* represent a project that is extreme and destructive, and which threatens the essential character of our nation. It is because this faction is in the ascendancy that Cameron is actually failing; he remains captive to an economic reductionism that could well destroy conservatism – in the proper sense of valuing and conserving the nature and assorted institutions of the country.

Cameron is not one of this crew. Tactically, in the short term he might survive; but in the medium term he is toast.[6]

Cruddas was right about the fate of Cameron, but was less perceptive about him being 'not one of this crew'. Imagine if a relatively left-wing government had been in power and a book published by Labour MPs well to the left of that administration. Almost certainly all hell would have broken loose within the media and a large part of the Labour Party, and the MPs would probably have been vilified and marginalized. The opposite happened to the authors of *Britannia Unchained*. Cameron gave most of them prominent ministerial posts.

By 2014, two years after the publication of this right-wing polemic, Truss was a member of Cameron's cabinet. Apart from Truss and Kwarteng, the other authors were Dominic Raab, Priti Patel and Chris Skidmore. By 2015 Patel was employment minister under Cameron. In the same year Cameron made Raab his minister for human rights. George Osborne appointed Skidmore as his parliamentary private secretary in 2015. Later Raab was the most senior campaigner for Rishi Sunak in the 2022 leadership contest. The gap between the like-minded Cameron, Osborne and Sunak and the apparently different-minded Truss and her fellow authors was not as gaping as it appeared to be.

The language adopted in the coalition era was also similar to the provocative words in *Britannia Unchained*. The self-proclaimed centrist, Osborne, defended the real-terms cuts in benefits while he was chancellor by framing some recipients as lazy in the same way as the *Britannia Unchained* authors wrote off a significant proportion of the population. Osborne argued that his policy was about 'being fair to the person who leaves home every morning to go out to work and sees their neighbour still asleep, living a life on benefits . . . we have to have a welfare system that is fair to the working people who pay for it'.[7]

The welfare secretary at the time, Iain Duncan Smith, was livid about the proposed cuts and the framing to justify them. But in the Alice in Wonderland world of British politics and the media that mediates on the voters' behalf, Duncan Smith was portrayed as the right-wing voice while most commentators and some on the right of the Labour Party accepted Osborne's judgement of himself as being a 'centrist'.

Truss continued to soar under successive leaders to the extent that by the time of the 2022 leadership contest she was foreign secretary and the longest-serving cabinet minister. Sunak had risen even more speedily to become a youthful chancellor under Boris Johnson. Truss had been a cabinet minister for much longer than Sunak. Yet in the 2022 leadership contest, Truss managed to embody the 'change' candidate, as she apparently rejected the orthodoxies of recent decades. The gulf between the two candidates seemed vast. Truss had an almost Keynesian faith in the power of borrowing to generate growth, although she planned to spend the money in a way that was far removed from the ideas of Keynes.

Even so Truss's successful bid to become Conservative Party leader and prime minister had two significant virtues alongside the fatal flaw of shallow thinking. They were overlooked amidst the chaos. One positive element was that she wanted to be a change-maker and was willing to cause trouble in the pursuit of growth. Trouble-makers raise questions, they challenge complacent orthodoxies, of which there are many in the so-called 'liberal' establishment. They have a role and purpose but nearly always struggle with the complexities of power. Jeremy Corbyn was another such example, but the political and media establishment were never going to let him near power. In

Britain, there is much more space for trouble-makers on the right. Unlike Corbyn, Truss had the misfortune to become prime minister and for her ideas to be tested by reality, but her assessment about the 'consensus' of recent decades contributing to the UK's poor economic growth had merit. Her simplistic solutions were the problem.

She displayed another virtue, although a self-interested one: she was honest, knowing honesty would help her win a leadership contest in which a small number of right-wing Conservative members had a vote. No one had an excuse to be greatly surprised by what she did when she became prime minister. During the contest she said what she meant and meant what she said. Tax cuts were more or less her only proclaimed weapon although she promised increased spending as well. She did not even pretend that her approach commanded wide support amongst economists, although again being candid worked for her as she was positioning herself as a consensus-breaker.

During the leadership contest, when she was asked by the BBC's Nick Robinson whether she could name any economists who thought cutting taxes was the right medicine for the economy, she replied with almost comical openness: 'Patrick Minford.'[8] She knew what she was doing. The exchange came four decades after the same question was put to another Conservative prime minister, her hero Margaret Thatcher. After 364 economists wrote to *The Times* attacking the 1981 budget as reckless and deflationary, the Labour leader, Michael Foot, asked Thatcher whether she could name two economics professors who supported her strategy. Thatcher named Minford and her adviser Alan Walters, later joking in the car taking her back to Downing Street: 'Thank goodness he did not ask for three!'[9]

But even Minford, aged seventy-nine at the time of Truss's *Today* programme interview, had enjoyed little contact with Truss. Minford revealed that, 'I haven't got an arrangement with her. I met her when she was at the Department for International Trade and she mentioned that she agreed with a lot of things I'd been trying to say – how we need to get away from tax rises and have proper supply-side reform, and not be bothered with very short-term rules that are quite inappropriate to addressing solvency.'[10]

Even though Truss had told him she agreed with his views, that is by no means the same as a testing exploration of ideas over many years between an economist and an aspiring leader. But Truss was not a fan of testing ideas. Her preferred political dynamic was conversations with people she agreed with. The Institute of Economic Affairs and the Taxpayers' Alliance were her favourite right-wing think-tanks or pressure groups. The think-tanks were vibrant and self-confident during her rise and after her fall. During her ascendancy she and senior figures from these bodies would meet and agree on the virtues of tax cuts, light regulation and a smaller state. As the leadership contest intensified, the only question they asked each other was whether she was going far enough. Figures on the left soon find their ideas being scrutinized to destruction by a critical media and internal as well as external opponents. Their equivalents on the right endure no such levels of scrutiny and often wallow in intoxicating praise; an advantage in some respects, but also a cause of deep fragility.

In some ways, Sunak's campaign was unrecognizably different. In the first televised debate of the leadership contest he was brutally frank, turning to Truss and declaring: 'Liz, we have to be honest. Borrowing your way out of inflation isn't a plan, it's a fairy tale . . . The best way to help everyone, the best way to make sure that they have money in their pocket, is to get a grip of inflation – and that should be everybody's priority, because that's the thing that's going to erode everyone's living standards.'[11] This was Sunak's persistent theme. He also was being honest, but unlike Truss, his candour was less politically astute. For Conservative Party members the promise of tax cuts was the route to victory. They did not want to hear about fiscal responsibility. Apparently here was a contest between two candidates with entirely different visions, the Tory equivalent of Jeremy Corbyn taking on a figure from the right of the Labour Party. Some in the media portrayed the battle as Truss from the radical right versus Sunak from the technocratic centre ground.

Once again this was not an accurate portrayal. The contest in the summer of 2022 was rooted on the right of the party. There was no candidate from the party's one-nation tradition, unsurprising as Johnson had purged many of them during the Brexit battles in the autumn of 2019. Both Truss and Sunak worshipped at the altar of Margaret Thatcher, unable to leave behind the 1980s and the leader who was a product of a different era. When he was chancellor, Sunak had a photo of Nigel Lawson on his desk, his predecessor in the Thatcher era. Truss cited the Lawson tax-cutting budget of 1988 as if it were a biblical text. As we saw earlier, at the start of the campaign Sunak and his wife went to Grantham, the town of Thatcher's birth, and were photographed paying homage to her statue in the centre of the town. Truss appeared to wear similar clothes as Thatcher and as foreign secretary was photographed in a tank as Thatcher had been several decades before. The spell that Thatcher continued to cast over the Conservative Party was without precedent. She had left office in 1990. More than three decades later and no longer alive, she was dominating another Conservative leadership contest.

Sunak described himself persistently as a 'fiscal conservative', as Thatcher had done. Earlier in the year when he was still chancellor, in his spring statement, he made a bizarre pledge to cut income tax in 2024 without knowing what the economic situation would be by then and at the same time naively confirming by implication an election would not be held until this tax-cutting budget:

> I can confirm, before the end of this Parliament, in 2024, for the first time in sixteen years . . . the basic rate of income tax will be cut from 20 to 19 pence in the pound. A tax cut for workers, for pensioners, for savers. A £5bn tax cut for 30 million people.[12]

The move was nowhere near as reckless as the plans of Truss but pointed in the same direction. He made a similar broader point in his Mais Lecture delivered a few weeks before the spring statement.

> I firmly believe in lower taxes. The most powerful case for the dynamic market economy is that it brings economic freedom and prosperity. And the best expression of that freedom is for all of us to be able to make decisions about how to save, invest or use the money we earn. The marginal pound our country produces is far better spent by individuals and businesses than government.[13]

The divergence between Truss and Sunak was significant but narrow: how best to reach the promised land of lower taxes and a smaller state. Sunak wanted to balance the books first, closer to Thatcher's instincts. Truss wanted to go for growth and borrow to finance tax cuts. Neither candidate showed much interest in an active state or 'the good that government can do', the short-lived slogan that Theresa May adopted as prime minister before she was buried by the Brexit avalanche. May's words, written by her joint chief of staff, Nick Timothy, were an attempt to move the Conservatives towards a one-nation tradition and closer to the Christian Democrats in Germany. Both Sunak and Truss were a million miles from such an ambition.[14]

After Truss won the contest, all she could see was the narrow time-table to the next election, around two years away. She did not reflect on the need to build a coalition of support at least within the parliamentary party. Sunak had secured the backing of considerably more MPs than she had done in the early rounds of the leadership contest, always a recipe for trouble ahead. It did not seem to cross her mind that Thatcher had been in power for nearly nine years when Lawson delivered his totemic budget that she and indeed Sunak so revered. Instead she told allies, 'I've got two years – I've only got two years.'[15]

Change and Consequences

The consequence of Truss's restlessness was Kwarteng's budget with Truss sitting next to him in the Commons as a political and ideological ally. Afterwards, the Conservative-supporting newspapers were at least as ecstatic as their ardent followers in the Commons and the think-tanks. The *Daily Mail*'s front page the following day reflected the enthusiasm of right-wing colleagues and columnists when it proclaimed: 'At last! A true Tory budget.' Allister Heath, editor of *The Sunday Telegraph*, wrote in a column that it was 'the best budget I have ever heard a British chancellor deliver'. Of its content he said, 'The tax cuts were so huge and bold, the language so extraordinary, that at times I had to pinch myself to make sure I wasn't dreaming, that I hadn't been transported to a distant land that actually believed in the economics of Milton Friedman and F. A. Hayek'. He went on to predict 'a new big bang in the City' and 'dozens of new Canary Wharfs on steroids'.[16]

The newspapers and the supportive columnists proved to be unreliable allies. When the economy hurtled towards the cliff edge, they soon turned on Truss and Kwarteng without acknowledging their own culpability in the fiasco that followed and crucially without arguing that they had been wrong in terms of the fundamental policies. Irrespective of what happened in the immediate aftermath, they had played their role in the build-up to the budget. Truss felt she had more political space than she did, waking up to the exuberant support of many in the media in the fatal days between her rise to the very top and the mini-budget.

Comparisons were made with the so-called 'Barber boom' of the early 1970s when the chancellor, Anthony Barber, borrowed in a dash for growth only to deepen the economic crisis whirling around the UK at the time, but Barber was moving in slow motion compared with Truss and Kwarteng. After Kwarteng sat down at the end of his mini-budget speech the reaction was as speedy as the preparations for the mini-budget. There was the familiar sterling crisis that tends to erupt around a fragile British economy. Borrowing became frighteningly expensive, not least for those with mortgages. By 29 September, a few days after Kwarteng's statement, 40 per cent of mortgage products had been withdrawn from the UK market. Early the next month, the interest rate on a typical two-year fixed-rate mortgage had risen above 6 per cent for the first time since 2008, the year of the global financial crash. On 1 November, the Nationwide building society reported the turbulence caused by the mini-budget had led to a 0.9 per cent fall in house prices during the previous month, the largest since June 2020 during the pandemic.

Meanwhile pensions were on the edge of collapse, a cliff edge as potentially dramatic as the near closure of banks in the autumn of 2008. Soon after the budget, the Bank of England was forced to trigger an emergency £65 billion bond-buying programme in order to protect pension funds at risk of insolvency. At around the same time, sterling reached an all-time low against the dollar. There was speculation that parity was possible, that totemic humiliation when the pound becomes worth the same as a dollar.

Truss and Kwarteng also faced internal political pressures that they should have envisaged before opting for a revolutionary swagger. On the Sunday of the Conservative Party conference at the beginning of October, the former cabinet minister Michael Gove was a guest on the BBC's main political programme. Another of the guests was Truss. Before her interview Gove warned that he could not support the cut in income tax for high earners. He argued mischievously that the cut was 'not Conservative', a potent message when Truss had wallowed in the 'At Last a true Tory Budget' headline a few days earlier.[17] Another former minister, Grant Shapps, wrote in *The Times*, 'This bolt-from-the-blue abolition of the higher rate, compounded by the lack in communication that the PM acknowledges, is an unforced error that is harming the government's economic credibility.'[18] These comments were echoing around the party conference in Birmingham, Truss's first as prime minister. The debut conference for a new prime minister elected a few weeks earlier might have had a celebratory air. This one was insurrectionary. Truss was losing control to the extent that she received a visit in her hotel suite from the chair of the powerful 1922 Committee, Sir Graham Brady, warning that she would lose a Commons vote on cutting the top rate of the tax.

This is where the turning point began, on the Sunday evening in Truss's conference hotel suite. She summoned Kwarteng and informed him that the U-turn on the top rate of tax was required. The following afternoon at the party conference, Kwarteng walked onto the main stage having given many interviews about the tax

U-turn and declared, 'What a day.' Such words can follow a triumph or a calamitous setback. Kwarteng did not utter the words
jubilantly. He sought to offer further reassurance by announcing that
the Office of Budget Responsibility would be publishing its assessment of the implications of the new tax-and-spend plans 'shortly',
another U-turn. Following his announcement of a reversal of the
plans to scrap the higher rate of income tax, the pound rose to pre-
mini-budget levels. But these were days of wild, nerve-shredding
oscillations: the pound soon fell again after Andrew Bailey, the governor of the Bank of England, confirmed the end of the scheme to
buy bonds. A cascade of negative verdicts on Truss's plans erupted
around the globe, from President Biden in the US to the International Monetary Fund.

Prime ministers in the deepest holes dare to hope there is a way
out. Truss made her one available move on Friday 14 October by
sacking her old friend Kwarteng. That afternoon she appeared briefly
as if in a daze at an awkwardly presented press conference during
which she confirmed the government was not going ahead with the
planned cut in corporation tax, the third major U-turn after the
mini-budget. 'I met the former chancellor earlier today. I was incred-
ibly sorry to lose him . . . he is a great friend and he shares my vision
to set this country on the path to growth',[19] she said. But Truss was
in no position to realize their joint vision, as Kwarteng had warned
her when she sacked him.

At one point during the Truss-induced storm, some polls put
Labour thirty points ahead. Voters in England tend to be forgiving of
a Conservative government. After the introduction of the disastrous
poll tax following the 1987 election, seen widely at the time as a fatal
move, England returned the Conservatives to power in 1992 with
the biggest percentage of the vote in their four successive election

victories. After Johnson's haphazard approach to the pandemic, the Conservatives gained Hartlepool in a by-election in the early summer of 2021, a victory that made Johnson even more mighty as a vote-winning prime minister. Conservative governments can survive quite a lot.

But even voters in England do not forgive a currency crisis that impacts immediately on their lives. The Conservatives never recovered in popularity from the UK's humiliating departure from the exchange rate mechanism in September 1992. In the aftermath of the mini-budget the Conservatives crashed similarly in the polls. It was time for the defeated candidate in the leadership contest to have a go.

Sunak and Hunt were similarly minded, both keen to return to the dance that Cameron and Osborne had begun in 2010. In his autumn statement delivered in November with Sunak now sitting next to him, Hunt announced tax increases and spending cuts spanning several years into the future. The markets were much calmer now, but the UK economy still tottered precariously, the poorest-performing in the G7.

This apparently stark turning point continued to be ambiguous. One of *Britannia Unchained*'s authors, Dominic Raab, was made Sunak's deputy when he first became prime minister. In April 2023 Raab resigned, not over any ideological differences with Sunak but because of allegations from senior civil servants of bullying. Several admirers of the Institute of Economic Affairs were in Sunak's cabinet. A senior adviser for Sunak, Nerissa Chesterfield, originated from the Institute of Economic Affairs and had also worked for Truss. This was unsurprising. Sunak and Truss broadly agreed on the virtues of a smaller state, the primacy of markets and the positive benefits of Brexit. Indeed, Sunak was a supporter of Brexit during the 2016 referendum whereas Truss only became a convert later.

The More Things Change . . .

The turning point from Truss to Sunak took an extremely limited form. Sunak sought a degree of stability before cutting taxes by exercising a tight control on spending and borrowing. Truss assumed that tax cuts would bring about economic stability. For both, the smaller state took priority over a search for a modern agile state. The dividing line between both leaders was less apparent than the split in the Conservative government after 1979, when the so-called wets in Thatcher's cabinet opposed her monetarist policies and yearned for higher levels of public spending as part of a return to one-nation Toryism.

Nor was there any inclination amongst Truss's more ardent followers to learn lessons from the saga of her premiership. Supporters of Truss formed the Conservative Growth Group in 2023 in which demands for tax cuts took centre stage once more. On its formation, around fifty Conservative MPs were members. Almost as if nothing had happened, Truss was back on the public stage. She visited Washington to speak to Republicans with like-minded views. Supporters rationalized that Truss's errors were around 'presentation' and failing to 'prepare the ground' – comforting excuses.[20] Not for a moment did they consider that they might have been misguided in terms of the substance and ideological verve that underlined the policies. The former cabinet minister Lord Frost, a fleeting backer of Truss, was soon calling for the return of her agenda, if not Truss herself, in his *Telegraph* column. *The Telegraph* was not alone. The *Daily Mail* cried out for tax cuts from the end of 2022, forgetting that the announcement of tax cuts had caused the chaos. Tory MPs joined in. The former leader Iain Duncan Smith and several others argued that high taxes were the reason the UK economy was languishing at the bottom of the G7 league tables. Tax cuts were their solution.

By early February 2023, Truss's assertiveness was such that the *i* newspaper ran a front-page headline: 'Liz Truss Comeback Ignites Fear of Tory Civil War'.[21] She wrote a 4,000-word essay published in *The Sunday Telegraph*. She was wholly unrepentant:

> Fundamentally I was not given a realistic chance to enact my policies by a very powerful economic establishment, coupled with a lack of political support.
>
> I assumed upon entering Downing Street that my mandate would be respected and accepted. How wrong I was. While I anticipated resistance to my programme from the system, I underestimated the extent of it.[22]

The influential Tory newspapers were excited once again, as they were after the mini-budget. The *Sunday Telegraph* leader argued, 'The statist Tory establishment has had its turn and the party is cratering in the polls; the free-marketeers must now speak up.'[23] The *Mail on Sunday* leader suggested, 'The ideas she stands for may be due for serious re-examination.'[24] The demands for tax cuts implied a schism between Truss's supporters and Sunak. Yet the difference remained narrow. On the day her essay was published, Rupert Harrison, Hunt's recently appointed adviser and Osborne's previous confidant, tweeted revealingly, arguing that Truss had got the sequence wrong. Tax cuts should only come after the 'public sector reform and a sustainably smaller state'. For Harrison the destination was the same. Only the route and timing differed.[25]

In the UK, the ideological self-confidence of those on the right is around ten thousand times greater than anyone on the left. There had been a limited turning point from one group of small-state advocates to another, but those who had been left behind were ready to re-join the battle as if the mayhem they caused had been a bad dream. Even after the near economic collapse of the autumn no lessons had been learned.

But one dangerous lesson had been plucked from the wreckage. Borrowing became even more sinful. Truss wanted to borrow to pay for tax cuts on the assumption that economic growth would follow. There was no evidence to suggest such a sequence would arise. But what about borrowing to pay for capital projects and other forms of public spending? The ascendancy of Sunak and the nervy caution of the Labour leader, Keir Starmer, more or less cut off a grown-up discussion about when governments should borrow and for what purposes. Labour politicians had always struggled to make the case that borrowing could sometimes make sense as a means of boosting economic growth. They had sought to do so erratically since the financial crash of 2008. But they were always open to criticism, typified by the accessible slogan George Osborne coined about the outgoing Labour government, 'Maxing out the credit card'.

At the start of 2023 the BBC published an illuminating review on its reporting of economic policies, written by independent experts Andrew Dilnot and Michael Blastland. They stated clearly that 'too many' BBC journalists lack an understanding of 'basic economics'. This particularly affects reporting on the central political issue of government debt, with 'some journalists' apparently 'instinctively' believing all debt to be inherently bad – and therefore failing to appreciate that the role of government debt is 'contested and contestable'.[26] This was a dream media context for George Osborne.

The tragedy for an increasingly dysfunctional UK was that after 2010, borrowing for governments was absurdly cheap. It would have been a smart investment to borrow for capital projects given the country's creaking infrastructure. That would have been a substantial turning point in the course of modern Britain. Osborne even appeared to recognize this opportunity in his budget held weeks after the coalition was formed in 2010. Amid deep real-terms spending cuts, he observed insightfully: 'I think an error was made in the early 1990s when the then Government cut capital spending too much— perhaps because it is easier to stop new things being built than to cut the budgets of existing programmes. We have faced many tough choices about the areas in which we should make additional savings, but I have decided that capital spending should not be one of them. There will be no further reductions in capital spending totals in this Budget.'[27]

And yet in the details of even that budget, there were cuts in capital spending and Osborne took no opportunity to borrow significantly in a long era of low interest rates. Later, the deputy prime minister and leader of the Liberal Democrats, Nick Clegg, looked back and admitted that one of the errors in this period was the failure to increase capital spending. By implication, many Conservative MPs came to the same view, as they pleaded for the government to spend more in their constituencies on road, rail and other infrastructure projects while being instinctively against higher public spending in general. As Clegg wrote in his memoir: 'It is now broadly accepted that capital investment in the UK – public and private – has generally been insufficient and erratic. The considerable economic gains to be had from an ambitious renewal of roads, rail, energy, housing and telecoms infrastructure have been stymied . . .'[28]

Every word of Clegg's retrospective analysis was right beyond the opening phrase. There was no 'broad acceptance' about the virtues of borrowing for capital spending. In the post-Truss era, the case for borrowing became even harder to make even though she had made a commitment to borrow for tax cuts rather than public spending. She made the term 'borrowing' even more toxic. Yet with growth in the UK flatlining after the financial crash, Brexit and the pandemic, with a political and media culture that assumed US levels of taxation and European levels of public services were both possible and desirable, where was the money going to come from? Both Conservative and Labour parties thought of 'growth' and 'reform' as if they were magic wands that would make the UK 'world-beating', one of Johnson's favourite phrases. The will to make the case for borrowing to invest was limited. Truss had sought to borrow for tax cuts on the misplaced assumption that they would more than pay for themselves. Sunak responded by being even more determined to cut borrowing as Hunt surrounded himself with advisers from the Osborne era.

One of the most dramatic turning points in modern British political history, the reversal of an entire economic strategy, had led to a cul-de-sac from which there was no obvious escape. Indeed the turning point reinforced the prevailing orthodoxies in the UK which had held for decades. Borrowing was irresponsible except in the most exceptional of circumstances. Public services did not need significant further investment but required 'reform'. Tax cuts were desirable once moves were made to 'balance the books'. This was broadly the consensus between the leaderships of the Conservative and Labour parties following the dramas of the early autumn in 2022. Truss was there. Truss was gone. The UK had not really turned at all.

CONCLUSION

In his book *The Course of German History*, the historian A. J. P. Taylor argued that 'Germany had reached a turning point and failed to turn'.[1] Taylor was referring to the 1848 revolutions that swept across parts of Europe, though not the UK. Taylor argued that the initial success of the revolution in Germany discredited conservative ideas and its ultimate failure undermined liberal arguments, leaving only 'the idea of Force and this idea stood at the helm of German history from then on'.[2] The book was published in 1945.

The ten turning points in the UK since 1945 suggest that it also struggles to turn or to do so for a sustainable period. During times of crisis, senior politicians and many in the media suggest that 'lessons must be learnt'. But memories are short. Once a crisis is passed, previously established orthodoxies reassert themselves. In the UK this is particularly true in relation to foreign affairs and the role of the state in terms of its responsibilities for delivering public services and planning for future crises.

After the Suez crisis in 1956, questions unsurprisingly arose about the UK's place in the world. Was it still a great power capable of acting alone, if the US could in effect veto a military mission planned by a British prime minister? Once Eden resigned, the newly installed prime minister, Harold Macmillan, tried and failed to join the Common Market, recognizing that being an isolated power was almost a contradiction in terms. But even when the UK finally managed to join in 1973 it was a disturbed member, never wholly committed. Was it more enthused by the so-called 'special relationship' with the US or did Europe matter more? Heath inclined towards Europe. Thatcher looked to the US. Tony Blair sought a 'third way' in which the UK would be a 'bridgehead' between the EU and the US. Inevitably during the Blair era, issues arose in which significant EU powers disagreed with the US, the war in Iraq being the biggest. On Iraq, Blair had to choose and he sided with the US.

The UK's ambivalent relationships with the EU and the US continued until the Brexit referendum, when voters elected to return the country to where it was placed in the Suez crisis, a relatively small island unable to act alone and yet detached from more formidable institutions. If it was unsure of its place by the end of 1956 there was no greater clarity in the 2020s. During the Brexit referendum in 2016, there was no reference to Suez, the crisis that triggered the UK's long-drawn-out attempts to join the EU. Then again, there was no reference to very much of significance in the referendum campaign. Nor did the triumphant victory of the Brexiteers establish new forms of clarity and definition. Was the relationship with the US even more important now that the UK had turned its back on Europe? Was the Commonwealth the place where the UK exerted influence and derived strength? Was there much chance of closer ties to what Boris Johnson liked to call with a hint of mischievous menace 'our European friends'? Were Rishi Sunak's arduous efforts to make the Northern Ireland protocol work more smoothly a sign of a more constructive relationship or a pause in the UK's determination to keep its distance from Europe? There were as many questions in the aftermath of the referendum as there had been post-Suez and during the stormy era of Britain's membership of the EU.

Lessons in the UK were learnt and then unlearnt after two of the global turning points: the financial crash in 2008 and then the pandemic in 2020. Governments acting together to invest billions saved the world's biggest economies from falling off the cliff edge. But the brief return to a form of Keynesian economics was short-lived. Before long, spending cuts became the order of the day in the UK as they had been after the 1979 election. By 2023, lighter regulation for banks was being proposed once more by the chancellor, Jeremy Hunt, as if the crash had never happened. Following the pandemic, it looked as if the crisis in social care in the UK, exposed by the health emergency, was finally going to be addressed. Within months, plans for a social-care levy announced in the summer of 2021 had been dropped.

When power changes hands and the winning party secures a big majority, a new government has considerable freedom to bring about radical change. Such a switch is rare. Labour won a landslide in 1945, the first in the party's history. The speed of implementation after the election victory was one of that government's formidable strengths, but also a weakness. Britain was transformed but most of the changes and the ideas underlying them were challenged more quickly than those that underpinned the counter-revolution from the right in 1979. Were the models of public ownership established after 1945 the most effective that were available? Were there examples of welfare reform in Europe that might have been adopted in the UK?

The questions might have been asked again in 1979, when the long counter-revolution began. The immediate backdrop to the rise of Margaret Thatcher was the crises of the 1970s, fuelled by the quadrupling of oil prices in 1973, another turning point when the UK failed to turn. In 2022, after Putin's invasion of Ukraine, the UK was at least as vulnerable to soaring energy prices as countries far more dependent on gas from Russia. With the OPEC price rise a distant memory, UK governments had failed to invest in energy storage capacity when prices were much cheaper, a short-term saving with longer-term consequences.

After the chaos of the 1970s, the Thatcher revolution was unleashed with the insistence that 'there is no alternative'. Her assertion soon became fashionable orthodoxy. The only response to the failure of 1970s-style 'corporatism' was to regard the state as the enemy of innovation and 'freedom'. At a key turning point, there was little grown-up debate about why the clunky forms of state intervention failed in the 1970s and whether a modern state might be able to perform more effectively and if so what form it might take. There was little focus on models from other countries. The Labour Party collapsed into an inward-looking civil war. The Tory dissenters failed to organize in a way that challenged the Thatcherite juggernaut and were soon marginalized. Unlike Attlee, who was busy as deputy prime minister in the wartime government before 1945, Thatcher had time to frame arguments as leader of the opposition for nearly four years. Attlee had to make his case for a few weeks in the immediate aftermath of war and then get on with it. Arguably Thatcher had less sense of precisely what she wanted to do with power than Attlee and his senior colleagues, but more space to decide once she had got there. Her longevity and the support of powerful newspapers meant that Britain was still recognizably hers long after she had died. The UK had taken one particular turning and did not look back.

There were several attempts to break with the Thatcherite creed after 1979 but her ideas and policies reasserted themselves before long. In 2008, during the financial crash, the state came back into fashion, briefly. It saved the banks and acted in ways that avoided a deep recession or depression. But again, the UK failed to turn much beyond the duration of the crisis. David Cameron and George Osborne won the argument that the state was to blame for the financial crash, or specifically that public spending levels were the cause. With the blink of an eye, we were back to the 1980s, arguing over how the state could and should do much less. The same pattern arose with the pandemic that spread across the world in 2020. As the NHS creaked, with fewer beds and staff than equivalent countries across Europe and elderly patients taken out of hospitals to die in care homes, senior Conservative ministers were among those insisting on a near daily basis that lessons must be learnt. But soon, the planned social-care levy was dropped and the NHS went into a deeper crisis. As a youthful chancellor, Rishi Sunak presided over the biggest intervention in modern times to keep the economy breathing, with his multi-billion-pound furlough scheme. But the self-declared fiscal conservative was itching to return to Thatcherite economic policies as public services creaked and the economy failed to grow.

A partial challenge to the enduring might of Thatcherism was the New Labour government elected with a landslide in 1997, but even this administration adhered to Conservative spending limits and income tax levels set by the preceding Tory administrations. It also paid homage to the haphazard privatizations, even seeking to privatize additional industries. On one of the biggest post-war issues, ownership, Thatcher had won hands down even as most of the services provided by private monopolies were unreliable at best.

Her ideas were challenged more fundamentally but erratically by two Conservative prime ministers. When she became prime minister after the Brexit referendum in 2016, Theresa May proclaimed that it was time to talk about the 'good the state can do'. These words would not have been uttered by Thatcher or David Cameron. Under the guidance of her thoughtful chief of staff, Nick Timothy, she also argued the state had a duty to intervene in some failing markets. When a former Labour leader, Ed Miliband, made the same point, he was portrayed in some newspapers as a combination of Marx and Trotsky seeking to take the UK 'back to the 1970s', as if any Labour leader would take a look at that decade and conclude it was an election-winning model.

When Theresa May interrogated the role of the state in her early prime-ministerial honeymoon she was called 'strong and stable', as she put it with misguided repetition during the 2017 election campaign. Indeed that election, largely airbrushed out of history, almost became a turning point with the two bigger UK-wide parties debating how best to use the state to revive the economy and public services. The Conservatives won their highest share of the vote since 1987. Labour secured the highest since the landslide victory in 2001. But May became submerged by Brexit, the fate of Conservative prime ministers since 2010, and had no space to develop fresh ideas. The Labour leader, Jeremy Corbyn, failed to capitalize on the success and led his party to electoral slaughter in 2019. May was followed by Boris Johnson, who occasionally exclaimed that he was a 'Rooseveltian', a Tory leader who believed like Roosevelt in the benevolent consequences of higher public spending. Johnson's favourite theme, 'levelling up', had a 'Rooseveltian' echo. But on other days of the week Johnson could be an eager follower of Thatcher's. Most of the time he wanted to have his cake and eat it, asking his chancellor, the increasingly bewildered Rishi Sunak, for spending increases and tax cuts. Johnson's 'cakeism' was not a philosophy that disturbed those still worshipping at the Thatcherite altar.

CONCLUSION

In spite of the many seismic events that might have brought about lasting change, continuity is a more dominant feature of British politics. Of the ten turning points explored in this book, two have endured with little revision, the social reforms of the 1960s and the Thatcherite revolution unleashed after the 1979 election. Some of the 1945 government's visions are still in place, including the NHS, but quite a lot of the values espoused by Attlee and his colleagues were swept away when Thatcherism took hold. On the whole, turning points are reached, passed and the UK muddles on with the old familiar patterns still in place.

After Labour's landslide victory in 1945, the reforming Tory Rab Butler subtly persuaded his party to accept some of the sweeping changes that Clement Attlee's government had introduced. The initial instincts of his leader Winston Churchill, an erratic peacetime politician, was to attack virtually the whole set of policies that had made the 1945 election one of the biggest turning points in the twentieth century. A more textured politician than Churchill, Butler prevailed and the Conservatives adapted to the voters' expectations after the war.

Based on the post-war consensus between Butler and Labour's Hugh Gaitskell, the chancellor in the final phase of Attlee's government and then party leader in opposition, *The Economist* magazine coined a term, 'Butskellism'. The consensus between the two figures was exaggerated for journalistic impact. Butler tended to agree with Gaitskell when he was being tough on public spending, a Tory priority, while Gaitskell approved of Butler's reforming zeal that sometimes involved consulting figures outside his party. There were also big differences between a Tory and a Labour politician. So there should be. The idea that consensus between the two main parties in the UK is healthy undermines the entire notion of democratic politics. Healthy democracies require an eternal battle of ideas and the policies that arise from them. Thankfully there was still much that both sides disagreed about in the 1950s even if the gap between the leaderships of the Conservative and Labour parties was relatively narrow, a one-nation Conservative Party versus Labour led by Gaitskell, on the right of his party, and then Harold Wilson, an expedient magician.

In a different context there were similar patterns under the governments of Harold Wilson, Edward Heath and James Callaghan in the 1960s and 1970s. The three prime ministers were formed politically in the 1930s when high unemployment came to be regarded across the political spectrum as a social and economic evil. Again this is not to argue that they were 'all the bloody same' in the 1960s and 1970s. They were not. The reforms of the Wilson government in the 1960s have been undervalued, as were those implemented amid the seismic crises of the 1970s. To take one example, the creation of the Open University in 1968 was a life-enhancing innovation that no Conservative government would have introduced. In 1973, Heath's wilful determination managed to secure the UK's entry into the Common Market when Labour opposed such a move. Few want the equivalent of a one-party state in which policies are virtually the same whoever is in power, even if in the decades after the war England showed a willingness to elect Conservative governments most of the time.

The dominance of Conservative rule from 1951, with occasional interruptions from Labour, partly explains why familiar patterns persisted after what appeared to be significant turning points. Mainly accustomed to losing, Labour governments after Attlee's often felt like imposters with a desperate need to reassure voters and the newspapers they read. One-nation conservatism ran its course after the traumas under the leadership of Edward Heath, leaving the field open for Margaret Thatcher to cast her spell.

Turning points can be an opportunity as well as a threat. The Suez crisis and the war in Iraq raised big, thorny questions about the UK's role in the world. Questions can be healthy for a democracy if they are answered. There were no clear answers. The UK is still stuck awkwardly between the US and Europe, both geopolitically and also in terms of its political culture. With the ideological triumph of Thatcherism from 1979 the country has moved closer to the US in terms of its politics, with the Conservative Party close to the Republicans, even echoing the same internal tensions between fiscal conservatives and nationalist populism. New Labour overtly imitated Bill Clinton's third-way politics in the 1990s while Keir Starmer kept a close eye on how President Biden made his pitch in the 2020 presidential election.

Yet Europe is still on Britain's doorstep, in some cases providing potential models for public-service delivery that are worth exploring. It likewise still has a single market that was partly designed with the UK's interests in mind. The unresolved ambiguities feed on themselves. How to plan for a modern economy with growing demands on public services, a question raised by the quadrupling of oil prices in 1973 as much as by the pandemic in 2020? How can the UK economy become more productive, a question made all the more urgent by Brexit?

Explosive events erupted more often from the financial crash of 2008 onwards and the breakdown in trust that arose from it, with the rise of the SNP, the brief ascendancy of Jeremy Corbyn in the Labour Party, and Brexit. Then there were the pandemic and the war in Ukraine. The consequences of each are still being played out. They will bring new turning points. But will Britain turn?

ACKNOWLEDGEMENTS

Thank you to the brilliant Andrew Gordon and Mike Harpley . . . and to all Mike's colleagues at Macmillan: Nicholas Blake, Jiri Greco, and Lindsay Nash.

NOTES

CHAPTER 1: LABOUR WINS A LANDSLIDE

1. 'Some Aspects of the Inequality of Incomes in Modern Communities', 1920, and 'Principles of Public Finance', 1922, were published when Dalton was a lecturer at the London School of Economics.
2. Nicholas Timmins, *The Five Giants: A Biography of the Welfare State* (William Collins, 2017), p. 7.
3. The broadcast is on YouTube and opens with a morale-boosting fanfare closer to a party election broadcast.
4. BBC Archive. Originally broadcast 2 December 1942.
5. Ibid.
6. Nicholas Timmins, London School of Economics talk, 19 February 2018.
7. Peter Hennessy, *Never Again: Britain 1945–51* (Penguin, 2006), p. 134.
8. Churchill's speeches, YouTube.
9. nationalarchives.gov.uk/cabinetpapers
10. *Clement Attlee* by David Reynolds on the History Room YouTube channel. Available at https://www.youtube.com/results?search_query=clem+attlee+david+reynolds
11. David Marquand, *The Unprincipled Society* (Jonathan Cape, 1988), pp. 210–11.
12. Cited in *The Guardian* editorial, 8 April 2003, in the midst of another Labour internal crisis.

13. Gresham Lecture by Vernon Bogdanor, 'The General Election of 1945', 23 September 2014. Available at https://www.gresham.ac.uk/watch-now/general-election-1945

14. Winston Churchill's Gestapo speech, broadcast on 4 June 1945. Available at https://www.youtube.com/watch?v=7TY7oUNobsY

15. Clement Attlee, *As It Happened* (Sharpe Books, 2019), p. 143.

16. Part of the introduction to Labour's 1945 manifesto.

17. Quoted in Vernon Bogdanor's Gresham Lecture, 23 September 2014.

18. David Kynaston, *A World to Build* (Bloomsbury, 2008), p. 136.

19. Peter Hennessy, *Never Again*, p. 140.

20. Ibid., p. 132.

21. Ibid., p. 140.

22. The words are one of thirteen vivid Bevanite quotes in the *Oxford Dictionary of Quotations* but the precise source is unclear. Apparently Bevan uttered the words to a friend, but some consider the much-repeated quote to be apocryphal.

23. Peter Hennessy, *Never Again*, p. 119.

24. He did so in a conversation with the author in October 1997.

25. Douglas Jay, *The Socialist Case* (Faber and Faber, 1937), p. 43.

26. This is explored in more detail in Chapter 9.

27. Kenneth O. Morgan, *Labour in Power: 1945–1951* (Clarendon Press, 1984), p. 191.

28. Correlli Barnett, 'The Audit of War', *Journal of the Royal Society of Arts*, vol. 134, no. 5364 (November 1986). Available at https://www.jstor.org/stable/41374248

29. Kenneth O. Morgan, *Labour in Power*, p. 141.

30. Christian Wolmar, *British Rail* (Penguin Books, 2022).

31. 'Rebuilding after the Second World War', Economics Observatory (2020). Available at https://www.economicsobservatory.com/rebuilding-after-second-world-war-what-lessons-today

CHAPTER 2: THE SUEZ CRISIS

1. http://www.conservativemanifesto.com/1951/1951-conservative-manifesto.shtml

2. *The Guardian*, 16 June 2010.

3. The argument that Eden was being more subtle at the beginning the crisis is outlined most persuasively in Jonathan Pearson, *Sir Anthony Eden and the Suez Crisis: The Reluctant Gamble* (Palgrave Macmillan, 2003).

4. Blair and Iraq are explored in Chapter 7.

5. Dominic Sandbrook, *Never Had It So Good* (Little, Brown 2005), p. 9.

6. D. R Thorpe, *Eden* (Chatto & Windus), 2003, p. 502.

7. The broadcast is on YouTube.

8. Dr Thorpe Eden p. 500.

9. Letter from President Eisenhower to Prime Minister Eden, Office of the Historian, 31 July 1956.

10. 'Falklands: Reagan phone call to Thatcher', 31 May 1982, Margaret Thatcher Foundation. Available at https://www.margaretthatcher.org/document/110526

11. *The Guardian*, 6 July 2016, quoting from a memo from Blair to Bush published in full in the Chilcot report on the war in Iraq.

12. Hansard, 12 September 1956.

13. Hansard, 12 September 1956.

14. Hansard, 30 October 1956.

15. Hansard, 1 November 1956.

16. Hansard, 3 November 1956.

17. Eden TV broadcast, 3 November 1956.

18. 'Perfidious Albion again', *The Economist*, 22 May 2010. Available at https://www.economist.com/europe/2010/05/20/perfidious-albion-again

19. Rhiannon Vickers, 'Harold Wilson, the Labour Party, and the War in Vietnam', *Journal of Cold War Studies*, vol. 10, no. 2 (Spring 2008). Available at https://www.jstor.org/stable/26923428

CHAPTER 3: THE 1967 ABORTION ACT AND A CIVILIZED SOCIETY

1. Pete Paphides, 6 October 2022. Available at petepaphides.co.uk

2. Dominic Sandbrook, *White Heat* (Abacus, 2009), p. 699.

3. David Steel, *Against Goliath* (Pan Books, 1991).

4. 'The Abortion Act 1967', Institute of Contemporary British History, 2002.

5. Ibid.

6. Ibid.
7. Roy Jenkins, *Life at the Centre* (Macmillan, 1991), p. 208.
8. Andrew Adonis and Keith Thomas (eds), *Roy Jenkins, A Retrospective* (OUP, 2004), p. 64.
9. John Campbell, *Roy Jenkins* (Jonathan Cape, 2014), p. 299.
10. Conversation with author, 27 August 2022.
11. Hansard, 14 July 1967.
12. Roy Jenkins, *Life at the Centre*, p. 107.
13. Malcolm Muggeridge in *The Sunday Times*, 2 February 1975.
14. Hansard, 27 July 1989. All the quotes from the debate are from Hansard on this date.
15. 'Report of the Committee on Homosexual Offences and Prostitution', October 1957, Parliamentary Archives. Available at https://discovery. nationalarchives.gov.uk/details/r/C1386377
16. *The Guardian*, 27 April 2017.
17. Woodward defected in December 1999.
18. Interview with author, *The Cameron Years*, BBC Radio 4, 15 January 2018.
19. Ibid.
20. Anne Perkins, *Red Queen: The Authorised Biography of Barbara Castle* (Pan Books, 2004), p. 292.
21. Ibid., p. 275.
22. *The New Statesman*, July 2003.
23. Anne Perkins, *Red Queen*, p. 297.

CHAPTER 4: THE PRICE OF OIL QUADRUPLES

1. He made the observation to the author in the summer of 1997 when he was having to decide what to do about electoral reform for the Commons, the plans for the Millennium Dome and other matters that seemed thorny at the time.
2. John Campbell, *Edward Heath: A Biography* (Jonathan Cape, 1993), p. 531.
3. Hansard, 18 December 1961.
4. *The Observer*, Sunday 31 July 1966.
5. John Campbell, *Edward Heath*, p. 564.

6. John Campbell, *Edward Heath*, p. 566.
7. Edward Heath broadcast, 13 December 1973. Available at https://www.youtube.com/watch?v=bj9OlIiHFo4
8. Harold Wilson, Labour Party conference, November 1974.
9. Denis Healey, *The Time of My Life* (Penguin, 1990), p. 427.
10. James Callaghan, Labour Party conference speech, 28 September 1976.
11. Interview with author, *Rock & Roll Politics* podcast, 26 September 2022. Available at https://podcasts.apple.com/in/podcast/the-return-of-the-truss-era/id1384867286?i=1000580010849
12. Thatcher deployed the phrase during her speech to the 1980 Conservative conference.
13. *Oil: A Crude History of Britain*, BBC Radio 4, 7 September 2015.
14. Anthony Barnett, Open Democracy, 8 April 2013.

CHAPTER 5: 1979

1. This was her theme at the Conservative Women's Conference 1980. Subsequently some referred to her as 'TINA', as in 'There is no alternative'.
2. Ian Gilmour, *Dancing with Dogma: Britain under Thatcherism* (Simon and Schuster, 1992).
3. Interview with Matt Forde, *The Political Party* podcast, 27 September 2017.
4. *The Times*, 2 October 1981.
5. 'Working Together for Britain', Liberal/SDP manifesto 1983. Available at http://www.libdemmanifesto.com/1983/1983-liberal-manifesto.shtml
6. 'Foreword' to the Conservative Party manifesto 1979. Available at https://www.margaretthatcher.org/document/110858
7. Peter Jenkins, *Mrs Thatcher's Revolution* (Jonathan Cape, 1989), p. 62.
8. Ibid.
9. Hansard, 12 June 1979.
10. Ibid.
11. Hansard, 26 March 1980.
12. Hansard, 29 March 1980.
13. Ibid.

14. Charles Moore, *Margaret Thatcher: The Authorized Biography, Volume One* (Allen Lane, 2013), p. 623.
15. *Daily Mail*, 28 October 2022.
16. Charles Moore, *Daily Telegraph*, 26 November 2022.
17. 'Speech Opening Nissan Car Factory', 8 September 1986, Margaret Thatcher Foundation. Available at https://www.margaretthatcher.org/document/106470
18. David Marsh, 'Privatisation Under Mrs Thatcher', *Public Administration*, vol. 69, no. 4 (December 1991).
19. D. R. Thorpe, *Supermac: The Life of Harold Macmillan* (Pimlico, 2011), p. 602.
20. Charles Moore, *Margaret Thatcher: The Authorized Biography, Volume Two* (Allen Lane, 2015), p. 240.
21. Ibid., p. 188.
22. David Marsh, 'Privatisation Under Mrs Thatcher'.
23. *The Guardian*, 10 November 2022.
24. Conor Burns, Conservativehome, 11 April 2008.

CHAPTER 6: LABOUR WINS THREE ELECTIONS IN A ROW

1. At least that is what he said to the author at the time.
2. Labour Party conference, Brighton, 29 September 1995.
3. Channel Four, 'Fact Check – Labour's Election Pledge Card 1997'. Available at https://www.channel4.com/news/articles/politics/domestic_politics/factcheck+labours+election+pledge+cards/507807.html
4. Ibid.
5. Ibid.
6. Ibid.
7. This is how Blair and others in his office explained the move to the author at the time.
8. 'SureStart Evaluation Report', May 2018. Available at https://www.etini.gov.uk/sites/etini.gov.uk/files/publications/surestart-evaluation-report-may-2018.pdf
9. *The Guardian*, 31 May 2004
10. This is what he told the author on the evening before the budget.
11. He noted this to the author.

12. BHF, *Heart Matters* magazine, April 2016.
13. Conversation with author in July 2007.

CHAPTER 7: IRAQ

1. Donald Macintyre, *Mandelson and the Making of New Labour* (Harper Collins, 1999), p. 107.
2. 'Clause 4 at 20', *The Guardian*, 29 April 2015.
3. Cook told me about his visit to the Beaconsfield by-election in one of several conversations during which he showed a greater understanding of Blair than any other cabinet minister, in my opinion. His views are explained in his book, *The Point of Departure* (Pocket Books, 2004), one of the best from the New Labour era.
4. *The Guardian*, 4 August 2003.
5. Interview, *On the Record*, 15 February 1988.
6. 'President Clinton and PM Blair Joint Press Conference (1998)', Clinton Digital Library. Available at https://clinton.presidentiallibraries. us/items/show/15944
7. Ibid.
8. Paddy Ashdown, *The Ashdown Diaries Volume Two: 1997–1999* (Allen Lane, 2001), p. 169.
9. Hansard, 17 December 1997.
10. 'The Blair Doctrine', 22 April 1999, Global Policy Forum. Available at https://archive.globalpolicy.org/empire/humanint/1999/0422blair.htm
11. 'President Delivers State of the Union Address', 29 January 2002, The White House, President George W. Bush Archive. Available at https:// georgewbush-whitehouse.archives.gov/news/releases/2002/01/20020129-11.html
12. Chilcot Inquiry, July 2016. Available at https://assets.publishing. service.gov.uk/government/uploads/system/uploads/attachment_data/ file/535407/The_Report_of_the_Iraq_Inquiry_-_Executive_Summary. pdf
13. *The Guardian*, 3 September 2002.
14. *The Guardian*, 12 May 2011.
15. *The Sunday Times*, 13 January 2003.

16. Michael Portillo's columns in *The Sunday Times* were supportive of Blair in the build-up to Iraq but he turned soon after. He is a barometer figure on the issue. On 8 June 2003 he was expressing doubts, writing in the anti-war *Independent* that Blair had 'disappointed' him by claiming the toppling of Saddam justified the war when the original aim was the removal of WMD.

17. 'Chirac says no to any second resolution authorising war', 10 March 2003. Available at https://www.youtube.com/watch?v=7R9Q9yopHAU

18. 'The Price of My Conviction', *The Guardian*, 20 February 2003.

19. *The Sunday Times*, 13 April 2003.

20. *Financial Times*, 29 April 2003.

21. *The Mail on Sunday*, 1 June 2003.

22. Hansard, 29 August 2013.

23. Ibid.

24. *The Guardian*, 30 August 2013.

25. BBC *Today* programme, 30 August 2013.

26. Hansard, 29 August 2013.

27. Ben Rhodes, 'Inside the White House During the Syrian "Red Line"', *The Atlantic*, 3 June 2018. Available at https://www.theatlantic.com/international/archive/2018/06/inside-the-white-house-during-the-syrian-red-line-crisis/561887/

28. Ibid.

CHAPTER 8: BREXIT

1. Hansard, 28 October 1971.

2. Ibid.

3. Hansard, 21 October 1971.

4. Hansard, 28 October 1971.

5. Roy Jenkins, *Life at the Centre*, p. 337.

6. Nick Thomas-Symonds, *Harold Wilson: The Winner* (Weidenfeld and Nicolson, 2022).

7. 'Bruges Speech', Thatcher Foundation.

8. Jeane Kirkpatrick, 'Thatcher's Europe: The Major Difference', *The Washington Post*, 19 March 1991. Available at https://www.washingtonpost.com/archive/opinions/1991/03/19/

thatchers-europe-the-major-difference/504b7feb-f9f6-4b03
a448-52d51938f9e1/

9. *The Independent*, 6 October 1992.

10. Ibid.

11. Andrew Adonis, 'Tony Blair and Europe', *Prospect*, 11 November 2017. Available at https://www.prospectmagazine.co.uk/politics/45315/tony-blair-and-europe-shattering-the-ming-vase

12. *The Independent*, 26 January 2016.

13. *The Independent*, 20 July 2019.

14. *The Cameron Years*, BBC Radio 4.

15. Interview, *Andrew Marr Show*, 21 January 2018.

16. BBC *Today* programme, 27 February 2018.

17. Hansard, 30 December 2020.

CHAPTER 9: THE STATE TO THE RESCUE

1. Hansard, 16 April 2002.

2. *The Times*, 5 April 2004.

3. Interview with author.

4. *Financial Times*, 18 March 2008.

5. He published *Beyond the Crash* after he left office.

6. Cameron's victory speech, 6 December 2005.

7. Gordon Brown, *Beyond the Crash* (Simon and Schuster, 2010), p. 41.

8. Ibid., p. 52.

9. *The New York Times*, 8 October 2008.

10. *The Times*, 3 April 2009.

11. The author was one of those who saw Brown in Number 10 on the Monday following the summit. The prime minster was downbeat. His next guest was Neil Kinnock, who embraced him like a proud, supportive relative. The embrace was both celebratory and yet initiated in a way that suggested Kinnock sensed Brown needed cheering up.

12. *Sky News*, 24 October 2019.

13. 'PM Speech in Greenwich', 3 February 2020. Available at https://www.gov.uk/government/speeches/pm-speech-in-greenwich-3-february-2020

14. 'Prime Minister's Statement on Coronavirus (COVID-19)', 16 March 2020. Available at https://www.gov.uk/government/speeches/pm-statement-on-coronavirus-16-march-2020

15. YouTube, 20 March 2020.

16. Kate Bingham, Oxford Romanes Lecture, 24 November 2021.

17. Nicholas Timmins, 'Never Again? The Story of the Health and Social Care Act', The King's Fund, 12 July 2012. Available at https://www.kingsfund.org.uk/publications/never-again

18. I attended this meeting and several others that took place regularly in 2007 and 2008 as the Conservatives prepared the ground for their election manifesto.

19. *The Guardian*, 4 October 2006.

20. At one point during the contest Ed Miliband had such a conversation with the author. Brown and his team were used to forensic policy-making, producing endless budgets and other heavily scrutinized statements. They read the columns and the editorials in detail and could not discern any clear 'reform' policies being advocated beyond a vague commitment to greater use of the private sector and a wariness of investment in the NHS.

21. Conversation with author and Ian Birrell, then deputy editor of *The Independent*, 8 November 2006.

22. The author had coffee with Clegg on the day the white paper was published. He was exuberant, arguing it was a conflation of Conservative and Liberal Democrat values.

23. Nicholas Timmins, 'Never Again? The Story of the Health and Social Care Act'.

24. Conversation with Jeremy Hunt, December 2014.

25. Hansard, 5 February 2013.

26. *The Andrew Marr Show*, 5 July 2020.

27. The King's Fund, 'The Health and Care Act: six key questions'. Available at https://www.kingsfund.org.uk/publications/health-and-care-act-key-questions

28. *The Andrew Marr Show*, 4 September 2011.

29. Interview with author broadcast in *The Brown Years*, September 2010, and on BBC Sounds.

30. *The Guardian*, 9 December 2022.

31. ONS report, 27 September 2022.

32. *The Guardian*, 2 June 2022.
33. Ibid.
34. Treasury Select Committee, 1 March 2011.

CHAPTER 10: LIZ TRUSS AND RISHI SUNAK

1. Hansard, 23 September 2022.
2. Ibid.
3. Hansard, 17 November 2022.
4. Liz Truss et al., *Britannia Unchained* (Palgrave Macmillan, 2012), p. 12.
5. *The Guardian*, 12 August 2012.
6. *The Guardian*, 27 September 2012.
7. Hansard, 5 December 2012.
8. BBC *Today* programme, 21 July 2022.
9. *The Guardian*, 6 September 2022.
10. *The Daily Telegraph*, 27 August 2022.
11. *The Daily Telegraph*, 15 July 2022.
12. Hansard, 23 March 2022.
13. Rishi Sunak, Mais Lecture, 24 February 2022.
14. Nick Timothy, May's joint chief of staff, told the author on his podcast in January 2022 that this was the objective of the new, more statist agenda.
15. Harry Cole, James Heale, *The Times*, 29 October 2022.
16. Allister Heath, *The Daily Telegraph*, 22 September 2022.
17. Laura Kuenssburg interview with Michael Gove, BBC 1, 2 October 2022.
18. *The Times*, 2 October 2022.
19. *The Guardian*, 14 October 2022.
20. This was Truss's own analysis in an interview with Spectator TV on 6 February 2023.
21. *The I Newspaper*, 6 February 2023.
22. *The Sunday Telegraph*, 5 February 2023.
23. Ibid.
24. *The Mail on Sunday*, 5 February 2023.
25. Rupert Harrison, Twitter, 5 February 2023.
26. James Meadway, *The Guardian*, 31 January 2023.

27. Hansard, 22 June 2010.
28. Nick Clegg, *Politics: Between the Extremes* (The Bodley Head, 2016), p. 239.

CONCLUSION

1. A. J. P. Taylor, *The Course of German History* (Hamish Hamilton, 1945), p. 71.
2. Ibid.

INDEX

INDEX

Divorce Act 81

Drakeford, Mark 308

Duncan Smith, Iain 223, 226, 233, 236, 271, 338, 348–9

Dyke, Greg 245–6

Eadie, Alex 86

Economist, The 299

Eden, Anthony
    becomes PM 44, 46–8
    Blair and 48, 50–51, 54, 56, 58–9, 62–3, 66, 69–70, 73–4, 205
    Britain's post-war role and 44, 47
    Churchill and 45, 46–8, 51, 53, 58, 59, 64, 67, 68, 70, 74
    domestic policy and 51
    expert in foreign affairs 48–50, 51, 57
    fall of 44, 48–9, 53, 69–71, 120, 354
    general election (1955) and 48, 51, 56
    health 56–7, 70–71, 120
    media and 53–4, 67, 120
    prime-ministerial successors 72–5, 354
    Second World War and 9, 48
    Suez Crisis and 44, 45–75

Education Act (1944) 15–17, 18, 37

Education Training Inspectorate 185–6

Eisenhower, Dwight D. 53, 55–60, 62

Elizabeth, Queen 326, 328, 330, 332

Emergency Medical Scheme 18, 35–6

Equal Pay Act (1970) 75, 102, 116, 141

euro 174, 175, 178, 182, 195, 197, 217, 221, 255, 262, 264, 265, 268, 269, 270, 280

European Coal and Steel Community (ECSC) 46

European Commission 261

European Economic Community (EEC) ('Common Market')
    Benn opposes membership of 138
    Foot opposes membership of 259
    foundation of 46, 47
    Heath's driving mission to join 73, 360
    Macmillan seeks to join 72–3, 354
    Suez Crisis and 251, 292
    UK joins (1973) 253–5, 257, 354, 360
    UK referendum on membership (1975) 121, 154, 254–5, 257, 260, 267, 272–3, 286

European elections
    (1988) 290
    (2014) 272
    (2019) 285

European Reform Group 281

European Single Market 261–2

European Union (UN)
    Blair and 41, 191, 197, 354
    Brexit and 72, 74, 200, 251, 253–93, 328, 354 *see also* Brexit
    euro and *see* euro

INDEX

INDEX

INDEX

INDEX

Steve Richards is a political columnist, journalist, author and presenter. He regularly presents *The Week in Westminster* on BBC Radio 4 and has presented BBC series on Tony Blair, Gordon Brown, David Cameron, Theresa May and Jeremy Corbyn. He is the author of *The Prime Ministers* and *The Prime Ministers We Never Had*, the latter of which was named a 'Book of the Year' in *The Guardian* and *The Times*.

He writes for several national newspapers including *The Guardian*, *The Independent* and the *Financial Times*. He also presents a popular political one-man show each year at the Edinburgh Festival and across the UK.